A GREEK JOURNEY
With Fork and Pen

Two Sisters Find Their Roots

Georgia Sardonis Cone
and
Elizabeth Sardonis Songster

I was completely enthralled by *A Greek Journey with Fork and Pen,* caught up in the delight of travel and adventure in Greece, the joy of family and heritage, and the quest and enthusiasm for food, more food and more food! *A Greek Journey with Fork and Pen* invites you into the lives of good people and great cooks as the four journal-keepers share unique observations on their Greek journeys, and yet their stories blend to create an enjoyable and loving narrative of people, who rejoice in each other's company and embrace all that is around them.

Visions of delectable food offerings made with olive oil, lemons, tomatoes, oregano and wine while sitting by the Aegean against a backdrop of pure white buildings, persuaded me to get to Greece as soon as I could, and the treasury of family recipes in *A Greek Journey with Fork and Pen* stirred within the desire to get to my kitchen to create delicious, tasty Greek dishes. Joy, celebration, love, friendship, adventure and food. Greece and life are wonderful! Be warned: Have snacks at hand while you read this book!

—Cindy Lelliot
Cindy is a librarian and museum curator in Nova Scotia, Canada.

Part recipe collection, travel log, and memoir, this charming read recounts the adventures of Greek-American sisters Georgia and Elizabeth as they, with husbands in tow, tour the land of their immigrant forebearers, eating and gathering recipes and stories as they go. The joy of the journey—the beauty of the land, its people and its food—fills every page, making this an enticing book for anyone interested in travel and pleasures of the table.

—Holly Jennings
—Holly Jennings, founder of Dowdy Corners Cookbook Club

To our family—past, present and future

Αιωνία Η Μνήμη

May your memory be eternal

Cover and book design: Korongo Graphics
36 Highland Avenue, Randolph VT 05060
802-236-9854

Contents

153 MANI 1994, 1997, 2006

Our cousin at the homestead kills a chicken for dinner; how to tenderize an octopus; souvlaki on brown paper

Preface

It was on our first trip to Greece together on a ferry boat in the Gulf of Corinth that the idea for this book took shape. We wanted to capture the fun we were having traveling through Greece, the incredible food we were eating and the excitement of visiting our family homesteads. Throughout our travels, we experienced the focus of Greek hospitality, food and dining together. The generous spirit of sharing a meal is part of the notion of kefi, that magical quality that is undefinable but recognizable in the Greek personality that seems to reflect the joy of living. Kefi, some call it the Greek passion.

Since we've made several trips to Greece, we have combined all of them into this book for ease of writing and flow of itinerary. The table of contents shows each location we visited, the highlights of the place and the recipes of the delicious foods we ate there. Many of the recipes were ones we were nurtured on, recipes that were echoed everywhere in our travels along Greece's seaside and hill towns. It is in these places we find an unmistakable link to the sacred elements of ancient Greek cooking: bread, olives, and wine. These are the same elements we had handed down to us as we enjoyed our daily bread with our family. Along with some family stories, this book also includes wonderful poetry, historical references, ancient inscriptions—a feast of words too beautiful to leave behind.

Our adventures dance across the pages in our journal entries, identified by each of our names: Georgia and Elizabeth. Our husbands, Floyd and Dan, contributed some of their own journal entries as well. Oftentimes, entries may seem repetitive, but we thought it was important to include them all because the nuances of each one's perspective gave a fuller description of our experiences, all of which caught the moment. The recipes we have here are a combination of those we grew up with, those of new friends we met on our travels, and those of chefs we interviewed at the tavernas where we ate. It's the cooking in these ubiquitous, casual dining and gathering places that we savor. We consulted many cookbooks both from our own collections and from Greece to make some adaptations for the sake of accuracy of measurements and clarity of directions.

Concerning the recipes

In our index we have listed the recipes in alphabetical order according to the main ingredient.

As easy as Greek cooking is, there are a few tips on techniques of preparation using filo dough and making egg-lemon sauce that are important to know before beginning. We have included a number of pie (*pita*) recipes, both savory and sweet, that use commercial filo dough. There are important instructions for use on the package (which is usually found in the freezer section of your grocery store), such as thawing the filo in the refrigerator overnight, then removing from fridge and bringing it to room temperature. After unrolling, remove as many sheets as needed to complete the recipe, then cover with plastic wrap to prevent drying out. Return unused sheets in original plastic bag to the refrigerator. When sealed tightly it can be used for up to fourteen days. The usual one-pound package has either one roll of 20 to 24 sheets (about 12 inches by 17 inches) or two 8-ounce rolls of 20 sheets each (about nine inches by 14 inches.) In our recipes using filo, we have tried to describe how to layer and butter the sheets but it can be confusing. It basically is a matter of using a pan about the size of the filo sheets and then fitting the filo to the pan. Do not worry if it tears while you are handling it since most recipes call for many layers and no one will see it once it is done. Filo dough in Greek cooking serves as a base for many dishes similar to the use of pasta in Italian cooking, both versatile and essential in each cuisine.

When using syrup in the dessert recipes, please note that it is essential to cool the syrup (by preparing it ahead of time) before pouring it onto the hot dessert whether it is made with filo dough or is a cake.

The most famous sauce in Greek cooking is egg-lemon sauce, used in many of the recipes we have included. The most important technique is to temper the beaten eggs and lemon juice with liquid from the recipe you are making. It is important to slowly add that hot liquid while continuing to beat the eggs, then just as slowly, add it all back to the pot. Continue to cook on low heat and stir until it thickens slightly, but do not boil or it will curdle.

We have included serving sizes for all the recipes, but they are approximate and to be used as guidelines.

Introduction

Come, let us dance and make a feast of joy.

—*Ancient toast*

Elizabeth

On November 25, 1993, our beautiful mother, Poppy Sardonis, passed from this earth after a long illness, to join our dad, Jim, who had died on April 29, 1980. Among the many lovely cards of condolence was one I received from a very dear family friend. She related how shortly after her mother's death, while she was making kourambiethes, a Greek cookie, one of her friends dropped by. They sat down together to enjoy a few pieces with a cup of coffee and the friend said, "These kourambiethes were made with your mother's hands. She will always be with you." When I read these words, they were very comforting. Even now, each time I mix the feta and spinach ingredients for spanakopita, spinach pie, or pour warm honey over my baklava, that famous Greek nut pastry, I feel my mother here with me, encouraging and inspiring me as she always did.

Our dear parents celebrated life through the enjoyment of food with family and friends. They were both wonderful cooks. Dad had a restaurant when we were growing up and did most of the cooking there. My mother's father, our Papouli Petro, was a baker, and her mother, our Yiayia, was cooking long into her nineties. I still remember her beating the eggs for avgolemono soup, the best I ever had, with Mum's a close second. And so there is a thread that connects us all to the kitchen, from her parents to her and her six siblings, all great cooks, to me and my four siblings. Now our children, at home in the kitchen as anywhere, creative and inspired, are sharing our legacy of love and food, so entwined you can taste it.

In 1997, my sister, Georgia, and her husband, Floyd, invited me and my husband, Dan, to join them on a trip to Greece where they had been a few years before, wanting to bring us to visit the homestead of my mother's side of the family. Thus, our great adventure began, and it was on this trip that we decided to write this book.

It started out as a cookbook, but by the end of our month-long adventure it had evolved into a travel journal filled with recipes passed down through our family, as well as recipes given to us by new friends we met during our travels. We had so much fun on our first trip that we went back two years later with the intention of asking taverna cooks and people we met for some of their own family recipes, hoping to learn a new twist on an old recipe. This time, Georgia and I went to a dance seminar in the tiny village of Roustika on the big island of Crete for ten days, while our non-Greek-speaking husbands had their own adventure, traveling without reservation to the Samarian Gorge and places beyond, returning ten days later to pick us up.

We want to encourage you to go on your own adventure, without worrying about whether or not you speak the language. As long as you have the spirit of adventure and one small (yes, small) suitcase you can go almost anywhere. Since we traveled without reservations, we might have been more willing and open to experiences of all kinds. We engaged people in conversations and shared our stories with one another. We wanted to get to know our roots, which meant getting to know the people. Sensing our sincerity, they responded by bringing us into their world, making us a part of it, and in turn, we got a real sense of who we were. They gave us so much in their generosity of spirit, their kefi.

This book comes from that place in our hearts where our parents and grandparents still live and share their secrets to enjoying life. While cooking family recipes, I often slip back into my mother's kitchen or my father's restaurant, where the wonderful aromas connect to happy memories. Now new recipes connect to generous people who shared them with us. We hope to weave some of these memories in with the recipes of this book. And so the tradition of the Greek kitchen continues. It is always a Greek feast of joy.

Georgia
"A time to mourn and a time to dance..."

I have bittersweet memories of both my daughter's and my mother's comings and goings, their life dances. The young dance of my daughter, the seasoned dance of my mother: the spirit is the same, the steps are different. The grace that comes with age or the exuberance of youth, like a regional difference, creates variation in the pattern of dance steps. Both women's courage is a constant reminder of their attitude to learn, in fact, to seek new adventure, new steps to their dance. I, in the middle, look both ways to the comfort of the old steps and the excitement of the new. I will be attending the Fifth Annual Greek Dance Seminar on the island of Crete. This will be my first trip to Greece, a place sacred to me because of our family's heritage. A place to heal after mourning my mother's death, a place that will touch my soul like no other and connect me with the Greek spirit, the kefi, that will lead me on a new journey, a new dance.

I thought I knew how to dance. I thought I knew how to cook. The childhood memories I have of growing up in New Hampshire are still bright in my mind and warm in my heart. Both sets of grandparents arrived in America from Greece in the early 1900s. Here on Ellis Island the paternal family name, Sardounis, only lost its "u" to become Sardonis. The maternal family name, Kakakos, became Comas, an adulterated transliteration for the Greek word for "baker" (psomas), which was the profession of our grandfather. My earliest memories were created in the home of our paternal grandparents, Papou and Nona Sardonis; a little house surrounded by gardens and grapevines. My dad had respected the customary Greek tradition of bringing his bride to the home of his elderly parents. Dad's two older brothers had died young before he was married and we knew only a younger brother who lived far from us. We five children were very young when Papou and Nona died, but those early impressions of life there are imbedded deeply in each of us. Later it was with my mother's very large family in Maine that we spent all our holidays and many Sunday dinners playing with the clan of eighteen cousins and all of us feasting with the sixteen aunts and uncles–aunts who would often break into harmonies of Greek ballads while cooking, uncles who could twirl in a few steps of dance in the living room. Oh, how I loved to listen to the stories at bedtime! It was with this family that we shared so much time and learned about the homestead on the Mani peninsula of Greece, where all the adults had visited.

We were always told that the relatives waited to welcome the next generation of the Kakakos-Comas family, so we made it a mission to visit on our first trip to Greece in 1994. In 2006 as we were preparing another visit I happened to be looking at my baby book and noticed for the first time the tiny print of my mother's writing in the genealogy, the village name, Kertezi, in the northern Peloponnese. This was the home of our grandfather Sardonis. I knew only that he had met his wife in Patras and lived nearby. It was very exciting to think about finding this homestead, a place where no family member had ever visited.

Having gone to every Glendi, party, in our Greek church community, I loved being a part of the ever spiraling circles of Greek dances at summer picnics, urged on by the sounds of the bouzouki and clarinets marking the familiar Oriental rhythms. We all, some longer than others, went to Greek School on weekday afternoons to learn to read and write the Greek language. At home the food was always delicious and Greek. The house was fragrant with roasts seasoned with oregano and mint, or the sweetness of honey syrup, simmering on the back burner. These perfumes were occasionally interrupted by the acrid smells wafting up from the cellar where Papou brewed Retsina wine and ouzo, fire water, in his mysterious laboratory, the wine cellar. In his gardens, which flanked our home, I helped him weed the onion patch and plant the gladiola bulbs; my rewards were strolling through the rows of pole beans towering above me and snacking on their bright greenness! He tactfully employed me to guard the cherry trees by scaring away birds with the rag top sapling he had made for me and promised the reward of the little ruby red fruit that tasted as good as candy.

Surrounded by family cooking and feasting, and singing and dancing, it was natural for me to think I knew how to cook and how to dance! But I began to learn while traveling through Greece where the regional variations in both cooking and dancing, like facets of a gem, each reflect a different taste, a different step. In cuisine, the recipes are familiar but the variations are in the herbs of a particular hillside on an island, or in the oil of the olive groves of the sandy arid south, or in the butter from the shepherd's country of the north. In dance, the circles may move sprightly up and down, mimicking the movement of waves near the sea, or be slow and steady like the ancient movement around a millstone threshing the grain. And still there can be more variation in local combinations and individual flourishes, and even different words for the same dish! What stays the same is the kefi, the spirit that permeates and unites all life in Greece. As we move in our own circle of travel, we begin to taste the origins of the familiar cinnamon touch in tomato sauce of our Peloponnese roots, rice-and dill-stuffed veggies, and leaves wrapped around a hundred different fillings, a very ancient tradition indeed! Nut-filled pastries and layered pastas! All these are Persian, Arabic, Turkish, and Italian pieces of the culinary mosaic of Greece.

In each generation, starting with our grandparents in America, non-Greeks married into our family, so that the authentic Greek traditions, an important part of our Greek-American experience, have been passed down primarily through the foods that we prepare.

Our travel adventures were truly an exciting experience of discovery of new culinary delights, new variations of dance, and, most important, finding the final link to our ancestral roots, the ties that bind our family.

Georgia

The Ties That Bind

These few lines poignantly capture the sentiment of our family meals then and now:

"So the meal came to an end and they were knit together again by it. Their lives parted now and each went his way, but three times a day they were knit together bodily. The body was their tie, the sameness of their blood and flesh. They met together and ate and drank and they renewed their flesh and their blood. They rose refreshed and ready to live apart for awhile. In the search for what they wanted beyond the body, they lived alone. But they would come together again and again so they were never lost in loneliness."

— *The Time Is Noon,* Pearl S. Buck

Our Family

GEORGIA

While the journey of generations slowly moves through our kitchens, we connect good food with good memories. There is something magical that can happen when we, as children, stand by the apron strings of our mothers or fathers, grandmothers or grandfathers, aunts or uncles. By a cultural osmosis we absorb the techniques of cooking. Our senses are tuned to these defining nuances by holding the beater for avgolemono sauce, fingering the texture of dough for phoenekia, seeing the color for the perfect golden brown baklava, smelling the intoxicating aroma of onion-dill-laced spanakopita, rolling the tidy packets of minted dolmathes, even listening to the discussion or debate about the proper herbs for keftethakia or the best béchamel for pastitsio.

We are still part of what our grandparents and parents were. Those first family travelers came to America from the Peloponnese and that almost-island-blood flows like a torrent through our beings. We're embraced by the memories of grandfathers who baked bread and brewed wine, a grandmother who sang the past and one who whispered the future, all celebrations of life.

Our parents, the first generation of our Greek-American family, passed on the culinary secrets without necessarily knowing they were planting the seeds for our Greek feast of joy. Now, we give to our children and grandchildren the gifts of recipes and our memories, keys to unlocking the timeless dance of our family circle as it spins from the past to the present to the future.

So the dance continues.

Nona
Andriana Philepeou Sardounis

I remember the family story of our Papou Elias Sardounis, from Kertezi in the mountains meeting our grandmother, Nona Andriana Philepeou, a city girl from Patras by the sea. They made a striking couple, as he was a tall, lanky six-footer and she was petite and very short. He always used to say that he just picked her up and put her in his pocket to come to America in 1911.

In a storage room behind our kitchen the tin-covered travel trunks from Greece were tucked away. Every now and then I would sneak in and lift the lid of one and stare at the carefully folded linens: a white curtain with pale green designs and tiny stitches, pillowcases with embroidered pastel edges, a heavy gold and ivory woven coverlet, white cotton nightgowns with wide crocheted straps, a rosy magenta brocade tablecloth. All these treasures, probably part of her dowry, seemed to be still too precious to use, these remembrances of her other life left behind.

As Papou's wine cellar was his private domain, hers was the finished room in the basement. Here in the corner by the window stood her old treadle Singer sewing machine with the shelf covered with giant spools of coarse black and white threads, ready for mending or creating new aprons and house dresses. For me she'd fashioned tiny pockets of soft red cloth filled with crushed seashells, then closed up with tiny stitches. These were amulets pinned to my clothing to protect me from the evil eye. I wonder if she was the one who first taught me to thread a needle and make the long, lusciously fragrant necklaces by stringing small single blossoms of lavender lilacs from the bushes that guarded our front door.

After having four sons she delighted in her first two granddaughters, Elizabeth and me, little baby girls to decorate with ribbons and ruffles and roses! There are many photos of us with big round Rugosa rose blossoms pinned in our hair. These same rosebushes from our gardens provided the flowers for her to make rose-petal glyko, the spoon-sweet offered to every guest.

I used to think it was very special to go with her across the street to her friend Kyria Eleni's house to make filo. I watched in amazement as they rolled out paper-thin sheets of dough, growing large enough to drape like a tablecloth almost to the floor. Then they cut the filo into squares and stacked them into covered piles, ready for the

14

making of the week's pites and pastries. Later they shared "kouventoules," little chats, as they'd enjoy their Greek coffee in the pale green and yellow demitasse cups. Kyria Eleni, after finishing her coffee, would carefully turn her cup upside down on a saucer. Nona then assumed her role as the neighborhood "kafetzou," the reader of the patterned coffee grounds as they slithered and hung on the inside of the cups. With her hands still aglow with the traces of olive oil, she turned the cup over and twirled it round and round reading what the future would bring: Travels? Illness? Joys? Funerals? Weddings? Visits? Naturally, I listened and believed every word, especially when she would lift me onto her lap, point to my forehead and remind me that my destiny was written there. She was our family's Delphic oracle.

Papou
Elias Sotiri Sardounis

Our paternal grandfather, a towering six-footer even at his slightly stooped age of ninety-four, came from the village of Kertezi in the northern mountains of the Peloponnese. We discovered from our visit there in 2006 that it is known for wonderful beans and glorious wine. Papou introduced us to his homemade wine, Retsina, at Sunday dinner, when, employing an ancient ritual, he'd mix a small amount of wine with water and present it to us when we turned ten. We loved his coq au vin (kotopoulo methismeno, "drunken little chicken"), made with pheasants he trapped in our backyard and braised for hours with his own glorious Retsina. I can still picture him stirring the stockpot of fasolatha (bean soup) with a long wooden spoon sampling every now and then until he finally exclaimed, "Nostimo!" (tasty!), He created our cold medicine, too, a soup concocted with noodles and wine!

He was a splendid gardener, flanking our family home with carefully tended vegetables, flowers, fruit trees and his precious grapevines. He provided the family with that universal and ancient essential, a gift from the gods, wine.

Yiayia
Maria Stelianakou Kakakou/Comas

Our Yiayia was born and raised in a hillside village near Gythio, the seaport for ancient Sparta on the southern Peloponnese. A blue-eyed, red-headed beauty, Maria was famous in the region for her singing of lamentations for the deceased person's life. These songs were improvised at the gravesite and were performed by women only. Called *Mirologia* ("words of destiny"), this ancient tradition dates from Homer's time but now is largely extinct in parts of Greece.

The story of her meeting our grandfather, Pieros Kakakos, is not one of love at first sight, but rather love at first song. Pieros, who lived in a neighboring village, had walked the hills to Yiayia's village to attend a funeral. As he approached the gathering he heard an angelic voice singing the dirge. He fell in love with that voice before he had even seen the lovely young woman with the sky-blue eyes and rose-pink beauty who owned it.

To us Yiayia was a wonderfully inventive cook, perhaps because of the challenge she faced raising twelve children with limited means. An example of her inventiveness and a family favorite through three generations is Hot Dog Stew, which originated in her kitchen at the pleading of her children, who wanted to eat hot dogs on Saturday night like all their Yankee friends. Having been warned by her husband, who'd worked in a meat cutting factory upon arriving in America, that the mysterious ingredients in hot dogs were less than healthy and even unknown, she assured him that her way of cooking them would render them "sterilized" as well as delicious. She braised her concoction of onions, tomatoes, potatoes, hot dogs and peas for hours. Her husband relented, and Hot Dog Stew became the Saturday-night staple for the children in this Greek kitchen.

Though Yiayia was a widow for thirty years, she was fortunate to live independently until the last few months of her long life. When we visited her in the nursing home, she was happy to show us what was in her night table drawer: a jar of Greek oregano and a yellow plastic lemon full of juice that she kept to season her food.

Papouli Petro
Pieros Kakakos Comas

Our Comas grandfather, known as Little Grampy Peter, grew up in Neo Hori, another hill town near Gythio. He loved school but when his father made him quit to work in the olive groves, he ran away to Athens to become a baker. Then as the father of a large family, he could always provide the basic source of nourishment for body and soul, fresh and fragrant soft Greek bread. The children were taught at an early age that bread was precious, and if a piece of bread fell on the floor they were to immediately pick it up and kiss it in appreciation. Lynne Rossetto Kasper, author of *The Italian Country Table*, notes in her research a reference to this custom also in Sicily, an early colony of the ancient Greeks, for whom bread was even an offering to the gods!

Mom remembered how her father would entice her and her sisters to help in the bakery by telling stories from the *Iliad* and the *Odyssey*. While sitting on lumpy bags of flour (from whose flower-printed cotton sacks Yiayia would sew dresses for her four little girls) waiting for the dough to rise, they held their breath in dusty anticipation to hear the story's climax! Papouli Petro usually saved that for the next day's telling. The favorite bakery snacks he made for them were as tasty as today's trendy white pizzas. He rolled out scraps of dough, spread them with beaten eggs, crumbled feta cheese, sprinkles of oregano, drizzled with olive oil and baked them in his ovens. He'd also treat the children with another bread delight. On Friday nights, he'd seal the Yankee neighbors' bean pots with strips of dough (a tradition of sealing pottery casseroles used by ancient cooks), preparing them for the usual Saturday dinners. After the long, slow bake all night, these now crusty strips were soaked with the steamy juices of the flavors of Boston Baked Beans. These were the luscious rewards for his faithful helpers.

Mom
Penelope "Poppy" Comas Sardonis

One of four lovely Comas sisters, our mother, Poppy, was the family beauty. A strawberry blonde in her youth, she maintained a sparkle in her beautiful blue eyes and spirit throughout her life. As she gracefully grew older, she continued to make new friends and enjoy people of all ages, who were attracted to her strong but gentle spirit and youthful, optimistic personality. Sharing the treasures she created in her kitchen was a special pleasure!

She was the first true muse for me. She went about her marvelous cooking with a love and joy that was contagious. It was at her side I learned to add a strip of orange rind to the simmering honey syrup for pastries; to use lemon and tomatoes together, a combination particular to the Peloponnese; to ladle hot broth into the foamy beaten eggs and lemon juice before stirring the mix into chicken soup; to make angled slits in the leg of lamb for the slivers of garlic to slide into; to roll dessert dough with a long skinny wooden dowel for sheer thinness. The list of culinary secrets is long and quietly slipped into my consciousness without my knowing it. A gift for me.

What influenced me most was her flexibility in using leftovers for new creations and substituting ingredients for adaptations of old standards. To me this was a testament to her ease and ability to keep a dish authentic yet creative. Her love of sharing food, whether an appetizer or a feast, was a natural part of her, as well as a legacy of "Philoxenia," Greek hospitality.

She told us about this story she grew up with which was food folklore from Mani: Around Christmas, the children would put a chair by the door with a plate of tiganites, a fried dough called Lalangia. The fragrant aroma of these treats was to appease the mischievous imps who were said to prowl the earth during this time. In the morning the plate was empty. At Papouli Petro's bakery there was no shortage of bread dough. Yiayia would roll out big chunks of risen dough into long strips; cut them and tie them into knots before frying them in hot oil. Sprinkled with honey or grated cheese, these treats appeased both children and the other imps! The poem which the kids chanted as they arranged the Lalangia on the plate went as follows:

Ee aroritehs edhonteh	The little imps are coming
Ta pehthia geerevonteh	They're looking for the children
Tiganeetehs thelooneh	They really want some fried treats
Ee ta pehthia the parooneh!	Or else they'll take the children!

18

Dad
James L. "Jim" Sardonis

Our dad's first encounter with Mom's tradition of hospitality was after a youth-group meeting at her church, where he was a speaker. Her family of brothers and sisters invited him to their home for refreshments. Following the custom of a fine Greek hostess and already star struck by his handsome eloquence, she carried a silver tray with his tall glass of cool water and a spoonful of "visino," cherry spoon-sweets. In her nervous excitement she proceeded to spill the tray all over him. This inauspicious moment began their very long and loving life together. Our mother kept their love letters—Dad's tied in silver ribbon, hers tied in gold—in her cedar chest her whole life long.

Dad was an entrepreneur par excellence. In the middle of his varied careers, he owned, managed, and cooked in a restaurant he created and called Sardy's. It was a classic American diner, but he could not ignore his culinary heritage. Though he never cooked at home, at his restaurant he spiced the burgers with oregano, seasoned the chicken rice soup with splashes of lemon, and doused the coleslaw with olive oil and vinegar. The one fully Greek item and very popular entrée was lamb on the stick with sides of coleslaw and rice pilaf. The chicken croquettes, so trendy in the fifties, were much like the Greek tomato or squash fritters we ate in Greece. These were simply flour-dusted mixtures fried in oil at the perfect temperature.

Occasionally, he added a Greek dessert, his mother's recipe for Rizogalo or, rice pudding, which was very popular.

Aunt Emmy
Emilie Comas Cherry

Crooning melancholy Greek love songs or dulcet lullabies, Aunt Emmy has the most beautiful voice in the family. I remember her singing melodious duets with Mom and Aunt Effie, casting a spell of musical reverie. She always baked hundreds of crispy cookies each year for her church's Greek Festival and holidays. Her Greek biscotti-type creations, redolent with cinnamon, are the all-time best for dunking in coffee, tea, or milk.

Uncle Sam
Sarando Comas

I cherish the memory of Uncle Sam with his twinkling eyes, enchanting smile and quiet kefi. He could keep the intricate rhythm of a slow and steamy Greek circle dance while balancing a tray of ouzos on his head and never missing a beat nor spilling a drop.

He flourished his flamboyant terms of endearment on his wife, Aunt Effie, who was always dancing and singing by his side. "Agapoula mou" (my little love), "Chryso mou" (my precious one), "Lahtara mou" (my longing), "Trella mou" (my thrill). So romantic! His favorite dish was the Greek classic, braised celery with pork.

Aunt Lily
Lillian Comas Soffron

Aunt Lily, the first in the close band of sisters, had a regal style that glowed about her. This was a perfect quality for her hostessing the many guests at their family restaurant, the Village Pancake House. In her own home the fragrance of roasting chicken with lemon and oregano wafted through the kitchen to greet us as frequent Sunday dinner guests. My sister and I always insisted that hers was the best avgolemono chicken soup, while our cousin Peter insisted our mother's was the best. Was it because one used rice and the other orzo? Both were equally tangy, creamy and comforting. We, the cousins, kindly honored both mothers!

Aunt Helen
Helene Comas Giftos

Fun, flirtatious and feisty are three words that describe Aunt Helen. Her indomitable spirit guides her every endeavor. One of our favorite quotes that she taught us, once we became Yiayias, is "To paithi tou paithiou mou, thio fores paithi mou": "The child of my child, is my child, two times over"—a sentiment perhaps only a grandparent can understand.

In her hometown she has always been known for her community projects as well as her famous Moussaka, which she describes so deliciously that she tantalizes you before you even taste her scrumptious casserole

Uncle George
George Comas

George, the oldest Comas brother, had a very exotic career as a ship's steward cooking for the crew of an international freighter. Like most Greeks he was a marvelous story-teller, mesmerizing his audience with his raspy-voiced tales of his adventures at sea. Our favorite was about dining with a ruby-ringed maharaja in India. His wife, Aunt Bea, who lived to be ninety-three and still wrote poetry every day, described him best with these words:

"George is like Plato, who when offering advice on dietary matters, claimed that cheese and olives are essential to the attainment of a healthy old age. Feta cheese, Kalamata olives, tomatoes, yogurt, honey, olive oil, greens and an abundance of lemons and chicken stock are part of our perennial provisions."

It's always fun to listen to Aunt Bea's comments about their marriage as "a little bit Yankee and a lot Greek" working together in their ethnic kitchen. For Bea, discovering herbs and spices was a happy revelation. For Uncle George herbs and spices were meant to be blended from every cuisine! baked eggplant, onion, garlic, and tomatoes bathed in a rich, cheesy milk sauce.

We remember, above all, the signature recipes forever linked to these great cooks in our family.

Kali Orexi! Enjoy.

Seasoning: An Art I Had Not Learned

Day followed soggy
dumpling day . . . blobs of bland
flour paste . . . occasional
sugar-frosted holiday
gritty gravel sweetness on
Puritan coated tongue. Flavorless
my ways. Seasoning an art I
had not learned until
I curled my lips around those names:
Coriander, basil, fennel, thyme,
Ginger, curry, cardamom and clove.
Crushed red peppers hissed
their fury . . . spat their flame . . .
chilies dangerous as a wildcat's
purr. Sadistic claws nipped, pricked,
stabbed my taste. They twisted
slinky bodies around my legs
staring at me with unblinking
saffron gaze that dared
me stroke their fur.

—Beatrice H. Comas

23

Nona's Rice Pudding
Rizogalo
Serves 8–10

This is a creamy, vanilla flavored pudding, common in every Greek kitchen.

1½ c boiling water
½ c of short-grain white rice
¼ t salt
7½ c milk
4 T cornstarch

1 c sugar
1 strip of lemon peel
1 T vanilla
Ground cinnamon

Wash rice and drain. In a large saucepan add rice and salt to boiling water, stir, cover and cook slowly until most of the water is absorbed. Add the milk, stir and simmer for about 20 minutes. Dissolve the cornstarch in a little water and gradually add it to the rice mixture along with the sugar and lemon peel. Stir constantly over medium heat until pudding turns thick and creamy, about 15 more minutes, making sure the rice is thoroughly soft. Remove lemon peel and stir in vanilla. Pour into small individual bowls and sprinkle generously with cinnamon.

Papou's Simple Noodle Soup in Wine
Bigouli
Serves 4–6

This is our grandfather's own creation. He believed it to be the perfect cure-all at the first sign of a cough or sneeze.

½ lb very fine egg noodles (fideo)
2 quarts of water
1 t salt or to taste
2 c Retsina wine or Sauvignon Blanc

In a medium saucepan, bring water to a boil, add the noodles and salt and cook until noodles are done. Add the wine and heat.

Yiayia's Fragrant Stuffed Peppers
Piperies Yemistes
Serves 6

When we visited our Yiayia, we could depend on having these lamb-and herb-stuffed peppers that smelled so good, because they were one of our favorites.

6 large green peppers
2 medium onions chopped
½ c olive oil
½ lb ground lamb or beef
½ c uncooked long grain rice
2 T minced parsley
2 T pine nuts

2 T fresh dill
1 clove garlic minced
1 t salt
1¼ c tomato juice
Olive oil for drizzling
2 T Parmesan cheese
¾ c water or tomato juice for baking pan

Slice tops off peppers and remove seeds. Cut a thin slice from the bottom of each pepper if they won't stand upright in the pan. Cook onions in hot oil until soft. Add meat and cook until it loses its pink color. Add rice and stir until glazed with oil. Add parsley, dill, garlic, pine nuts, salt and tomato juice. Cook covered until most of liquid is absorbed. Cool slightly then stuff peppers with this mixture. If there is more filling left, put it in the pan around the peppers. Brush outside of peppers with olive oil. Place in oiled casserole and sprinkle cheese on top. Pour additional juice or water in pan and drizzle each pepper with olive oil. Bake for one hour in a preheated oven at 350 degrees F. with pan lightly covered with foil.

Papouli Petro's White Pizza [adapted]
Psomakia Me Feta sto Fourno
Serves 4–6

Papouli Petro was ahead of his time with a white pizza, using feta cheese and red pepper flakes to give his pizza its tang.

1 package oat bran, flax, and wheat flour pita bread or any pizza crust
1 c crumbled feta cheese
½ c olive oil, plus some for drizzling
2 T dried Greek oregano
Red hot pepper flakes to taste
¾ c Italian peppers, chopped and fried (optional)
Salt and pepper

Brush each pita with olive oil and season with salt and pepper. In a small bowl mix the feta, olive oil, pepper flakes, oregano and divide and spread among the pita breads. Sprinkle with the chopped fried Italian peppers, if using. Drizzle each pita with a little more olive oil. Bake in a preheated oven at 400 degrees F. until feta softens and bubbles, about ten minutes.

Mom's Spinach and Cheese Pie
Spanakopita
Serves 12 or more

Mom's use of lots of onions in this famous, buttery pita makes it extraordinary.

2 10-oz bags fresh spinach
2 large onions, chopped
1 bunch green onions, chopped
1 lb feta cheese, crumbled

5 eggs
½ c fresh dill, chopped
½ t each salt and pepper
1 lb butter, melted
16 leaves filo dough

Preheat oven to 400 degrees F. Wash spinach and drain very well. Chop spinach coarsely. In a large bowl, mix spinach with onions, green onions, feta cheese, dill, salt, pepper and eggs. Toss to mix all ingredients. In a buttered 10- by 15-inch pan place eight filo sheets, buttering each one. Spread the spinach filling, then cover with eight more sheets, buttering each one. Tuck in edges of sheets to fit pan, making sure to butter edges well. Lightly score top of the spanakopita to release steam. Place foil over top of pan for the first half hour of baking. Then remove foil and continue baking for another half hour or until golden brown all over. Cool slightly before cutting into squares to serve.

Mom's Chicken, Potatoes and Peas
Kotopoulo me Patates ke Pizelia
Serves 4–6

Instead of hot dogs which her mother used to use in this stew, Mom substituted chicken. We especially loved the leftover potatoes and peas of this casserole the next day.

2 lb chicken pieces
5 T butter
1 c chopped onions
½ c dry white wine
2 c canned tomatoes
1 c tomato sauce

1 c chicken broth
5–6 potatoes, quartered
1 package frozen peas
1 clove garlic, minced
Salt and pepper

In a large skillet, season chicken with salt and pepper and brown in butter; remove to deep saucepan. Sauté onions in pan drippings then add garlic and pour over chicken. Add wine, cover and simmer for ten minutes. Add tomatoes, tomato sauce, broth, and potatoes. Cook slowly for about one hour until chicken and potatoes are cooked and sauce has thickened. About ten minutes before hour is up, add peas and continue to cook for ten minutes more until peas are done. Serve with feta cheese on the side if desired.

Athenian Chicken in Filo
Kotopoulo Aromatiko se Filo
Makes 10 rolls

When Mom's friend gave her this recipe, it instantly became a family favorite. The combination of the baked feta and wine in the filling makes it fabulous.

5 skinless, boneless chicken breasts,
    halved and pounded flat
Marinade:
1 c white wine
½ c olive oil
3 cloves garlic, chopped
½ t dried oregano
1 bay leaf
¼ t each salt and pepper

Filling:
1 lb feta cheese
2 T grated Romano cheese
1 egg
¼ c white wine
¼ c chopped scallions
20 leaves of filo dough
½ lb melted butter

Marinate chicken in wine, olive oil, garlic, oregano, bay leaf, salt and pepper. Refrigerate overnight. Bring the filo to room temperature (about thirty minutes out of refrigerator). Mix feta, Romano, and egg. Bring ¼ cup of white wine to a boil with the chopped scallions. Simmer for about three minutes, then cool. Add to the cheese mixture. Place a chicken breast half on a flat surface and put two tablespoons. of cheese mixture in center and roll up. Set aside until all the chicken breasts have been used.

Place two filo leaves on the flat surface on top of each other, buttering each one. .Fold the bottom up about two inches and put one rolled chicken breast on this little "apron." Fold both sides in and roll up creating a rolled package. Continue with each chicken breast. Place rolls in buttered baking pan and brush with melted butter.

Bake in moderate oven preheated at 350 degrees F. for one hour until golden brown.

Mom's Egg-Lemon Chicken Soup
Avgolemono Soupa
Serves 4–6

This is the most famous Greek soup. The egg-lemon sauce transforms it into creamy magnificence.

2 quarts chicken broth
1 c orzo pasta
3 large eggs
½ c lemon juice
Salt and pepper to taste

Bring broth to boil and add orzo. Cook, partly covered, over medium low heat for about 15 minutes, or until the orzo is cooked. Remove from heat. In a medium bowl, beat the egg whites until very frothy. Add lemon juice and continue beating. Add egg yolks and beat. Take about one cup of warm broth and add to the egg mixture, beating gently. Pour into the soup. Put the soup back on medium low heat, stirring constantly in a figure 8 for about ten minutes until soup thickens slightly and gets creamy yellow. Do not boil or it will curdle. Season with salt and pepper.

Mom's Custard Baked in Filo with Honey
Galatoboureko
Serves 8

The contrast between the crisp filo crust and the silky custard with the bath of honey syrup makes this an elegant special dessert.

Syrup:
2 c sugar
1 c water
3 thin lemon slices

1 cinnamon stick
1 c honey

Custard:
4 c milk
¾ c farina (cream of wheat)
5 eggs
1 c sugar

1 t lemon zest
1 t vanilla
16 sheets of filo
1 c butter, melted

Combine all ingredients for syrup except honey and bring to a boil. Reduce heat; simmer for ten minutes. Remove lemon slices and cinnamon stick and stir in honey and blend. Allow syrup to cool.

In a deep saucepan heat milk and farina, stirring constantly until it thickens and barely reaches the boiling point, being careful not to scorch it. Remove immediately from heat; cool five minutes. In a bowl, beat eggs and sugar until fluffy; add to farina mixture. Add lemon zest and vanilla; blend well. Place eight filo sheets in a buttered 9- by 13-inch baking pan, brushing each sheet generously with butter. Allow filo to extend up sides of pan. Spread filling evenly over filo; fold overhanging filo over the filling and brush with butter. Cover with eight more buttered filo sheets, which have been trimmed to fit the pan. With a sharp knife, score only through the top filo layers, making four equal rows lengthwise.

Bake at 350 degrees F. for 45 minutes until golden. Pour cold syrup evenly over hot pastry. Let stand 2 hours before serving. Cut into diamonds or squares. This pastry is best served the day it is made. Refrigerate any leftovers.

Dad's Lamb-on-the-Stick at Sardy's
Souvlaki Arni
Serves 6

It was such a treat to go have dinner with Dad at his restaurant. He always made extra of this marinated lamb dish when he knew we were coming.

1 lb boneless lamb cut into 1½-inch cubes
2 medium white or red onions quartered
2–3 green peppers seeded and cut into 1½-inch squares
Several small tomatoes quartered
    or whole cherry tomatoes

Marinade:
¼ c lemon juice
½ c olive oil
1 T dried Greek oregano
½ t each salt and pepper
2 cloves garlic minced

Marinate meat in a plastic bag for several hours before broiling or grilling. Reserve marinade. Slip chunks of lamb onto eight inch skewers with onion, tomato, and pepper pieces alternating with meat. Brush with marinade and broil 8 inches from heat, or barbecue over medium coals. Brush with marinade while cooking.

Dad's Coleslaw at Sardy's
Lahanosalata
Serves 6

We grew up never having mayonnaise in coleslaw.

4 c of green cabbage finely shredded	4 T olive oil
1 c carrots finely shredded	4 T apple cider vinegar
¼ c green onions chopped	1 T sugar
¼ c fresh dill chopped	¼ t each salt and pepper
1 clove garlic minced	3 T fresh chopped parsley
1 T celery seed	¼ t stoneground mustard

In a bowl, combine all vegetables. In a small container combine the vinaigrette and shake. Pour over the vegetables and toss well.

Uncle George's Almond Pilaf
Pilafi me Amygthala
Serves 4–5

Because Uncle George traveled the world, he often came back with a different twist on an old classic.

2 c water	¼ c melted butter
1 c rice	3 T lemon juice
1 t salt	¾ c toasted almonds
½ t turmeric or a few pinches of saffron	¼ c minced parsley

In a large saucepan, bring 2 cups of water to a boil. Add salt and rice. Cover and return to a boil. Cook over low heat for 25 minutes or until tender. Mix in turmeric or saffron. Stir in butter, lemon juice, almonds and parsley. Heat through. Serve sprinkled with additional almonds if desired.

Uncle Sam's Braised Pork with Celery in Egg-Lemon Sauce
Selino Me Kreas Avgolemono
Serves 6

The rich taste of the pork and the soft feel of the celery create a perfect balance for this lemony stew.

1/3 c olive oil
1½ lb boneless pork cut into stewing pieces
4 c celery cut into 2-inch pieces with leaves
2 bay leaves
3 c chicken broth or water

1½ c dry white wine
Salt and pepper to taste
2 eggs
½ c fresh lemon juice

In a large stewing pot, heat oil over medium heat. Add pork cubes a few at a time, season with salt and pepper and brown on all sides. Add celery, broth or water, wine, bay leaves and bring to a boil. Reduce heat and simmer for about 1 hour and 45 minutes, until pork is fork-tender and celery is very soft. If necessary, add more liquid to maintain at least a cup during simmering.

To make sauce: Beat 2 eggs with lemon juice until thick and frothy. Still beating, very slowly add 2 ladles full of simmering liquid from the stew pot, one at a time, to the egg mixture . Slowly pour sauce over pork and celery. Stir well on the lowest heat for about a minute. Remove bay leaves. Serve with rice.

Aunt Lily's Roast Chicken and Potatoes with Oregano
Kotopoulo Riganato
Serves 4

On the way to visit Aunt Lily, our mouths watered just thinking about her roast chicken and potatoes.

2 lb roasting potatoes,
   quartered lengthwise
1 whole chicken (4–5 lb)
½ c fresh lemon juice
½ c olive oil
½ T salt or to taste

Black pepper to taste
6 cloves crushed garlic
¼ c dried Greek oregano
3–4 bay leaves
1 T butter
2 c chicken broth or water

Preheat oven to 375 degrees F. In a small bowl mix lemon juice, olive oil, salt and pepper, then brush the chicken all over with the mix. Place the chicken in a deep heavy baking dish and surround with potatoes, garlic and bay leaves in a single layer. Sprinkle the chicken with oregano and dot with butter. Pour the rest of the oil mixture and the broth or water over the potatoes and roast uncovered for 15 minutes. Reduce temperature to 350 degrees F. and roast until very tender and the potatoes are soft when pierced with a fork, about 1½ hours. Baste chicken and potatoes, occasionally adding more liquid if necessary.

Aunt Helen's Baked Eggplant Casserole
Moussaka
Serves 8–10

This scrumptious casserole emphasizes the rich flavor that eggplant adds to a dish.

4 medium eggplants
1 large onion, chopped
2 cloves garlic, minced
½ c olive oil
4 T butter
2 lb ground chuck
1½ t each salt and pepper
½ t cinnamon

3 T tomato paste
Fine cracker crumbs
½ c chopped fresh parsley
½ c water
½ c dry red wine
4 c milk
4 eggs
1½ c grated kefalotiri or Parmesan

Slice eggplants into half-inch slices, salt heavily and let stand for an hour. Rinse thoroughly and squeeze between paper towels until dry. Brush both sides with olive oil and bake until soft. Sauté onion in oil and butter, add garlic and meat, salt and pepper and cinnamon. Cook until redness is gone. Add tomato paste diluted with water and wine. Let simmer uncovered until most of the liquid is absorbed, about 20 minutes, then add all the parsley. Butter a 13- by 10- by 3-inch pan and sprinkle lightly with the cracker crumbs. Line with a layer of eggplant slices. Sprinkle with half-cup of grated cheese. Spread meat mixture over this and sprinkle with another half cup of grated cheese. Cover with remaining slices of eggplant. Beat eggs, milk and remaining cheese together until foamy and pour over the casserole, shaking pan so milk mixture spreads. Dot with a little more butter and bake uncovered in a preheated oven for one hour at 350 degrees F. Turn off oven and allow to finish cooking in oven. Cover with foil which has been pierced all over with a fork. Better if served the day after it's cooked. Remove from refrigerator two hours before, heat with foil on for about 30 minutes at 300 degrees F.

Aunt Emmy's Greek Cinnamon Twice Baked Cookies
Paximathia
Makes about 48

We loved dunking these crunchy cookies in milk.

½ c butter
½ c shortening
1½ c sugar
3 large eggs
1 t vanilla extract

2 t baking powder
½ t baking soda
4 cups all-purpose flour
1½ t ground cinnamon

In a large bowl with mixer at low speed, beat butter, shortening, and one cup sugar until blended. Increase speed to high; beat until light and fluffy, about five minutes. At low speed, add eggs, one at a time, and vanilla, and beat until well mixed.

Gradually add baking powder, baking soda, and three cups flour and beat until well blended. With a wooden spoon, stir in remaining one cup of flour until soft dough forms. If necessary, add more flour (up to ½ cup) until dough is easy to handle.

Divide dough into four equal pieces. On lightly floured surface, shape each piece of dough into an eight-inch long log. Place two logs, about four inches apart, on each of the two ungreased large cookie sheets. Flatten each log to 2½ inches wide.

Preheat oven to 350 degrees F., place cookie sheets on two oven racks and bake logs 20 minutes or until lightly browned and toothpick inserted in center comes out clean, rotating cookie sheets between upper and lower racks halfway through the baking. In a pie plate, mix cinnamon with the rest of the sugar.

Remove cookie sheets from oven. Transfer hot loaves (during baking, logs will spread and become loaves) to cutting board; with a serrated knife, cut diagonally into half-inch thick slices. Coat slices well with cinnamon sugar. Return slices, cut side down, to same cookie sheets. Bake slices 15 minutes. Turn slices over and return to oven, rotating cookie sheets between upper and lower racks, and bake 15 minutes longer or until golden. Remove cookies to wire racks to cool. Makes about 4 dozen cookies.

GREECE

Travel Itinerary

1. Athens
2. Skopelos
3. Tinos
4. Santorini
5. Crete
6. Mani
7. Olympia
8. Zakynthos
9. Kalavryta and Kertezi
10. Delphi
11. Meteora
12. Volos to Skopelos

Athens

"O glorious Athens-shining,
violet-crowned, worthy of song."
— Pindar

DAN

Last day to shop for odds and ends, then tomorrow is the final day of packing. We will then go to sleep knowing the next time our heads touch a "real" pillow, we will be sleeping in Athens.

ELIZABETH

We are on board a 747 British Airways plane in LAX bound for London. Jeb drove us to the airport. We will miss all the kids and our darling new first grandson, Jack.

DAN

At 10:20 a.m.—London time, Heathrow Airport—we have found a McDonald's near the Olympic Airways counter (our flight to Greece) that advertises "The Lamb McSpicy." It's a lamb patty with tzadziki sauce on a bun…we have to try it, of course, and it's surprisingly good! We have 1½ hours before the plane leaves for Greece, so Elizabeth is checking out the shops.

GEORGIA

We have landed in Athens and tomorrow Elizabeth and Dan will join us. At the airport we made comments that might have offended the gods. Hubris descended upon us when we said, "Could this be too easy?" So the Greek "thing" happened.

FLOYD

We were excited to be in Athens again, more determined than ever not to be taken by cab drivers, etc. We got in line for a cab and I kept asking, "Poso kahni? How much" (to Athens)? The cab driver who said the magic words, "It's according to the meter" got our luggage and we left for the Thission Hotel. Georgia began talking in Greek and the driver became more and more friendly and relaxed. We got to the hotel fairly quickly and easily, unloaded bags, and walked in to meet our old friend Maria, the young concierge, and our first disaster occurred. I forgot my travel bag with air tickets, passport, and cash in the back seat of the cab. We had a brief moment of panic. Maria and a hotel worker joined in the panic and tried to tell us what to do next, both talking at once. We were just about to take another taxi to the driver's apartment, which he had pointed out to us on the way, near the Dimitrios Hotel, where we had

41

stayed our first time in Greece. Maria was sure she could find the wife by buzzing every apartment and explaining our plight. The wife would next contact her husband by phone, tell him to search the back seat and return our bag to the Thission. Of course, this would be a miracle. Just as we were going out the door, our airport cab came swerving around the corner, the driver madly waving the travel bag. Everyone started crossing themselves, exclaiming, "Thavma! Thavma! A true miracle!" I tipped the driver 2,000 drachma and we breathed easy again.

GEORGIA

Since our room wasn't quite ready, we walked to a nearby familiar café for a drink, then down the block to a market where we bought our traveling staples, olive oil, vinegar, oregano, some Greek tomatoes fresh from a garden, bread, and feta for lunch. We returned to the hotel to find our room was ready. Settling in was leisurely and cool with the new air conditioning. We got our lunch ready and went out to the shady balcony to enjoy it. Competing with the view of the Acropolis was a gypsy family's pickup truck below our balcony. The father, who was inside bartering for his melons and tomatoes, had left the mother and little girl in the back of the truck. It was the sweetest thing to watch the lovely young mother singing and clapping while her tiny girl danced and twirled among the bright green watermelons and shiny red tomatoes. It was complete happiness in the moment.

A very noisy night for sleeping, but the view of the Acropolis is stunning from our balcony. Floyd was up early walking to our old favorite stomps in the Plaka. He came back with a warm Milopita, a sweet apple filling enveloped in golden, buttered filo leaves, from our friend at the corner coffee shop who remembered us. We were showered and out by 11:00 a.m., wandering through the Plaka to Eleni's for lunch. This is the taverna where on our last visit we met a British family on their way to their island vacation home on Alonissos. As we exchanged personal information, the three little girls were enchanted by my story of learning regional Greek dances in a village in Crete and wanted me to show them. I asked the guitar player to play a dance tune and in a minute I was leading these three little English beauties in a circle of happy dancing as the parents clapped and smiled. Because of this memorable moment, Eleni's Taverna will always be a favorite. Today the grilled fish, Tsipoures, and village salad were perfect. The magenta bougainvillea overflowing the walls across the patio formed a lovely enclosure for our long and lazy lunch.

FLOYD

Today we walked a few blocks to the Museum of Cycladic and Ancient Greek art. The small elegant building houses the exquisite collection of Stavros Niarchos, owner of an international shipping company. We lingered over neolithic figurines, pottery, bronzes, and Georgia, of course, can't get her eyes off the jewelry, entranced by the still colorful beads and carved stones of those very ancient times. This museum closes at 3 p.m. on Saturday, but the guard said we could come back tomorrow on the same ticket. Good.

GEORGIA

An ancient museum guard on the second floor stood in the window behind the drapes gazing outside and singing softly with such a sweet voice. I wondered where in his mind he was, certainly not doing his job, a lucky thing for the few who heard him. I told him that was a lovely song. He said "What song?" "Weren't you singing?", I asked. "Who me? Not me," he said with his eyes twinkling. We continued to chat and only when we learned both our families were from the Peloponnesos, that rather isolated, fiercely independent region called Mani, did he accept my compliment. We bonded as patrioti, almost family!

Floyd has been practicing his language skills. The newest terms of endearment for me in his unique Greek are Karpouzi mou, my watermelon; Peponoula mou, my little melon; and Varka mou, my small boat! He said he's feeling quite confident now. "I feel so much more assertive about using my Greek. But, of course, I might end up in "preezone"!

Floyd's Melon Poem

Eho peponya; eho kala peponya!
You can have peponya, if you really wannya!
If you're really choosy, you can have karpoozee.
If you're really lahkee, you can have souvlaki.
It's a surah betta, you can have good feta!

Eho kala – I have good
Peponya – melons
Karpoozi – watermelon
Souvlaki – skewered meat
Feta – Greek cheese

FLOYD

While walking back to the platia it started pouring. We stood under cover for a while then hurried on during the lighter sprinklings. We stopped at a taverna, which will become a regular and favorite, for sure, the Byzantino on Kythathineon Street. That afternoon the sight of a rude American tourist, arguing that she knew better than the waiter what a gyro was, made us cringe. We apologized to the waiter for her rudeness. "Then beerazee," he said it doesn't matter. He brought us two ouzos and shook our hands. Finally the rain stopped and we gingerly climbed the slippery stone staircases out of the Plaka and found our way back to the Thission Hotel.

GEORGIA

After a long siesta we left the hotel in the evening and walked one block away to a grill whose tables were all scattered over the outcroppings of rock in the yard that slopes down from the observatory and St. Marinas Church, facing the Acropolis. We were hardly hungry but forced ourselves to eat juicy, grilled chops, braised zucchini, fresh bread and Retsina before walking to the Phillepeou Theater to watch the famous Dora Stratou Dance Troupe perform the folk dances of every region in Greece. Great beauty and magic here!

"And the sweet singing pipe was mixed with the lyre and the sound of cymbals ..."
—Sappho

ELIZABETH

We are in a cab, telling the driver where we wanted to go. We began to worry because he had no idea where the Thission Hotel was located. Fortunately, I had written down the two cross streets, which he recognized and he knew that was across from the Thission Temple. Still not feeling total confidence in the driver, we tried to see the names of streets we were passing. Suddenly the cab stopped and looking out the window, we were thrilled to see Georgia and Floyd on the balcony across the street, waving to us frantically. We had arrived! We read in a Berlitz guidebook to Greece that the Thission became the popular name for the Temple of Hephaistos, because of the sculpture portraying the Theseus and Hercules legends on the temple, even though the temple was dedicated to Hephaistos, the goldsmith of the gods and god of all metalworkers portrayed on its frieze along with other stories of Hercules.

DAN

After a warm reunion with Georgia and Floyd, we went to our room, excited and happy to be here. Then a shower and clean clothes before we went downstairs to the outside garden café and had warm bread, Retsina and a Greek village salad that tasted so fresh the vegetables must have just been picked.

Village Salad
Horiatiki Salata

This is a simple salad that appears on every menu. The intense flavor of the local tomatoes and cucumbers is what makes it so incredible, so use the freshest produce you can find.

Tomatoes cut in wedges   Kalamata olives
Cucumbers chopped   Feta cheese crumbled
Green bell peppers sliced   Olive oil
Onions sliced

Mix all vegetables and drizzle olive oil over all. Sometimes it is served with lemons or vinegar, salt and pepper to taste.

GEORGIA

The wine, Retsina, has an exotic crisp taste of resin, reminding us of our dad's father, our Papou, who made it in giant oak barrels in our cellar in New Hampshire. He always let us have a tiny glass of it mixed with a lot of water at the Sunday dinners of our childhood. He used to tell us the ancient Greeks lined the porous ceramic wine jars with resin to keep the Persians from wanting to steal it, because it made the wine taste so strong. Over the years the Greeks became accustomed to that flavor and enjoyed it enough to continue using the resin in some of their wines.

"Get hold of the big embellished cups, mix one with water to two of wine, fill them to the top, let one cup follow hard upon the other."
—Alcaeus

ELIZABETH

The only reservation we ever made was for our rooms here at the Thission Hotel on Apostolou St. and Agias Marinas, in the Thission district. We had decided to go here because early in the '70s our Aunt Effie and Uncle Sam had discovered it and loved it. That first night in Athens we found out why. We went up to the roof garden, called

"Tapatsia", for wine and appetizers. Once we were seated under a very black night sky, we looked beyond the vine-covered rail and saw the Parthenon in the golden glow of a full moon. That huge moon looked as though it had been placed there permanently – as though it was tied to this magnificent place drenched in history and light. It was hard to tell if the moonlight was, in fact, reflecting the glory that was Greece or the Acropolis was reflecting the glow of ancient fires witnessed and held onto by the eternal moon. Words caught in my throat along with a sob. I felt a sense of coming home. I turned to my sister and said, "Pinch me."

We raised our glasses to toast not only this splendid sight, but to the memory of our parents, whose loving hearts we feel here with us tonight.

"Aionia Ee Mneemee": May your memory be eternal.

Just then our food arrived and captured our attention. The deep purple edges of the eggplant, "Papoutsakia," which means little shoes, were barely discernible in the melted cheese, golden as the moon. It covered the savory blend of ground meat, ripe juicy tomatoes, onions and herbs all sizzling on the plate before me. The juices bubbled and spilled over the edges of the eggplant as I pierced it with a fork. In unison, we clinked our glasses and toasted "Kali orexi": Enjoy,"

Stuffed Eggplant
Papoutsakia
Serves 6–8

Deep purple eggplant shells holding the perfect blend of ground meat, ripe juicy tomatoes, onions and herbs all sizzling on the plate.

4 large eggplants
¾ c salt for soaking
2 c canola oil for frying
2 T extra virgin olive oil
2 onions finely chopped

1½ lb ground beef
¾ c dry white wine
Salt and pepper to taste
Pinch of cinnamon
1 ½ c tomato sauce

Béchamel Sauce: see recipe below

Wash the eggplants and trim the stems. Cut them in half lengthwise. Fill a large bowl with about 2 quarts water and add the salt. Soak the eggplants in the salted water for about one hour to remove bitterness. Drain and pat them dry.

With a sharp knife, remove enough pulp to leave a half-inch shell and set pulp aside.

Heat the canola oil in a large skillet. Fry the eggplant halves, cut side down, over medium heat until they are soft and brown. Remove the shells and drain on paper towels. Set aside.

In a fairly large saucepan, heat the olive oil and sauté the onions and the pulp over medium heat about five minutes. Add the ground beef, turn the heat to high and continue sautéing until the meat browns. Pour the wine into the pan and stir over high heat until it evaporates, about five more minutes. Season with salt, pepper and cinnamon. Add tomato sauce and stir. Simmer, covered, over medium-low heat, stirring frequently about 30 minutes until sauce thickens. Set aside.

Béchamel Sauce
1 stick unsalted butter
½ c flour
4 c milk

3 large eggs lightly beaten
Salt and pepper to taste
1 c grated Kefalotiri or Romano cheese

To make this sauce, melt the butter in a large saucepan over medium heat. Whisk in the flour until smooth. Add the milk a little at a time, whisking constantly. Simmer over low heat, stirring until mixture has thickened. Remove from heat. Add the beaten eggs, salt and pepper and half the cheese, stirring until smooth.

Arrange the eggplant shells on a large baking sheet and stuff with the meat filling. Top with the béchamel sauce, sprinkle with the remaining cheese, and bake in a preheated oven at 400 degrees F., until the eggplant is very soft and the top golden brown, about 30 minutes. Serve hot.

After dinner, to cap off our first night together, we ordered glasses of 7 Star Metaxa and toasted once again.

DAN

Elizabeth and I woke up at 4 a.m.—our bio clocks were still in California. We could not go back to sleep so we read a bit and watched a rosy dawn creep up on a still-lit Acropolis. As soon as we gave up trying, we both fell asleep until 9 a.m. and met Georgia and Floyd downstairs for breakfast in the hotel's garden patio.

ELIZABETH

We were then energized enough to venture back out to the Plaka, where we roamed for a few hours until the many wonderful aromas of food beckoned us. We wandered into the Ouzeri-Kouklis, where we ordered a tray of mezethakia (appetizers). In an ouzeri, only ouzo, wines and mezethes are served, and many people are seated together at large tables. While waiting for our order, we started talking with a couple seated at our table. When they learned we were sisters they told us there is a specific word to describe two men married to sisters, more than brothers-in-law: "batzanaki." We thought this would be a great time to give our husbands Greek names to use on our travels. Thus Stavro (Floyd) and Niko (Dan) were "born." Just then, our tray arrived overflowing with stuffed grape leaves (dolmathakia), sausages (loukanika), fried cheese (saganaki), and feta dip (htipito). The saganaki had a golden coating that held the lovely, rich creaminess inside, while the feta dip had that perfect hot and salty combination we loved.

Fried Cheese
Saganaki
Serves 4

A sizzling chunk of cheese with a golden coating and rich creaminess inside.

1 8-oz chunk of Kefalotiri, Romano, or any hard cheese
1 c flour
2 T butter and ¼ c olive oil combined
Lemon wedges

Cut the cheese into slices about one-third inch thick. Coat the slices with flour. In a large nonstick skillet, heat the butter and oil and fry the slices until both sides are golden brown and crisp and cheese starts to melt. Place them on a platter and squeeze lemon juice over all.

Fiery Feta Dip
Htipito

The red hot pepper flakes add fire to this cheese dip.

1 lb crumbled feta cheese
2 large red peppers for roasting
(or 2 canned roasted red peppers)
1 clove garlic crushed

1/3 c olive oil
3 T fresh lemon juice
½ t red hot pepper flakes,
   or to taste

If roasting your own, line a baking pan with foil and place peppers in it. Broil in oven until peppers are soft and skin is blistered. Put into paper bag for 20 to 30 minutes. Peel them and remove seeds. Whether using freshly roasted or canned, chop roasted peppers and place in food processor with cheese and garlic and process until creamy. Slowly add oil, red hot pepper flakes and lemon juice and continue to process until thick. Transfer to a serving bowl and chill. Serve with pita wedges, chips or crackers. Makes about a cup of dip.

ELIZABETH

On to Alexander's Taverna—the nightlife is here! It was already 9 p.m. and people were just beginning to fill the tavernas. We climbed a flight of stairs and found everyone in there was dancing. Georgia and I immediately joined in while Dan and Floyd found a table. We requested music for one of our favorite dances, the Tsamiko. The musicians were happy to comply and when word got out that we were Greek-American sisters, people started throwing money at us while we danced, which seemed to be this taverna's custom. When we returned to our table, the lovely people behind us had sent over two wonderful bottles of wine and toasted us. We in return sent them the "liquid silk" Greek brandy called Metaxa and raised our glasses to them! Having filled ourselves with mezethes, we were not planning to order meals, however, the waiter who came to take our order had a bit of an "attitude" when we told him that, so we compromised and ordered bowls of olives, feta and bread to go with our wine. This seemed to satisfy him.

It is now 3 a.m. and we must get some sleep. Long after we get back to our hotel there are people in the streets. Tomorrow we will attempt to see the Agora, the once throbbing heart of the ancient city where all activities from political to religious to trading and entertainment took place. The modern Greek meaning of agora is merely a place to shop. We will visit the Agora Museum, which includes incredible finds from ancient graves as well as beautiful pottery, weapons, jewelry, frescoes, figurines, etc. We also look forward tomorrow night, to seeing the Acropolis Sound and Light Show high up on Pnyx Hill where the historical council took place. But for now I slip into sweet dreams of a haunting bouzouki, that stringed instrument that creates the quintessential sound in Greek music.

"I shall never turn aside from the muses, who rouse me to the dance."
—Euripides

ELIZABETH

The early morning sun helps us start our day. After breakfast we climb the Acropolis, the high part of the city. Among the temples there, the Parthenon, temple to Athena, for me, is the most stunning sight. Nothing prepares me for the majesty and magnitude of these ancient columns. It is overwhelming. The history swallows me alive.

GEORGIA

On our first trip to Athens, Floyd and I wandered through the ancient Agora. We stopped at the foot of the Acropolis to eavesdrop on a tour guide with an American-Southern accent speaking to a group of Americans. They all stood by the front door of a tiny Byzantine chapel, the Church of the Holy Apostles. He explained the prescribed architectural structure of the building and how the human voice of a priest or cantor would resonate as it bounced back and forth on the cross-shaped walls. As soon as they left, we went inside all by ourselves. Embraced by the light reflected from cool stucco and jewel-toned icons, I began to sing the three lines of Kyri' Eleison, a hymn remembered from my childhood church-going with Papou. I marveled that my voice sounded so melodious, almost ancient and sacred, an unforgettable moment for me.

ELIZABETH

Dan and I tried to visit the tiny church Georgia told us about but it was closed for renovations. We read that it was restored to its original form in the 1950s. It contains Byzantine frescoes which we would have liked to have seen. Georgia and Floyd were still talking about the experience.

DAN

We thoroughly enjoyed the Agora. The Thission there is the best preserved Doric Temple in Greece, with its graceful 34-column peristyle.

The Ancient Agora Museum founded in 1957 after the reconstruction of the Stoa of Attalos by the American School of Classical Studies in Athens was lovely.

FLOYD

After a few days in Athens we made the decision to begin our travels. We, as unofficial tour guides, have decided the best place to start would be our favorite spot in Greece, the tiny unspoiled harbor town of Agnonda, on the pine green island of Skopelos in the northern Sporades. So we found ourselves on Syntagma Square trying to arrange our travel to the island. We discovered we had to take a two-hour bus ride to Agios Konstandinos and then get either a ferry or a hydrofoil, also called dolphins, to Skopelos. The hydrofoil cost twice as much but was twice as fast so we opted for it over the ferry. We checked a number of the ticket agencies and I found one where we could get a bus and dolphin ticket together so I asked the girl selling tickets to sell us four fares. When she'd finished I handed her a credit card to pay for them, but she looked up a trifle annoyed and said, "No cards." I gestured to the credit card logos for MC and VISA colorfully displayed on the door, but she repeated, "No cards!" By then the others had joined me in the little agency and I told them the situation. Together we didn't have enough cash to pay for the tickets. Then I noticed a trapeza—a bank— across the street with an ATM window clearly in view. As I rushed out the door for the ATM my wife explained in Greek to the clerk what was happening. When I got to the ATM, I discovered it was in Greek but I figured I could navigate it without too much trouble. I put my bankcard in and managed to push the right buttons until I was looking at the amount I wanted to withdraw. The denominations were 5, 10, 20, etc., up to 200. I pressed the 200, thinking I'd get $200 worth of drachmas, which would more than cover the fares and give us some traveling cash as well. Then the machine began to spit out brightly colored notes in 1,000, 5,000, and 10,000 drachma denominations. The bills started piling up in my hands until I felt like I'd hit the jackpot on a Vegas slot machine. Finally, the machine stopped and I gathered my treasure in both hands and ran back across the street to the agency, convinced the ATM had made a colossal mistake. When the others saw me clutching my bills, they began laughing and questioning me about where I got all the cash. First, I paid for the tickets and then we counted the bills, which totaled 200,000 drachmas, including what we paid for transportation. I then decided to go back once more to the ATM to see if I could figure out my newfound fortune. This time as I looked at the screen more carefully, I noticed the "K" next to each of the denominations and realized I had asked the machine for 200,000 drachmas, not $200. Mystery solved, and we now have enough cash for our trip and I became the unofficial banker as well as tour guide.

ELIZABETH

When we first arrived in Athens we went over our previously planned itinerary that Dan had written out. Georgia and Floyd had told us about this little island they "happened upon" on an earlier trip, called Skopelos. From the sounds of it, we had all agreed it would be a good place to go at the end of our trip to ease back into the thought of leaving Greece. The more we talked about it the more it, felt like we should go now from here in Athens rather than wait. So that's what we did. We put it at the beginning of our island hopping after Athens.

DAN

A good night's sleep after Metaxa on Floyd and Georgia's balcony. We went to Syntagma Square to get tickets for the Skopelos trip. Having coffee now at the café around the corner by the hotel, Floyd and I split the last piece of tiropita, a little cheese pie. "Kind of hard to split four ways," I said, taking one half. "Let's eat on behalf of our wives." Later Elizabeth said, "Can you do that for the whole trip?" (meaning eat on their behalf). "Sure!" I said. Then there was much laughter over a diet imposed by us.

Skopelos

"When the divine voiced cicada is chirping his harsh song, sun-mad at the midday heat."
— Aristophanes

GEORGIA

We tell Dan and Elizabeth how we found Skopelos on our first trip to Greece. A friend of ours from Thessaloniki raved about their favorite island called Skopelos and urged us to go. We boarded a hydrofoil at Metamorphosis, a small port near Thessaloniki and arrived after three and a half hours over rough white caps and waves to the Northern Sporades. We stopped at Skiathos, before landing here in Agnonda, on the south side of beautiful Skopelos. This tiny summer community has three tavernas on the water. It is edged by colorful fishing boats, two caiques, sailboats and a long cemented pier where small ferries, private yachts, and the hydrofoils land when Skopelos Town harbor is too rough. Our hydrofoil, the *Ceres*, was like a 747 with no wings, funny looking but so fast! We talked with three ladies about rooms and finally found Maria, who rents lovely rooms over the seaside tavernas. We rented a room with marble-tiled floors, tiny fridge, small bathroom, and a little balcony to sit on and sip Retsina while watching the buses slink down the cement pier to drop off visitors from the capital, Skopelos Town. Boats dock in the small but deep blue harbor, boats from all over the world. We settled into our room then found our place on the beach surrounded by bare-breasted beauties of all ages and enjoyed lolling around the bright aqua warmth of the water. We took turns tasting in all these seaside eateries but started with the one directly below our room. Chilled local wine helped us decide on calamari and a special cheese pie, Skopelou tiropita, of the island. Thus began our first visit to Skopelos when we were on our own. That's how Floyd and I found what became our favorite island.

DAN

In Athens, the four of us wait for the bus to Agios Konstantinos, where we will board the hydrofoil for Skopelos. Before the bus arrived, I took a little side trip over to see the changing of the guards (the evzones) at the parliament building in Syntagma Square. Dressed in skirts, the traditional foustanella, fuzzy tipped boots and tights, their movements were precise and expressions unchanging. Unchanging, that is, until an inspection was begun. I thought I saw the slightest hint of a grin from one of the guards when his superior pulled at his sleeve, untangled his various black tassels, and adjusted his beret. It was as though his mother had just spit-wiped a mark off his face in front of his friends.

The bus ride was about two hours north from Athens. Once we arrive in Agios Konstantinos, we board a hydrofoil. In air conditioned comfort we skim the sea all the way to the island of Skopelos with one long stop in Skiathos, for a glimpse of white-washed houses with red roofs built on two low hills. In Skiathos town we enjoy excellent gyros at the No-Name Café, not far off from the main drag, while the ladies guard the luggage. Elizabeth and Georgia talk to a lady and got the name of the Alexandros Taverna for dinner and live music. We have eaten and drunk and enjoyed music as we kill time till we board the late hydrofoil to Skopelos. Bought a bottle of wine for the musicians and sit and wait as the minutes crawl by. Almost time to go to the ferry area. Practically slept in the chair; we actually did nap at the ferry landing.

ELIZABETH

We sit here at the Alexandros Taverna, at one of the tables set up outside under the trees and bordering the sidewalks. People pass through, seemingly oblivious to the music until we see a slightly stooped, elderly couple, both carrying grocery bags and walking slowly by. Suddenly the old, white-haired man stops in his tracks, puts down his bags and seems overtaken by the music. He begins with slow steps, arms out to the side, moving and turning in small circles, eyes closed and a smile on his lips, remembering some past moment in his youth that the music evokes. Then surprisingly, he leaps and slaps his heels keeping perfect time to the bouzouki beat. He lands on his feet, stops for a moment then bends and picks up his grocery bags and continues on, joining his wife who had stopped to watch this man, her husband, who is still filled with that Greek kefi, walking towards her while we all applaud and whistle in admiration. At last we board the hydrofoil.

DAN

The approach to Skopelos fills us with anticipation. The town is lovely, skirting a semi-circular bay and climbing steeply in tiers up a hillside.

When we begin our exploration, we are met with winding, steep stairs between white-washed homes,some with traditional blue stone roofs, some with Mediterranean tile. Everywhere are pots of flowers dripping from balconies and on each door step. Almost as lovely as the flowers, the doors are all painted in a colorful exclamation of each owner's preference. Halfway up the hill we stop for a lemonada. Relaxing under a shade tree, we hear a Tina Turner song in the background and watch the hydrofoils and ferries come into the bay. As we start our trek again, passing between houses with lace curtains, an occasional person calls out, "Yia sou," in the friendly traditional greeting.

From Skopelos Town we ride a bus to the small town of Agnonda, where Maria has two rooms for us above four tavernas overlooking the harbor. Agnonda is a jewel of my favorite colors: teal, aquamarine, lavender, pink, cobalt, indigo ... oh, the water! This is breathtaking here.

ELIZABETH

We landed in Skopelos on the hydrofoil. Georgia called Maria in Agnonda to find out if she remembered them from two years before when they had first rented rooms from her. She said of course she remembered them and had rooms available for us. We took a bus to Agnonda and looking out over the water, we could see fishing boats coming and going in the harbor as well as the beautiful sailing vessels docked at the quay for an overnight stop. This fishing village has four tavernas. Maria's rooms are over the top of three of them.

FLOYD

We have a happy reunion with Fotini and Yiorgo, but an even more emotional one with Maria and Tassos. We sat with them to chat and were served Maria's visino—cherry spoon-sweets—and cold water, and had flowers and sprigs of basil put into our hair, a sweet gesture of welcome. Most remarkably, we got a room at Maria's without reservations, though she fretted that we hadn't called to tell her we were coming! There is absolutely no question that this is our spiritual home in Greece.

Sour Cherry Spoon-Sweets
Visino
Makes about a quart

The red of these cherries is like shimmering jewels and this spoon-sweet is a traditional welcome to a guest.

2¾ lb fresh sour cherries   1 t lemon juice
6¼ c granulated sugar   ½ t vanilla (optional)
8 c water

Wash cherries well, removing stems and pits. Set aside to drain. Combine water and sugar in a pot and bring to a boil over medium heat, stirring at first to prevent sticking. When syrup thickens to consistency of maple syrup, remove from heat and allow to cool slightly. Add cherries to syrup and bring to boil over high heat. With a slotted spoon, skim off foam from the surface as it appears, then add the lemon juice. Allow to boil for another minute, add vanilla here if desired, to make it slightly sweeter and re-move from heat. When thoroughly cooled, store in airtight glass jars. Serve one heap-ing teaspoonful on a small plate with a glass of cold water.

ELIZABETH

Maria was waiting for us, excited that Georgia and Floyd had returned and brought us with them. They had a lot to talk about as she took us up the stairs to our rooms. They were simple but immaculate, each with a balcony side-by-side overlooking the peaceful, lovely harbor. They each had two single beds with night stands, two chairs, a small refrigerator, a small vanity table, and bathroom with shower. It suited us perfectly.

GEORGIA

By now, Maria seems like a sister. As we chatted in the shade of her beautiful garden, she suddenly shouts, "Ta loulouthia, ta loulouthia" *The flowers, the flowers!* Looking around at all the flowers, I soon realize she's referring to the zucchini flowers she has simmering on the stove in her outside kitchen. The flowers stuffed with rice, grated tomatoes, onions and herbs have sent their fragrance of "doneness" through the garden and Maria runs to rescue them from overcooking.

Later that afternoon, I saw Maria outside trimming her mother's hair and asked her if she would trim mine. "Se ligo, nai": *In a little while, yes.* We had a quick cold Amstel on the balcony and I went down to her little courtyard where she sells a few beach items by her front door. As she wrapped me in an orange plastic hairdresser's cape, she proceeded to snip, snip my hair and we exchanged vital information. Her husband, Tassos, is a fisherman, but alas, she herself does not like to go out in his boat or any boat! But she adores riding back and forth on the back of his very fast Vespa to their winter home in town where she has a garden larger than the one here. She has two teenage sons. Her husband's brother has one of the seaside tavernas. The families come here with both their mothers for the summer and move back to the town, where she has a big house and garden, in the off-season. I learned earlier from the "parea"— group of friends—of ladies who run the mini market next door that Agnonda closes down in October and reopens in May. Later that evening we all gather in Maria and Tassos' tiny yard to toast our friendship and to be serenaded by her son playing the bouzouki and singing! He will soon be of age to do his mandatory stint in the Greek army, so this is a bittersweet moment of family time and we are honored to be invited. Everyone is happy that we like this place so much.

ELIZABETH

Tonight, dinner at Fotini's Fish Taverna was truly an amazing experience. She remembered Georgia and Floyd from a previous trip and welcomed us all as if we were family. In addition to the incredible fresh calamari, we most certainly had a "message" from our parents we could only call a "thavma" (miracle). As we relished every perfect morsel of food, we talked to Fotini and her husband Yiorgo. When he heard Dan and I were from California he mentioned having a sister who lived in Upland, California, where she and her husband had a restaurant near a town that had many colleges (this was all in his limited English and my half-forgotten Greek). I still don't know why I asked her name but when he told me there was something familiar about it. He suggested we come back for breakfast because this sister of his would be visiting then. In the morning we walked to the taverna and met Vasso. Since her name rang a bell in the back road of my mind, I asked her if she had known our parents. When I told her their names were Poppy and Jim Sardonis she almost fainted and burst into tears. She said Kyrio Jimmy was like a second father to her. He had helped them with all their citizenship papers in 1977. He had walked her down the aisle at their wedding and they had even roasted a leg of lamb on a spit in my parents' back yard. She had had a premonition of his death a few days before it happened. We were literally speechless. What are the chances of such a meeting? Here on this tiny island, in a village with only four tavernas, one closet-sized market, and a six-room pension. We "just happened" to start talking to a complete stranger whose sister lives in California ... who "just happened" to have been taken under the loving wings of our parents twenty years before! Another connection to the "land of our fathers." A true Greek thavma. We can feel our roots!

And so we later toasted our parents again here at dinner with a great Retsina, Kourtaki Retsina of Attica.

DAN

Since our two small rooms have adjoining balconies, we all share a bottle of Retsina as the evening cools and the colors of the water change, pinks and mauves reflecting the sky.

62

GEORGIA

Every day our views from the balcony change slightly. On my right through the leaves of the tree, I spy a young fisherman and his wife and two tiny boys on their boat.

I watched her feed the boys a drink and bread and get two frappes ready, hers and her husband's, then she lit a cigarette and sat with her drink. Her husband stood on the box and stomped his feet for a long time before I realized he was cleaning and tenderizing the calamari. At some secret moment he knelt down and rinsed them by hand, draining the water by lifting the box to spill the dirty water out the hole in the side of the boat. When he finished that part, the wife joined him to continue cleaning. Then he carried a huge plastic bag full of calamari to the taverna in front of which his boat was tied. Returning to their morning rituals he and his wife together untangle the fishnets and lay them down in special folds. This whole time the little boys are practicing both things as they play: climbing carefully and speedily over piles of stuff, then hopping on top of the steering cabin where they both fit just right and watch their parents. They practiced fishing with a drop line off the side of the boat. You can tell they already know the proper way to pull the line up by the perfect miniature motions of hand over arm, hand over arm. The last thing I saw before noon was a huge, soft pile of new electric yellow net.

DAN

Sitting on the balcony of our room above the tavernas, early by Greek standards (8:00 a.m.), I see much activity on and near the quay. Two men are fishing with hand lines off the dock for small fish; below and to the left there are women cleaning last night's catch of squid at the boat ramp. Beneath us in the three tightly packed tavernas, tables are being set, silverware clanging, preparing for the day ahead. Across the way, Yiorgo and Fotini are washing the concrete, setting out fresh flowers on each table. A bright orange fishing boat pulls into its spot, husband driving and the wife still cleaning and arranging the nets, even as they approach. The first Vespa motorbikes head over the hill towards Limnonari Beach, as a huge seagull slides just in front of me and follows the shoreline out of the small harbor. The surrounding hills are cloaked in Aleppo Pine and I hear the distant sound of the ever-present cicadas. In spite of all the activity, this is a peaceful moment.

GEORGIA

I wonder if this was the same woman I saw another morning looking to the left on the balcony. She was barefoot and holding up her long flowered skirt bent over at the edge of the boat ramp where the cement meets water, rhythmically smashing octopus to tenderize it for the popular snack of ouzo and tidbits of grilled octopus.

It's evening now as I take up my watch. It's 7:30 p.m. and the sun is still hot on our balcony though the beach cove is shaded by the hillside of pines. The fisherman father is on deck now and he's been doing something magical with the new yellow net. Like the ancient Greek ladies crocheting a particular pattern, he counts strings and pulls together, then weaves a spindle through the mesh; puts the spindle in his mouth, counts strings, pulls together, weaves. He works under the long white awning that shades the boat-family from stem to stern. I can't figure out what the small triangular black flag stands for. Floyd says, "Pirates." Where's the rest of the family?

Along the concrete pier in front of a fish taverna, there are nine masts rocking back and forth, seven sailboats, a Catamaran and a good-sized fishing boat moving to the same rhythm. Fotini got a new haircut today. She was a Larisa beauty in her youth, still statuesque, especially next to her diminutive spouse, Yiorgo, the grill man. Her hair is still shining and dark though she's a grandmother, pearly teeth lighting her smile and black eyes darting warm and deep. She strides back and forth from kitchen to tables. Tied to her waist is a fanny-pack full of money and pad and pencil for orders and bill-figuring. She is constantly inviting passersby to stop and taste. "Ela, Elate! Come in, Come in!" Every now and then she bursts out singing a few lines from Greek melancholy love songs as she carries plates. She flits from table to table and sits with us singing a special verse and sharing bits of conversation about life's stew of worries—"Ta vasana!"—while simultaneously calculating all the dinner figures in her head, perfectly every time. As she visited at our table one time, I asked her if she also played a musical instrument. She explains she had wanted to be a singer and play the guitar, but in those days of her youth it was not a proper thing for a young lady to do. It seems as if she did get her stage after all, though, on the floor of her own taverna by the sea and an appreciative and intimate audience.

How could this be? I just looked up and the boat with the fishing family has vanished. Maybe he'll reappear in the morning. The sun slipped behind the pines so we

64

can close our balcony umbrellas. The sinking rays glint on the crystal cruets of the taverna tables. The sky is gathering its pinks and lavenders before nightfall. Time to think about dinner and which of the tavernas under our balcony to choose.

The days are long and lazy still but there is a difference in the air since the big wind storm when it almost rained Sunday. Our rooms at Maria's are situated perfectly in the center of this U-shaped intimacy of Agnonda's harbor. Yachts from London, sailboats from France, Italy, Cyprus, and the UK but mostly from Greece pulling in among the local fishing boats to eat grilled fish, fried calamari, cheese pie and toasting each other with Amstel beers, local wines or Tsipouro, an island fire-water! The boats all pull out at a regular rhythm that's noticeable here from the balcony.

DAN

This happened yesterday and the day before, and I know it will happen again tomorrow and all season long—a rhythm, like the seagulls following this boat in and snatching the small fish thrown overboard without landing, or the way the wind changes from our front door to the balcony side each day. Soon we will end our part in this rhythm as we continue our adventure.

DAN

Tonight I have been invited to go fishing for calamari by Maria's husband, Tassos. He told me, in his limited English, the squid do not come to bite the lure, only to "kiss it a little bit."

All my previous fishing experience was of no use here. As the squid rise from the depths they are as luminous as ghosts and you can see them clearly, shining from thirty-five feet down or more. There aren't any big tugs to tell you that you have one. I caught about five to Tassos' bucketful.

And here is a true fish story: A huge monster squid over three feet wide and longer took hold of the lure. Tassos came right over, took the line and tried to pull it up. He was too heavy for the luminous lure to hold and as he broke the surface, he expelled his load of water and was gone. Beginner's luck? Tassos said it was the biggest squid he has ever seen.

Looking up, I saw stars, stars and more stars filling the black sky, reflecting on the black water.

GEORGIA

We often walk to Limnonari Beach for our breakfast of Nescafe, yogurt and fruit at the new taverna there. The owner-cook talks with us for a long time and explains how she decided to go from a tiny kiosk under a tree on the beach to a full-fledged taverna. We rent chaises and an umbrella and spend the morning leisurely reading. At lunch we enjoy an order of fresh, crisp calamari and a few cool Amstel beers as we slip into a siesta by this turquoise cove.

DAN

Today Yiorgo let us use his small motorboat to explore. We stayed close to the shore-line and saw the wild goats dotting the rocky hillsides. Suddenly ahead of us was a small rocky island covered with wild onions. I just had to jump into the sea and swim over for a closer look. I climbed up onto one of the rocks and then wished I had my camera. When I got back to the boat we headed in the other direction to Limnonari Beach for swimming, sunning, reading, talking and, of course, eating. There was just one small taverna set amidst a shady olive grove which extends almost to the sand. Here we had the best calamari yet.

ELIZABETH

Oh, no! Dan just jumped into the water. He's swimming over to the rocks. It's the call of the wild onion, no doubt. He just can't resist.

GEORGIA

Tonight we met an extraordinary island couple who has been summering in this harbor-side community for over fifty years. The old man, Pendeli, lives with his wife, Eftihia, in a one room hut under the spreading arms of an ancient plane tree. On this beach side he sits in the middle of his boat in front of a taverna owned by Athenians. He is shaded by the green-and-white, striped awning of his boat of many colors, probably spruced up every spring with cans of leftover paint collected from neighbors with bigger paint projects going on. Pendeli often sits under the shade that covers the corner where he and his wife homesteaded fifty years ago for a little summer getaway to fish. He mends his nets there and greets his friends, neighbors, and tourists. She sits close to him crocheting and greeting people with her eyes. They refused to move or sell out to the Athenians who wanted that corner for their restaurant. They requested, instead, a flower trellis to hide their tin-roofed hut. He no doubt, will go out with all the locals who wait until dark to go out fishing. Last night we counted thirteen boat lanterns lighting the harbor like fireflies suspended in flight. While her husband fishes at night, Eftihia, takes her regular volta (a walk) with Maria, our concierge and stops and talks with old and new friends.

The very first night Maria introduced us to her she invited Elizabeth and me to come to her home for some sweets. Insisting that we follow her then and there she led us to her home under the tree and opened the door to a magical room. An oil lantern glowed just bright enough to warm the sight of a small double bed covered with a light embroidered coverlet on the one side; and icons shone above a candle flickering in a red glass holder. A one-burner hot plate rested on a short narrow counter with a one-door cupboard to the side of it. She opened the cupboard door and took down a shoebox-size container all wrapped with ribbons, which she quickly untied and smilingly showed us a variety of sweets; revani, kourambiethes, koulourakia and phenikia and the famous Skopelos tart. She stepped outside the door to bring in her two chairs, whose place is by the small dining table where she and her husband have their meals under the tree. For evening guests, though, she tells us we will sit in the lamplight inside. From a basket she puts linen napkins on our laps and begs us to take some and enjoy the sweetness of new friendship. Cool glasses of spring water complete this magical moment of Greek hospitality, a quintessential custom older by centuries than dear Pendeli and Eftihia.

FLOYD

We woke up to cloudy skies which have now cleared. We drink our Nescafé at our favorite taverna. Looks like a good beach day, but no hurry right now to do anything.

GEORGIA

I wake at eight o'clock this morning to the squawking of the Greek rooster and yes, it sounded like the Greek song I learned as a child, "Ki-kiri-ki-ki!" Looked off the balcony and saw a green-and-white-striped awning over a fishing boat docked at the fish taverna. Later we went over for Nescafé and loukoumathes, the mouth-watering fried and honey-bathed doughnuts. We stayed and stayed and read and wrote cards and eavesdropped on the Londoners from a morning-moored sailboat. Later I chatted with a man who loved it here, too, and he said, "You won't tell anyone about this place will you?"

I've been writing snippets of overheard conversation in Greek like this one: "Na ferees krasi na to pioume yia soupa!" One guy who wears a fishnet wound up for a belt, screams to his buddy, "Got any wine? Only four bottles? Bring it! We'll drink it as soup!"

Yiorgo and Fotini continued to run around opening up, readying for the lunch and dinner crowd. He checks the motor of every boat he rents. They're all lined up in front of the taverna along with a few other fishing boats of the locals. He then asked me to be the interpreter this morning for a German who is negotiating for a rental. Fotini stops her chores for a few minutes to sit down at our table, "Ti kanees?" I ask. How are you?". "You know," she says, "life is joy and sorrow. You must go face everything with joy in your heart! I lost my brother last year. I wore black for him but still I sang! People said, 'Look at that widow. She's singing because she's glad her husband's dead!' But no, life and death are all part of the big picture. We all have vasana, worries. But I was born with a great source of joy. My klironomiko—my inherited background—is good character! My mother was from here, my father from the elite in Asia Minor. Ta pedia na eene kala, Ne, ne! Let our children be well! That's all that matters."

FLOYD

Last night Fotini's daughter and friends came over from her coffee bar in Skopelos Town and reopened the fish taverna! They partied! Drinking, smashing glasses, toasting each other and jumping into the water. There was a little extra tidying up to do this morning.

Tonight we strolled to the fish taverna planning to eat fish till we saw a three–foot–long spit turning on the grill packed with seasoned lamb, tomatoes and pork. After a tomato and feta salad and warm bread, we ate the lamb and pork souvlaki with the best homemade fried potatoes. We vowed to eat only fresh potatoes fried in extra virgin olive oil from now on! Georgia got to talking with Fotini about dancing and within minutes we had made a date for Friday night. Her husband and she will take us into town for live music and dancing after closing time. Amazing! Walked back to our room looking for the pearl full moon I had glimpsed earlier, and there it was over our doorway when we went out on the balcony. Plans for many more meals at Fotini's.

ELIZABETH

Georgia and Floyd talk our ears off telling us a few of their adventures on their first trip, without us, to Skopelos. I wish I could have been there to join in the dance.

GEORGIA

This was one of our favorite adventures with Fotini and Yiorgo. It was 1:30 in the dark morning and finally the fish taverna had closed. We joined Fotini, Yiorgo and Eleni, the dishwasher, to drive to town. After dropping off Eleni we go on to a late-night bar housed in an old olive press building and find ourselves among the first and few. The band is warming up and Yiorgo orders us a round of brandies to warm us up, too. Soon a dance tune fills the room with that bouzouki sound. The singer, a lovely long-tressed woman, finishes her cigarette and adjusts her tiny finger cymbals. She starts to croon a sultry song, cymbals syncopating an Oriental rhythm and her arms actually dance to the music. I am mesmerized! One more brandy and Fotini and I are in the middle of the dance floor circling to the music. My dream come true! By now it's about 3 a.m., and we are exhausted. A platter of cool fruit quenches our thirst and we leave the club as the real revelers start to fill the jumping spot on this hot summer night. On the dark scary ride back to Agnonda, we learn about a famous musician who plays after midnight in a taverna at the top of the old Kastro back in town. This will be our next live-music adventure, I hope.

FLOYD

On our first trip here, Georgia and I had gone into Skopelos Town for a cruise to what we thought would be the neighboring island of Alonnissos. Instead, we were talked into a more expensive sail (7,000 drachma each) called Paradise Tours, to several islands and places. The price was right! It included snacks of fruit, biscuits, paximathia, and koulourakia. Also a great lunch of Greek salad, and such an abundance of fresh shrimp that they dumped the leftovers overboard after the cruise. The Retsina flowed and snacks of feta, olives and bread were munched on constantly! More important are the stops, the first of which was Alonnissos, with quite a community of Germans now,

69

who've restored many of the hill towns there. Here we took on a huge load of young people, touring campers, mostly French. Then, on to Kyria Panagia, an incredible old monastery on a rock cliff, overlooking where we docked. Some of the passengers went to the monastery while others, mostly the young, stayed by the boat and swam and snorkeled. We climbed the stairs, paths and rocks in the heat, from the boat to the hilltop, until we finally reached our goal, the monastery.

A rugged climb but well worth it. Monks had abandoned living there, but there was one lone man who stayed to tend flowers and herb gardens and tend the oil lamps in the chapel. He said occasionally a priest comes to bless the place. Its former liveliness has passed, but not its serene and lonely beauty.

GEORGIA

Our last swim stop was an isolated tiny island, farthest out in the Aegean, yet still part of the Northern Sporades group. We were told there were the remains of an ancient sunken city on the other side. A more amazing sight to me was the white and radiant lilies blooming directly out of the loose sand! They thrive on the sun, wind, and spray. We swam in the coolness of the water, guarded by the beauty of the lilies. After relating this adventure of our last trip to Dan and Elizabeth, we decided we should do it again with them, but sadly it was no longer available.

DAN

We had to go into the clinic in Skopelos Town for Elizabeth before leaving for Glossa. She has two ear infections from a cold she's been fighting. Maria recommended the clinic; it's free, and 1,300 drachma for prescriptions equals $4.20 total. Next stop is the Platanos Taverna for some gyros. Very good, as long as you can keep the guy from putting fries, mustard, and ketchup (imagine) on it! Now on the bus headed for Glossa.

Just finished the tour of the old town, a lovely hilltop community. That is what sticks with me. Families live here, kids play in the street, young girls eat ice cream, and the grandson helps his Papou at the restaurant. Rooftop gardens with lovely views of the harbor below. Exceptional food at the café, which they opened especially for us, since we arrived at siesta time. Kotopoulo souvlaki, as well as a very decent moussaka, the local beans as a meze. We also had great Amstel beers. Bill was 8,400 drachma, one of the best values so far. (Before the conversion to euros, the Greek currency, the drachma, ranged from 300 to 400 drachma per U.S. dollar).

ELIZABETH

We so enjoyed our meal here with great hospitality. One of the best dishes was the Greek baked beans. Because the chef–owner had time during this siesta break, he gave us his recipe. It is made with large, flat beans cooked in a beautiful tomato sauce made up of herbs, onions and celery all baked together in a casserole until all the juices are absorbed and only the tomato-tinged olive oil remains. Savory and delicious.

Baked Butter Beans in Tomato Sauce
Gigantes Plaki
Serves 6–8

The secret to the delicious tenderness of these buttery beans is a slow bake.

2 14-oz cans butter beans
2 c chopped celery
2 large chopped cloves of garlic
2 14-oz cans diced tomatoes
2 c shredded carrots
2 c chopped onion

½ c olive oil
2 bay leaves
½ t each salt and pepper
Pinch of sugar
¼ c chopped flat-leaf parsley

Preheat oven to 325 degrees F. Heat the oil in a sauce pan and sauté the onions and garlic until translucent. Add the tomatoes, carrots, celery, bay leaves and seasonings and cook about 10 minutes. Put the vegetables into a large shallow baking pan and stir in beans. Cover and cook in oven for about one hour until all the vegetables are soft. Occasionally check the pan and add hot water if needed. Add parsley and stir before serving.

GEORGIA

Looking down from these pinky orange tiles of the roof garden taverna, I spy, at the end of an alleyway, an old Papou, with his head leaning back in his straight, blue chair, resting against the wall of his house as his grandson whirls around flying his cicada-on-a-string. Haven't children been playing this game for millennia?

ELIZABETH

From high up in Glossa, we drive down to its seaport, Loutraki. The guys have already gone swimming, and we are now in the Phlisbos Café ordering pastitsio, fresh fried potatoes, and, of course, village salad overflowing the bowl with those indescribably sweet Greek tomatoes, crunchy cukes, purple Kalamata olives, and topped with a square of gleaming white feta drizzled with olive oil! A basket of warm bread waits for us to pull it apart. Soon we discover that our friendly waiter has a voice like the Janice character on the show, Friends. We try not to laugh at the sound of his voice as he explains the word *phlisbos* means the roaring of the waves as they crash against the seawall at the edge of the taverna's patio.

When we arrived at Fotini's Taverna this year we discovered that instead of being on the quay they had moved across the road. They still have a view of the harbor and the food is still exceptional. We told them we visited with George's sister Vasso, whom we had met on our previous visit in 1997 when we discovered her incredible connection to our parents. Adding to the amazing facts of Vasso having known our parents, we discovered when we visited them in California that she has photos of our father giving her away on her wedding day in 1977, as well as photos of two of my sons who were in attendance while I had stayed home with my youngest, recovering from the measles. Not only that, but when Georgia and Floyd got home from that last trip, Georgia found a photograph on her desk of our father and Vasso in his back yard turning a spit of lamb over a fire pit in the ground. Another thavma!

GEORGIA

When I found that photograph of Vasso with my father, it brought back a childhood memory of turning the lamb on a spit while our Papou stoked the embers for the cooking of the Easter lamb. As it roasted slowly over the fire, drippings crackled on the coals and the fragrance of oregano and garlic swirled up and around me. I was mesmerized watching as the lamb browned and became crisp. I could hardly wait for that first bite.

Roast Leg of Lamb
Arni Psito sto Fourno
Serves 6–8

This classic roast is the centerpiece of Easter dinner, filling the kitchen with its tantalizing aromas of garlic, lemon and oregano.

1 leg of lamb (8–10 lb), bone in
2/3 c lemon juice
4 garlic cloves slivered
½ c olive oil

1 t each salt and pepper
2 T dried Greek oregano or
    more to taste
1 c water

Preheat oven to 500 degrees F. Place the lamb on a cutting board. With the point of a sharp knife make deep slits all over and insert garlic slivers. Mix all ingredients except water for marinade. Marinate the lamb overnight either in a large plastic closable bag or roasting pan covered with foil. Turn lamb occasionally. Keep in refrigerator until ready to roast. Place lamb in roasting pan with marinade and water and reduce the heat to 350 degrees F. Roast for about 2 to 3 hours or until thermometer registers 170 degrees F. for medium to well-done (until skin is browned and crisp and juices run clear).

ELIZABETH
Fotini served us something we had never had before. She called it a sweet Skopelos tart. It was a crisp filo "cup" with a piece of honey-drenched walnut cake (karithopita) in the bottom. On top of that was a dollop of silky, pale yellow custard, crowned with fluffy whipped cream and a soft purple plum. While enjoying this outrageous Skopelos tart, we tell Fotini our plan to write a cookbook and that we would appreciate some of her recipes. She not only offered recipes, but invited us to come in the morning to watch her prepare the traditional Skopelos cheese pie.

Our last dinner in Agnonda began with calamari, kotopoulo, pork souvlaki and loukaniko with 2.5 liters of house white wine as a gift from Fotini. As we eat, a huge ferry with lights all over it comes into our little harbor and backs up to the quay. It looks like a magical fairy boat.

Already the daylight begins to fade but the memory of sun fluttering on fresh green is still there.

ELIZABETH

When we arrived this morning, we found Fotini in her vegetable garden. We walked with her as she told us how she uses the various herbs. We came to basil and she said, "Poteh!" Never! Basil is considered a sacred plant in the Greek Orthodox church, therefore it is never used in cooking. Most women plant a pot of basil with marigolds to set by the kitchen door and ward off the evil eye. This clarifies the fact that oregano, dill and parsley are the most common traditional herbs used in Greek cooking. We then went into her kitchen to begin our lesson. Watching her deft hands covered in flour roll out the dough, we were mesmerized by the speed and skill with which she completed her masterpiece. What would probably take us four or five practice runs to get it right in our own kitchen, took her only minutes.

Because Fotini made this from her long experience and second-nature, like many great cooks, she had not a single measurement to give us. It was "a little of this and a pinch of that."

We watched her make this simple dough without a bowl on her table. She kneaded it to make a medium dough. She rolled it out paper thin to about the size of a card table with a long, very thin wooden dowel. She told us to sprinkle it with corn starch so the filo dough won't stick to itself as you roll it. She used the hard Skopelos goat cheese, which doesn't melt easily. She sprinkled it all over, deftly rolled it up like a jelly-roll, sealed the edges with her fingers and coiled this into a spiral. She poured olive oil into a skillet and fried the whole thing in medium–hot oil on both sides until it was a buttery golden hue. She removed it, blotted it with paper towels, and gave us a steaming hot, delicious sample. It was amazing what these few ingredients created. This was a succulent cheese pie, unlike anything we had ever had before. After this incredible performance we hugged her with gratitude.

After our cooking session, the guys joined us at the bus stop. Fotini came running out with a bag of cheese pies wrapped in brown paper for us to take on the bus. They were still warm and smelling of melted cheese. We could hardly wait to eat them!

DAN

The day is once more perfect as we prepare to go to Skopelos Town to catch the ferry. We have to force ourselves to leave this idyllic setting. Cicadas sing in the surrounding forest of trees. We buy small seashells from children for about a nickel. We *ooh* and *aah* over their beauty. They understand these sounds without knowing our language and smile in agreement. Here comes the bus. Moments to go before we must depart. The cicadas will sing even after we are gone. Bye for now, Agnonda.

GEORGIA

We settle up front on the almost empty bus. Before we know it the bus driver pulls over on the side of the road in front of a modest white house. He turns and addresses us with "If you don't mind, I'll just be a moment," and jumps off the bus. We watch him open the gate to the courtyard and disappear. Within five minutes he's back carrying something behind him and presents me with a bouquet of oleander and sweet carnations. "From my own garden," he says. "I've been watching you go back and forth from town to Agnonda and remember you from your many trips here. I'm glad you love our island. This is a gift of remembrance." He sits back down in the driver's seat, glances at us in his mirror and gives a wink and a smile. A kefi gift, for sure.

DAN

Off the beaten path in Skopelos Town we found the Owl Restaurant. Here we had one of our best meals yet. WOW! It was almost beyond description.

ELIZABETH

When our meals arrived we were overwhelmed by the incredible aromas as each order was placed before us. Stavro and I had exohiko, which is lamb, vegetables and cheese wrapped in foil and baked until all flavors meld.

Country Lamb with Vegetables Wrapped in Foil
Arnaki Exohiko
Serves 6–8

Tender chunks of lamb, vegetables and cheese are wrapped in foil and baked to perfection.

¼ c olive oil
7 green onions chopped
3 T fresh chopped dill
3 lb spring lamb cut into
    large chunks
12 oz crumbled feta

1 lb potatoes peeled and
    cut in sections
Salt and pepper to taste
1 lb medium carrots thickly sliced
12 oz shelled peas
Water as necessary

Heat oil in large pan. Sauté green onions and meat over medium heat until meat is browned (about 10 minutes). Add vegetables and dill with one cup of water and simmer for about 30 minutes until liquid is reduced by half. Season with salt and pepper. Add feta and mix gently.

Place some of the meat-and-vegetable mixture on a square of foil, folding edges into a small parcel. Lay parcels on baking sheet next to each other until all meat mixture is used. Bake in a preheated 350 degrees oven for 45 minutes.

Niko and Georgia had the stamnato. Stamnato actually means "clay pot," which was filled with a savory blend of tender chunks of beef, potatoes, carrots, onions and three cheeses. The lids were sealed with bread dough. When we all unwrapped our lovely food "packages," we truly felt we had received a gift. In our exclamations over the food, we called our waiter over and asked if we could meet the chef. He disappeared for a few moments, and reappeared with the very flattered chef whose name was Dimitri. We offered him a glass of wine and asked if he would share his recipes and he was honored to do so. He explains that *exohiko* means "country," because in rural areas of Greece, people had their own gardens where they could hand-pick their vegetables and herbs, use their homemade feta and wrap this mixture in their homemade filo.

Beef Stew With Three Cheeses
Stamnato
Serves 4

This is a meat, vegetable and cheese dish slow-cooked in the oven in a clay pot, traditionally, but any covered casserole dish will do.

2 T olive oil
1 lb beef
2 onions chopped
4 cloves garlic chopped
3 carrots thinly sliced
3 bell peppers sliced

2 c water
Salt and pepper to taste
½ t cinnamon
1 c red wine
1 28-oz can tomato sauce
½ c feta, ½ c parmesan, ½ c Romano

Cut meat into cubes. In a frying pan, heat oil and brown the meat. Add onion and garlic, salt and pepper, and cinnamon. Sauté 6 or 7 minutes. Add red wine, tomato sauce, water, carrots and peppers. Bring to a boil and add the three cheeses to the mixture. Remove from heat and pour all into a casserole dish. Cover tightly with lid or foil. Bake for 2½ to 3 hours in a preheated oven at 325 degrees F., until meat is fork tender. Check for salt and pepper before serving with crusty bread.

GEORGIA

As we leave the Owl, still enjoying the flavors left in our mouths by that extraordinary meal, we notice the restaurant sign, portrays the same image of the owl as the one that appears on the ancient Athenian silver coins showing Athena's owl. We tell Dan and Elizabeth about our magical night listening to live Rembetika in Skopelos Town the last time we were here.

After a very late, great dinner in a waterfront taverna and a slow sipping of Metaxa, Floyd and I waited until midnight, then finally started up the hundreds of stone steps winding through alleyways and many levels of quiet darkness until soft, almost echoes of bouzouki seemed to be bouncing off the walls of houses where most people are sound asleep. Around every other turn a glow lights our pathway. The bouzouki is loud and clear now and after the last turn, the hilltop square opens up to us.

It's a vision of outside café tables crowded with people, some even standing around the perimeter riveted to the music of George, the bouzouki player, hypnotizing his audience with an old classic of Rembetika. This is an eastern musical genre created primarily by the Greeks from Asia Minor as they resettled in the cities of the mainland, Athens, Thessaloniki and Piraeus. The spirit of this music is often compared to American jazz with its lyrics of the blues. We slithered through the throngs and found a place to sit on the low stone wall edging the platia, where a waiter took our drink order. Soon our night-hike up to this spot was rewarded by the introduction of George's twin sons, about nine or ten years old, who sat on either side of their father and began to blend their Rembetika voices—lessons well taught and lovingly passed down to the next generation.

Tinos

"There is a temple in ruin stands,

Fashioned by long forgotten hands;

Out upon time! Who forever will leave

But enough of the past for the future to grieve

Remnants of things that have passed away,

Fragments of stone rear'd by creatures of clay."

— *The Siege of Corinth,* **Lord Byron**

ELIZABETH

The sunny morning ferryboat ride from pine-covered Skopelos south to Tinos was relaxing and invigorating at the same time. We highly anticipated this next stop on our island-hopping itinerary. Approaching the harbor, we can already see some obvious differences in the landscape of this first Cycladic island of our visit. These islands are arid and glisten with the whites of their geometric houses unlike the Sporadic islands farther north, whose stone houses with slate roofs and groves of walnut and plum trees among the pines cover the hills with shades of gray and green.

The island of Tinos is the home of the famous church of the Miraculous Icon of the Virgin Mary. It is a charming mountainous island with white sparkling villages, windmills, and farmers' terraces. The church's Greek name is the Panagia Evangelistria; it is at the top of a hill directly up from the harbor, where scores of pilgrims make their way, often on their knees, to venerate the icon. This icon is covered with jewels, offerings to conjure up its curative powers. Draped with strings of pearls and ablaze with shiny precious stones, the icon itself is almost hidden. I had never seen anything like the numbers of people lining up to get inside and have a chance to pray to the Holy Mother to take away their suffering. There is also a fountain with holy water coming from a hidden spring where the icon was found, and the pilgrims splash the water over themselves while praying. The island's serenity is disturbed twice a year by the pilgrimage, which comes in March and in August.

DAN

It is a pleasant thing to find a comfortable room near the town and the beach yet secluded enough to be quiet. Such is the one we found: Yianni's Pension, offering peaceful, lovely, airy rooms in a 75-year-old home with blue shutters. The doves coo above our window in the morning. We've read that on this island there are over 800 tall stone dovecotes built by the Venetians to attract doves for nesting.

FLOYD

Yianni showed us the communal kitchen where I'm making our morning coffee with my ever-ready filter. There's a great garden outside surrounded by a high wall to protect us from the howling winds of Tinos, which have been constant since we arrived. The weather overall has been lovely and remarkably cool. No question about the impact of the Kosovo Civil War going on now in 1999. Tourism is down noticeably and the dollar is strong against the drachma.

GEORGIA

After our siesta here at Yianni's Pension, I open our blue-shuttered window and his five-year-old grandson, little Stelio, hops up on the window sill. He's with his Yiayia, who begs him to recite her many-versed poem about the island. He does this well and jumps down. "Bravo!" I clap and say, "Efharisto! Thank you!" He corrects me with the proper "Parakalo." Then he hops back up for another poem. We see him again later in the garden, standing small among the flapping, drying sheets. He sings us a "Welcome to the house of Yianni. Enjoy your stay on Tinos." The multi-colored writing pad, a gift from me, delights him. Now he follows me and Elizabeth into the laundry, singing. I ask him to help me with my Greek because he knows so much. He says, "Ego xero ola! Esee xerees tipoteh!" I know everything and you know nothing! I ask if he's drawn anything on the pad yet. He flips the pages and says sadly, "Look at all these colors. No, my pencil is downstairs and I had a red pen but now it's lost."

"Let's see if I have one in my bag," I said. He squeals with laughter and claps and tells his Yiayia he can't help her right now because the Kyria, the lady, is looking for a red pen for him. Then I confess that I do know a little song, the Greek version of Twinkle, "Twinkle Little Star." We sing it together and in that moment I know we're friends. Yiayia is calling to him and he goes.

ELIZABETH

Yianni again assures us these winds that have been blowing since we arrived will stop today. Feeling optimistic, we find the tourist office to purchase tickets for the day to the nearby islands of Mykonos and Delos. The ticket agent warned us that the boat departure is still tentative. The Meltemi, warm summer winds from the north, are still strong and the water too rough to navigate. We will have to just wait and see.

In the cobbled back streets, the old iron balconies of the houses recall centuries of Venetian rule. As we wind our way back to our pension, we are lured into a sweetshop by its owner, who promised the most incredible loukoumi we'd ever tasted. Loukoumi, of Turkish origin known as Turkish Delight, is a taffy-like candy covered in powdered sugar and often flavored with rose water or orange blossom water. It was never a favorite of ours until we tasted this one. We were told this loukoumi was made with pure island butter and fresh cream as well as the most unexpected flavor of coconut! This definitely changed our minds. It was so creamy it melted in our mouths. Leaving here we passed the Tinos Bakery and couldn't resist buying a sweet bread called Tsoureki for breakfast tomorrow. As we left we passed two women having coffee and looking at their plate piled with an assortment of sweets. We heard one of them say, "Apopse thi-eta." *Tonight we diet.* So it's not just in America that we make this promise.

Sweet Bread
Tsoureki
Makes 2 round loaves

This sweet bread with special flavorings is baked for Easter.

Flavoring:
1 T cinnamon
1 T orange peel
Boil the cinnamon and orange peel in ½ cup of water for 5–6 minutes. Cool and set aside.

Bread:
2 envelopes of dry yeast
¾ c warm water
1 c milk
½ c butter
1¼ c sugar
1½ t salt

1 T cinnamon–orange flavoring, cooled
  (see recipe above)
1 t vanilla
1 T orange zest
3 eggs well beaten
6 c flour (approximately)
Topping:
Sesame seeds 1 egg and 1 t milk

Dissolve yeast in warm water. Scald milk and add butter, sugar, and salt to hot milk. Allow to cool and then add vanilla, cinnamon-orange flavoring, orange zest, and 3 well-beaten eggs. Add the dissolved yeast. Measure half of the flour into a large bowl; add milk, yeast and egg mixture to the flour and mix well, adding as much more of the flour as needed to make a dough easy to handle. Knead for about 10 minutes on a floured surface. Place dough in an oiled bowl and turn over to grease the top. Allow to rise in a warm place until doubled in size. Punch down and divide in two. Either place in two cake layer pans or separate each ball into three parts, elongate each part by stretching and braid, making two braided loaves; place these two braids on a cookie sheet. Let rise again about one hour. Brush top with another egg, beaten with a teaspoon of milk. Sprinkle with sesame seeds. Bake at 325 degrees F. for 45 minutes in a preheated oven.

DAN

We're on the small ferry, the *Tinos Star*, to Delos then hoping to go on to Mykonos. The seas are still not calm as the wind continues blowing, but this short trip should be okay. After landing and wandering through the ancient ruins, we sit at the gift shop drinking cold water, overlooking the ruins. If it wasn't for the tours which flood this place with hundreds of interested people, it would be one of the saddest places in the world. I read that two civilizations, the Minoans and the Classical Greeks, utilized Delos as its religious center because it was the birthplace of Apollo and his twin sister Artemis. Only five of the original nine lions in the famous Terrace of the Lions guard the entrance of the Sacred Lake, which no longer exists. All other islands and city states competed and contributed to the construction of the finest temples and art. Thirty thousand people once lived here, now all gone. This is now an island of stone, dry wildflowers and grasses, brown and bent in the scouring wind. Beneath a blue sky and blazing sun, Apollo stays nearly alone.

ELIZABETH

We toured the small museum, which felt cool on this hot, windy day. The best of the Delos sculptures are in the Athens Archaeological Museum. Outside, the lions remaining, sculpted from Naxian marble, are worn smooth by the incessant winds. They still hold a strange majesty even in their almost shapeless condition.

Our little boat, the *Tinos Star*, valiantly fights the wild sea and takes us to Mykonos, known for its windmills. We explored the shops, busy with cruise passengers' daily invasions. The town is lovely, with narrow, winding alleys and lanes. From here we walk to the nearby beach, where Dan and Floyd are trying to nap on the sand, in the midst of tame pelicans that have become island mascots. Exhausted from window shopping we take Stavro and Niko to lunch. We all order the same thing, which is highly unusual for us. A taste of home—hamburgers and fried potatoes, Greek style.

Greek Beef Burgers
Biftekia
Serves 6

The combination of ground beef, ground lamb and oregano makes these burgers Greek.

1 lb ground beef
1 lb ground lamb
1 c soft breadcrumbs soaked
    in ½ c wine or ½ c water
2 cloves garlic minced
Salt and pepper

2 T dried Greek oregano
2 T each fresh parsley and dill
2 beaten eggs
1 grated onion
1 grated tomato

Combine all ingredients and mix by hand. Form six thick patties. Heat broiler and broil for 4 minutes on each side or pan fry if desired. Sprinkle with a little lemon juice.

DAN

Floyd and I lay on the beach and started to snooze until all the Belgian girls from our boat ended up there, chatting uncontrollably. When Elizabeth and Georgia turned up, too, that was basically the end of our nap. A lovely, windy town full of jewelers and fashionable shops, along with our favorite stopping places—tavernas where the girls take us for well-needed nourishment.

FLOYD

We are waiting to board the *Tinos Star* back to Tinos, but we are still docked. The wind and seas are still too rough to head out. As all the passengers anxiously line up on the dock, the captain finally gets permission to leave.

85

DAN

WOW! The seas are rough for this little vessel. The waves are hitting the bow and spraying over the top, soaking everyone. The squeals of fun and excitement from the Belgian girl students soon turn to moans and groans as tummies are being tossed a little too vigorously along with our little boat. The usual hour-long trip took 1½ hours. Soaked to the skin, we were all happy to reach dry land.

"Unhappy daughters let drop the bright beams of their tears into the dark wave."

—Euripides

ELIZABETH

After changing into dry clothes, we all meet at the top of the stairs as the sun goes down. We suddenly become aware of a strange sound, like that of a flag flapping in the wind. As we look around we realize the sound is coming from Floyd's and Dan's nylon pant legs furiously flapping in the ever-blowing Meltemi winds, and we laugh ourselves silly. We go in search of a taverna for dinner where we try a Tinos potato specialty, the patatou, for the first time, then go back to the pension, exhausted by our harrowing, wild boat ride.

Potato Casserole
Patatou
Serves 6

This is a lovely, cheesy mashed-potato alternative. If you ever have leftover mashed potatoes (at Thanksgiving) this is a good way to use them.

1½ lb potatoes
1 c Kefalotiri or Parmesan
   cheese, grated
4 eggs lightly beaten

½ c bread crumbs
1 bunch parsley chopped
Salt, pepper and nutmeg to taste
2 T butter

Boil potatoes, drain and mash with cheese, eggs, bread crumbs and parsley. Combine well, add nutmeg, salt and pepper to taste.

Use 1 tablespoon butter to coat a 9 by 12-inch roasting pan. Spread mix evenly in pan. Make pattern on top using a fork dragged lightly across the mixture in rows. Melt and drizzle remaining butter over top. Bake 1 hour in a preheated oven at 325 degrees F. Cut in squares and serve hot.

DAN

This morning we decide to ride over to Panormos Beach. Yianni said the wind would stop today. Hah! It's more than ever, but when we saw him he said it is less by half! We plan to go to Panormos Beach, in any case.

GEORGIA

We take the local bus to the other side of the island to Panormos Beach. On the way there, the bus driver points out the site of an ancient school of marble sculpting that still operates today. The roads are rough and bumpy up and over the mountain ridges and soon we come to the lovely seaside village of Panormos. All along the way are the dovecotes we read about, the characteristic landmarks of the island. We have lunch the minute we get off the bus. At a psarotaverna, a fish taverna, we eat succulent fried fish with lemon and oregano and Greek fried potatoes after the waiter brought us the fish dangling from his two fingers through the eye sockets to show us how fresh it was!

Pan Fried Fish
Psari Tiganito

The classic way to cook a white fish fillet is to dust it with flour, salt and pepper, fry in olive oil on medium high heat until golden brown and drench in lemon juice and oregano.

DAN

The wind is howling and sand is stinging my back as I try to write this. Tamarisk trees line the road. There is a small town here with six tavernas. After lunch and a nice cold Amstel, Floyd and I swam and skipped stones even though it was windy enough to blow our stones off course.

ELIZABETH

After lunch, Georgia and I went window shopping. We were totally mesmerized by a display of beautiful dolls we saw in one shop. They each had a different theme, one was a Sea Nymph dressed in gauzy folds of fabric with shells and starfish caught in the folds; a Spring doll had a profusion of small flowers in the folds of her dress and in her long, curling hair. They were lovely. We were later annoyed at ourselves for not buying one on the spot.

GEORGIA

When we return from the beach, we dress for dinner at the taverna at the bottom of the stairway to our pension. The fabulous fragrance of garlic and tomatoes wafts over us as we enter. We order the special of the night, which is eggplant rolls stuffed with garlic and feta cheese and know at first bite we want the recipe.

The young woman chef, Miltini, is from Athens. She is complimented by the request and sits down at our table. Her words are accented by the tinkling silver wind chimes singing with the Meltemi winds—still blowing at midnight.

Eggplant Rolls
Melitzanes Mboukies
Serves 6

A young woman chef from Athens created this eggplant dish. Adding ten cloves of garlic and rolling the eggplant strips makes it her own.

2 large eggplants cut lengthwise
   into 3 slices each
3/4 c olive oil
10 cloves of garlic
1 c crumbled feta cheese

1 large onion, chopped
1 large can (28 oz) diced tomatoes
Salt and pepper to taste
½ c grated Parmesan

Wash and dry the whole eggplants and slice each one lengthwise into three pieces. In a large sauté pan heat a half-cup of olive oil and sauté each slice on both sides in two batches until soft. Remove to paper towels to drain and set aside. Finely chop eight of the garlic cloves and mix with the feta. Set aside. Make a tomato sauce as follows. In a saucepan, heat ¼ cup olive oil to medium-high. Add onions, remaining chopped garlic, diced tomatoes salt and pepper. Cook about 15 minutes.

Lay out each eggplant slice, sprinkle with feta-garlic mixture and roll each slice up. Place all rolls in a baking pan or casserole, side by side, and cover with tomato sauce. Sprinkle with grated cheese and bake in a preheated oven at 350 degrees F. for 25 minutes.

DAN
We finished dinner at Galera (the name means "ancient rowing sailboat")—our last dinner in Tinos. It has treated us kindly despite the winds that Yianni just told us will be cut by half tomorrow. Georgia is getting a recipe for eggplant rolls.

This morning we pick up our luggage and check out of Yianni's Pension. We walked along the waterfront to the boat dock and left our luggage there. Across the street is the Dockside Taverna which looks like an old filling station, so we cross and go in. We are all in the mood for a tomato-feta omelette, but it is nowhere on the menu. I asked the woman behind the counter, who said the cook could make anything we want. It was delicious as always and seeing our pleasure she said she might have to add it to her menu.

Tomato and Feta Omelette
Kayianni
Serves 2

This combination of tomato and feta, as well as its name, Kayianni, comes from our family homestead on the Mani peninsula.

4 t olive oil
Bunch green onions
2 tomatoes

Salt and pepper to taste
4 eggs
3 oz feta cheese

Heat olive oil in a large frying pan. Chop onions and tomatoes and sauté until soft. Sprinkle all over with salt and pepper. Beat eggs and pour over all. Sprinkle with feta. Cook on low heat until eggs are done.

ELIZABETH

I remember going into my Papou's garden with him when the huge red tomatoes started ripening. He had a bushel basket turned over in the middle of the garden with a salt shaker sitting on it. He picked a sun-warmed tomato, brushed it off, salted it and handed it to me. The first bite was heaven —so juicy it ran down my chin. I thought I could taste the sun in this tomato, and to this day, when I pick and eat that first tomato from our garden, I still think this is what summer tastes like.

DAN

The wild winds of yesterday have moderated a bit as we prepare to leave for Santorini. Departure was at 11:00 a.m., but they list the time as 10:15 to make sure you arrive on time. Very smooth sailing so far. This wind we've had is coming from a Thessaloniki storm, we've been told. Hopefully, we are sailing out of its path.

Santorini

Gyro means "something that turns in a circle."

DAN

We board the hydrofoil for a fairly fast trip to Santorini. What kind of bucking, bouncing dolphin is this? I thought the ride would have been smoother. I'll be surprised if I don't get seasick. I'll bet the captain is trying to make up time since he came in 45 minutes late. We arrive in the port of Athenios. We find a character running a taverna with a great attitude. His wife is from Pittsburgh, he from Athens but lived in the states for 21 years. The girls discuss pastitsio and béchamel sauce with his wife, the cook. He wants to open a Greek restaurant in California if we will back him! He serenades us with "California Girls" from the Beach Boys, and "New York, New York" to a girl, Robin, from New York who sits next to us. While we wait for the bus to take us up the volcanic cliff to the town of Fira, he buys us ouzo.

GEORGIA

This makes me remember Papou's special sanctuary. It was a small, narrow part of our cellar where he had his oak barrels for making Retsina wine and his copper still, the kazani, for making ouzo. We helped harvest the grapes from our backyard grapevine and watched him create the slurry of grapes from which he made, like magic to us, his wine and ouzo. As he distilled the ouzo from the dregs of the wine barrels, the horrible smell that wafted throughout the house was unforgettable. How could he drink something that came from that aroma?

We throw our bags on the first bus we see marked "Fira." We zigzagged up the sheer cliffs one thousand feet above the sea and we read in our guidebook that they plunge an equal distance into the sea. It was the biggest volcanic eruption in 1,500 BCE and created the crescent shape that Santorini is today.

I remember when Floyd and I saw this sight for the first time. It was at midnight and we were floating in on a cruise ship. The captain had told us earlier that we might want to be on deck for a spectacular view of Santorini at midnight. In that deep darkness it was impossible to distinguish the stars from the caldera of lights both creating the twinkling vision of scattered diamonds.

DAN

We got into town at 5:30 p.m. and went directly to the Poseidon Restaurant, which we had read about in one of our guidebooks. Once again, unusual as it was, we all ordered the same entrée, Yiouvetsi. This was the recommendation of our waiter, Thanassi, whose aunt is the cook.

ELIZABETH

We were very hungry from our long journey, and when the food arrived we were thrilled at the generous serving on each plate. This popular wine-baked meat and pasta dish, Yiouvetsi, arrived steaming in heavy white ceramic bowls. The contrast of the large chunks of browned meat mingled with the rice-shaped pasta and rich tomato sauce was irresistible. When Thanassi came back to ask how we liked it we begged him for the recipe. He was very proud to bring his Aunt Maria to our table, and she was more than willing to give us every detail of this delicious entrée. Dan left us having our coffee and ran off to find us a place to stay since we had no reservations. Thanassi sat with us and bemoaned the lack of marriageable women in his life. Soon Dan returned victorious, happily waving the key to the Petros Pension on the street below this restaurant.

Pork with Orzo Casserole
Yiouvetsi
Serves 4

Large chunks of browned pork mingled with orzo, a rice-shaped pasta, and rich tomato sauce.

1 lb cubed pork
2 onions chopped
4 cloves garlic chopped
¼ c olive oil
¼ c butter
1 c dry white wine
2 T tomato paste
1 c water or chicken broth

¼ t Tabasco sauce
1 t salt
2 bay leaves
½ cinnamon stick or a
   dash ground cinnamon
4 c water
½ lb orzo
Grated cheese

In an oven-proof pot, heat oil and butter together. Brown the meat well. Add onions and garlic and cook until transparent. Add wine and simmer a few minutes while mixing tomato paste and first cup of water or broth. Add salt, bay leaves, cinnamon stick and Tabasco to tomato-water mixture and pour over meat mixture. Stir, cover and place in the preheated oven at 325 degrees F., until meat is very tender, approximately an hour. Remove casserole and add four cups of hot water and the orzo to the pan and stir. Cover and continue to bake for about a half hour (add more water if liquid is absorbed before pasta is al dente). Adjust salt, remove bay leaves and cinnamon stick. Serve hot with grated cheese if desired.

FLOYD
Spent the morning walking in a postcard-beautiful section of the town center. Saw the cruise ship *Marco Polo,* a tiny dot below in the water bringing back memories of when we were on the same cruise two years earlier. Planning to go to Kamari Beach with Dan this afternoon.

DAN

Black sand at Kamari Beach! Black pebbles more like it. A very long beach, at least a mile of umbrellas, chaise lounges, blow-up rafts and people. Too crowded for me although the water is lovely. Floyd is now in it, too. It's not easy to get into this weird, rocky, slippery bottom. The girls are continuing this morning's shopping-gawking spree in Fira.

FLOYD

Refreshed by our swim we returned to the pension, showered and dressed for the evening. Petros' wife, Eugenia, offered us a bottle of homemade Nectari wine, which was excellent. With the wine we enjoyed a plate of her warm, fresh baked pita bread and the yellow split-pea dip, fava, similar to hummus. She gave the girls her recipe. I'm writing now on our patio just off our lovely room and relaxing. The evening breeze is picking up a bit.

Yellow Split-Pea Dip
Fava
Makes about 3 cups (serves 6 to 8)

A quick, easy, and richly flavored dip

½ c extra virgin olive oil
1 large onion finely chopped
4 c water
2 c dried yellow split peas
3 bay leaves
1 T salt

Black pepper to taste
¼ c lemon juice
1 T capers
4 green onions for garnish
1 t dried Greek oregano

Heat ¼ cup olive oil in a saucepan and soften the finely chopped onion in it. Add the water and bring to a boil; then add the split peas and bay leaves. Boil gently, removing any scum as it appears. When the water has been fully absorbed the peas will be mushy. Season with salt and pepper, remove bay leaves and quickly process with a hand-held blender or with a wooden spoon. Leave the puree in a cool place to set. Before serving, stir in the lemon juice and the remaining olive oil. Transfer to large bowl, garnish with capers, chopped green onions and sprinkle with oregano.

ELIZABETH

Tonight we walk to a gyro stand for gyro and fries, simple but very good. According to *Culinaria Greece*, we read an interesting paragraph about gyro, which means "something that turns in a circle." Broiling meat on a spit is a very old method of cooking in many cuisines. The Greek style is to season the meat mixture with salt, pepper, oregano, ground cumin, and olive oil, sometimes enhanced with rosemary, thyme and onions. Shape the meat around a spit to spin and cook. The outside crispy edges are then sliced off and piled on pita bread with sliced onions, tomatoes and tzadziki sauce.

FLOYD

Up and out for early coffee at 8 a.m. Dan and Elizabeth are off to Akrotiri while we relax here for the day and later go to the village of Oia, perched at the farthest cliff side of the island, to watch the sunset. The dollar strength is growing, much to our advantage.

DAN

Elizabeth and I just had a snack as we waited for the bus to Akrotiri. The heat is supposed to reach 95 degrees today as we head for that hot and dusty archaeological dig rivaling Pompeii except that the inhabitants seem to have known it was coming (possible theory), because no artifacts were left behind, just an empty city.

ELIZABETH

Akrotiri was quite amazing. I felt like I was in an ancient city here more than I have anywhere else, although Dan said, much work has been done, but without personal items it doesn't seem like much in the way of people really having been here. The few frescoes were the only things that felt personal. On our way back to the bus we found a hose that was watering plants and took the opportunity to spray ourselves to cool off from the dusty, hot tour we just took.

DAN

Six-thirty p.m. and we are waiting for the bus to Oia, reputed to have the most beautiful sunset in the world. There are no cars allowed here on the pristine cobbled streets so we walked to the terrace where everyone goes for the sunset view. The soft guitar was played by a young Greek man who obviously loved American rock, while the sun set in all its pink and apricot glory with streaks of purple across the sky.

GEORGIA

To me it's magical, almost prehistoric, to be here in a gathering of people who've come together to watch a sunset! In spite of the soothing strumming of the guitarist, the tension builds as the sky is painted with stripes of color. The horizon blurs to lavender, and a shining silver sea frosts the still water. The sun, hiding behind a veil of blue haze, appears now, but in seconds sinks its entire glowing peach orb below the silver. The gray silhouette of a nearby islet emerges. The guitarist is silent. The quiet is deafening. The people clap.

ELIZABETH

Then we wandered slowly towards the street again, looking at every taverna we pass until we found the Alkyon Grill. We savored several delicious dishes of cheesy pastitsio, pork chunks sizzling from the rotisserie, dripping lemon and oregano, and an herb-tomato fish fillet from the grill. To our surprise, once the waiter had cleared our table, to the tune of many compliments, the cook appeared with the gift of revani, Greek honey cake. This was a dense but light honey-drenched cake, so wonderful we pleaded with him for his recipe. Once we told him we were writing a cookbook, the recipe spilled from his lips and he said he was honored.

Greek Honey Cake
Revani
Serves 8–12

The farina in this cake gives it a unique texture and helps it to absorb the honey syrup. Make the syrup recipe below while cake is baking.

1 c flour
2 t baking powder
1 c farina (cream of wheat)
¼ t salt
¼ lb butter

1 c sugar
3 T milk
6 eggs separated
1 t vanilla
¾ c ground almonds

Sift the flour, baking powder, farina and salt into a bowl. Cream butter, then add sugar and beat. Add milk to egg yolks and beat, then add this to butter-sugar mixture as you beat. Now add vanilla and flour mixture a little at a time and beat. In a separate bowl, beat egg whites until stiff but not dry, and carefully fold into batter. Grease a 9- by 12-inch baking pan, distribute the batter evenly in it, and sprinkle with ground almonds. Bake on the middle shelf for 40 minutes in a preheated oven at 350 degrees F. or until top of cake is golden. Remove from oven. Cut into squares and pour cool syrup evenly over hot cake. Cover with wax paper and dish towel and let sit overnight.

Syrup:
2 c water
2 c sugar
1 c honey
1 cinnamon stick

5 T butter
Juice of 1 lemon
1 T Metaxa or brandy

Boil water, sugar, honey and cinnamon stick together for 10 to 15 minutes. Remove cinnamon stick and add butter, stirring to melt. Add lemon juice and brandy (optional) and stir. Let syrup cool.

DAN

We wish we had stayed overnight in Oia, lovely, busy but restrained, each shop a work of art, each space having been restored from what was formerly a cave home, typically carved out of the side of the caldera. The air is pure Aegean and we walk back to the bus stop, the views all astounding.

ELIZABETH

We ended our relaxing evening back at the pension on the patio, drinking Metaxa and playing our favorite word game, Stinky Pinky, which always evokes gales of laughter. We must have been louder than we realized because a young lady leaned out of her window and asked us to please be quiet. We were especially surprised because it was only 10 p.m., early by most Greek standards.

DAN

We have checked out of Petros pension and just had breakfast at Mama's Cyclades Restaurant, home of the best, and so far only, American breakfast we've had in Greece, where the usual is a continental breakfast of coffee and a roll. Today we had bacon, eggs, hash browns, and homemade French toast, which seems to be unheard of any-where else in Greece. Known only as "Mama," she's quite a character and a bundle of pure energy. "Mama loves you, Babies" is her favorite saying. She brought us over an Athens newspaper and the headlines were all about record heat of 107 degrees that day! We were grateful to be on the island, surrounded by water, where the tempera-tures were slightly cooler than that! We will be getting a ride to the ferry dock later this morning from Petros, who was kind enough to offer. Our next stop? Crete!

CRETE

Dear Friends,

Welcome to Crete for the Mazoxi '99 dance gathering. As in previous years we have chosen authentic teachers from several areas of Greece to teach us dances and songs in their authentic forms. For this reason we have chosen the village of Roustika, named a traditional heritage village by the Greek Tourist Organization, especially for the architecture of the houses and great number of 13th and 15th century churches. The residents are hospitable and openhearted. During the length of the Mazoxi, along with learning traditional dances and songs, we will have the opportunity to taste local cuisine of Crete and enjoy this special hospitality. We hope your stay will be full of nature, tradition and everything Greek.

> Sincerely,
> Kety & Andrea Fragiakis
> Seminar Sponsors and
> Former Members of the
> Greek National Dance Company

We spoke with many Greeks from the mainland about Crete and they all agreed that Crete, the largest of the Greek islands, is like its own country: so authentically Greek.

Historically it is the oldest civilization in Europe, between the Middle East and Western Europe, a true crossroads of cultures.

ELIZABETH

Our decision to go to Crete had everything to do with these two things: to attend a Greek dance seminar in the mountain village of Roustika and our husbands' plan to hike the Samarian Gorge.

As we settle ourselves on the top deck of the ferry to Crete, our eyes are washed with incredible blues of the sea and sky. Soon over the PA system we hear a little music and an exuberant voice announcing that the dining room is open for lunch. We're surprised that the menu offers almost as many choices as the tavernas we've visited on land. The four of us share the pleasures of different dishes. Our favorite was shrimp with feta, which had a heaping bed of rice-tomato pilaf on a plate with huge, juicy, perfect shrimp tumbling over the top of it, sprinkled generously with melting pieces of pure white feta.

Shrimp and Feta
Garides Yianni
Serves 4

The shrimp do not take long to cook, so be sure to prepare your rice ahead of time.

1½ lb of raw shrimp, peeled and deveined
2 T olive oil
1 c chopped onion
2 cloves chopped garlic
½ bunch chopped green onions
3 chopped fresh tomatoes
1 6-oz can of tomato paste
2 c chicken broth or water

½ c dry white wine
1 T butter
1 t dried Greek oregano
1 T flat-leaf parsley chopped
1 t each of salt and pepper
1 c feta cheese, crumbled
½ t hot red pepper flakes (optional)

Heat oil in pan, add garlic and onions and sauté until translucent. Add oregano and pepper flakes, salt and pepper. Add tomatoes and wine and sauté 5 or 6 minutes. Mix tomato paste in broth or water and add to pan. Simmer for 15 minutes. Add parsley, butter and shrimp and simmer until shrimp turn pink. Sprinkle with feta, cover with lid until feta softens or melts, from 5 to 8 minutes. Serve with crusty bread and rice.

DAN

Today we're on our way to Crete on the ferry, which lands in Chania, the city on the extreme west side of the northern coast. I ran sweating through the beautiful, narrow streets of old Chania built with the Venetian and Ottoman influences of the seventeenth and eighteenth centuries. I came back to find that while they waited with the luggage, Floyd had found a very suitable hotel fifty yards from the square I set off from! The hotel Arkadi is 10,000 drachma per night with breakfast and air conditioning.

GEORGIA

Settling into our rooms, we have a quick siesta and then stroll through the alleyways until we reach the harbor, softly lit with both the sunset and the tavernas' patio lights, a kaleidoscope of colors. We stop to have dinner at the Harbor-side Taverna. Eggplant salad, bread, lamb chops, fresh-cut fries, horta, and kotopita, the ultimate Greek chicken pie: flavorful chicken, onions and cheeses blended into a rich, herbed filling, accompanied by a light pink Cretan Rose wine. It was here that we had our first taste of raki, one of the popular liqueurs of Greece. Unlike ouzo, it is not flavored with anise. Cool and smooth, a welcome gift from our waiter!

ELIZABETH

This brings back a memory of our Papou, who lived with us until his death at ninety-four, when I was twelve. There seemed to be a rite of passage at a certain age, when we would get our turn at filling his ouzo glass when it was empty while he read his afternoon newspaper. My turn came at the age of ten, after watching my sister carry out this little ritual. I was always curious about that clear, white liquid that smelled of black licorice. No wonder he likes it, I thought, if it tastes sweet as licorice; however, that bubble was soon burst the day he called out his nickname for me, "Sahvah," to fill that little glass. I took the glass over to the fridge, full of secret anticipation, poured the magic liquid into it, and while the refrigerator door was shielding me, I stuck my tongue into what I thought would be liquid licorice. The shock of what I tasted must have been etched on my face as I turned around to take his glass to him, for there he was, having a good laugh, knowing exactly what I had done! I was never tempted to try it again (to this day, in fact).

Chicken Pie
Kotopita
Serves 6–8

Flavorful chicken, onions and cheeses blended into a rich herbed filling, baked between layers of flaky filo.

1½ sticks butter
2 stalks of celery finely chopped
4 bunches of green onions, thinly sliced
3 c cooked chicken, chopped
2 eggs, lightly beaten
2 c ricotta or cottage cheese
12 oz feta cheese
8 oz Parmesan, coarsely grated

½ c fresh dill, chopped
3 T chopped Italian parsley
¼ t ground nutmeg
1 T dried mint
1T dried oregano
1 t each salt and pepper
12 sheets of thawed filo dough

Melt the half stick of butter in a large saucepan. Add the celery and onions and sauté over medium heat until soft—about 5 minutes. Combine well with the chicken, eggs, cheeses, dill, parsley, nutmeg and the remaining dried herbs. Season with salt and pepper. Using a small pastry brush, grease a 9- by 13-inch baking pan with a little more melted butter. Line the pan with six sheets of filo, brushing each sheet lightly with melted butter from the remaining stick and letting filo overlap the sides of the pan. Spread the chicken filling over the filo. Cover with the remaining filo sheets, and fold in all edges to fit pan, brushing each with the melted butter. With a sharp knife, make lengthwise cuts 2 inches apart through the top layers of filo, then cut across, forming squares. Bake for 45 minutes in a preheated oven at 350 degrees F. or until top is golden brown. Serve hot, warm or at room temperature.

DAN

We are now ready to leave Chania behind and get to Rethymnon. What a wonderful bus ride on the northern coast of Crete! Windows open, lovely ocean vistas below, beaches, resort villas, cliffs, blue sky, green water—an amazingly swift trip to the bus station of Rethymnon. Like Chania, Rethymnon is a mix of Venetian and Turkish architecture: minarets punctuating the skyline, Arabic inscriptions on stone walls, tiny Venetian balconies in profusion and a fortress guarding the harbor.

FLOYD

We arrive in Rethymnon and begin walking to the center from the bus station. Along the way we came to a beautiful plush hotel, the Fortezza, only a block from the seaside. A lovely room with air conditioning, patio and pool, which I went to almost immediately. Dan and I swam and visited with a German man and his two little sons, while Georgia and Elizabeth sat at the poolside terrace chatting and enjoying a cool drink. Soon we join them for a light lunch of feta and olive salad, fried zucchini, and crusty Greek bread.

ELIZABETH

For dessert we indulged in a plate of assorted Greek cookies usually prepared for special occasions. Kourambiethes are shortbread cookies especially eaten at Christmas. Melomacarona, honey-dipped cookies, are for Easter; they are a very old tradition. Some say the recipe came from the Phoenicians, which is why they are sometimes called Phoenekia.

Honey-Dipped Cookies
Phoenekia or Melomacarona
Makes about 40 cookies

These cookies melt in your mouth.

1 c butter softened
1 c vegetable oil
¾ c sugar
¾ c orange juice
7–8 c flour
1 T cinnamon
3 egg yolks
3 t baking powder
¼ t baking soda

Syrup:
2 c sugar
1 c water
1 c honey
1 strip orange peel
Juice of ½ lemon
Topping:
1 lb finely ground walnuts
1 T sugar

Prepare the syrup before making the cookies. Combine sugar, water and honey and bring to a boil. Add orange peel and simmer for 10 to 12 minutes. Remove saucepan from heat and add lemon juice and let syrup cool. While syrup is simmering, combine the ground walnuts and sugar in a bowl.

To make the cookies: Beat butter, egg yolks, oil, and sugar together for five minutes. Slowly add orange juice and blend well. Sift about 7 cups of flour with cinnamon, baking powder and baking soda, and stir into mixture. Knead until mixture forms a ball and leaves sides of the bowl, adding more flour if necessary. Pinch off small pieces of dough, about the size of an egg, roll into oval shapes and flatten slightly in the palm of your hand. Place on ungreased cookie sheet; bake in the center of a preheated 350 degrees oven until golden, about 20 to 25 minutes. Remove cookie sheet from oven. Place cookies on a wire rack for just a minute. Dip four or five warm cookies in cooled syrup with a slotted spoon and allow them to soak up the syrup while turning them several times. As you remove cookies from syrup, sprinkle them with the nut mixture and place them on a serving plate. Store in tins or cookie jars at room temperature.

GEORGIA

Afternoon siestas refresh us for our evening stroll and meal. We walked the lovely arched streets of Old Town and finally came to rest at a wonderful taverna called the Old Tavern.

We had a mouth-watering beef stew, salad, jacketed potatoes and Cretan white wine. We struck up a conversation with a Greek dance instructor, who invited us to go with him to a family-run tavern, O Gounas, known for its hearty, no-frills food but especially for its nightly authentic Cretan music and dancing. We entered this dark, stone cavern-like taverna and could see through the smoky atmosphere to the back of the one room where the lone musician was playing the lyra, an old three-stringed instrument played like a violin held on the knee. We were told that the circle of dancers was being led by the family patriarch. He was a striking figure with a shock of white hair, a bristly white mustache and dressed in men's traditional jodhpur-like trousers, shirt and vest, black head-band scarf, and Cretan knee-high boots of white leather rather than black. This might have indicated he had been part of a dance troupe in his youth.

He still had the posture and stance of a great dancer and his Greek gusto, his kefi, was still in evidence as he hissed and whistled through the intricate steps of the Cretan Syrto. We fortified ourselves with a little raki and crusty, lemony oven potatoes, then joined the circle for a dance before heading back to the Fortezza. The end of a splendid day!

A Beef and Onion Stew
Stifatho
Serves 4–6

This beef stew has more onions than beef and a sprinkling of spices that makes it unusually delicious.

1½ lb beef (or chicken) cut in pieces
½ c melted butter
2 T olive oil
2 lb pearl onions
1 t each salt and pepper
3 garlic cloves chopped
1 c dry red wine
1 6-oz can tomato paste

2 c water
3 T wine vinegar
1 T sugar
2 bay leaves
½ t ground cinnamon
½ t ground cloves
¼ t cumin

In a large saucepan heat butter and oil. Brown the meat on all sides, add the onion and garlic and sprinkle with salt and pepper. Cook for 2 to 3 minutes. Add the red wine and simmer for one minute. Mix tomato paste with water, vinegar and sugar. Add to pan with the remaining ingredients. Bring to a boil, remove from heat and pour all into a covered casserole dish. Bake in a preheated oven for 2 hours at 350 degrees F., until meat and onions are fork tender. After one hour check pan and add more water if too much liquid has evaporated.

DAN

Breakfast at the Hotel Fortezza. To get our money's worth we ate and ate! Every time someone got a cup of coffee Floyd said, "Cha-ching," indicating our savings! By the time we had eaten our room's worth we left the table. It's already very hot and we look forward to heading up into the hills tomorrow to the mountain village of Roustika, where the girls will stay for a week at the dance seminar.

109

ELIZABETH

As we wander over towards the center of town we discover the annual Rethymnon Wine Festival begins tonight so we decide to spend one more night here. And here at the bus station where taxis also gather, we meet our first man named Eleftherios — "Freedom" — or Lefty for short. He's a very friendly cab-driver and pension owner who offers to show us his bargain rooms only a short cab-ride away. We decide after having indulged in the Hotel Fortezza, tonight we needed a bargain. Piling our luggage in the trunk which won't close, Lefty flies through the narrow streets and alleyways, losing one of our suitcases but safely retrieving it after a couple of blocks, and stops in front of the Pension Kallergi, one of his three establishments, whose signs read "Friendly Atmosphere!! Cheap Rates!!" The rooms were immaculate, Lefty was very friendly and the rates were cheap. We vowed to remember Lefty and look him up next time in Rethymnon.

That night we walked over to the municipal gardens, which are furnished with tables and benches for the Cretan Wine Festival. For a nominal entrance fee, we are given a souvenir wine glass each and invited to sample as much wine as we'd like. Canteens offer souvlaki, crisp roast chicken, fresh cut fried potatoes or whatever your palette demands. Other stands provide more refreshments, beverages and beer. The festival's specialty, however, is the variety of wines produced in Cretan vineyards. Many varieties of wine of different taste and bouquet are available. It is organized by the local Touring Club in Rethymnon which gives special attention to the entertainment and fun for children. The festivities in the children's program within the framework of the festival are very carefully chosen and take place daily from 7 to 9 p.m. After 9 p.m. the scene is taken over by dance groups and singers.

Greek Fried Potatoes
Patates Tiganites
Serves 6

They used to be called Drachma potatoes because they were cut into rounds like the silver coin centuries before the Euro. They remind us of our Mom's potatoes. Fresh, crisp and delicious.

6–8 potatoes
¾ c olive oil
Salt to taste

Cut potatoes into quarter inch rounds. Heat oil to medium high and fry the rounds until golden, turning once. Drain on paper towels and salt to taste.

GEORGIA

Along with our first glass of wine, we were thrilled to purchase our favorite snack, fresh hand-cut fried potatoes. We finally accept the fact that fries are indeed a Greek staple, served with everything. Not too much variety in our dinner menu tonight: fries, souvlaki, and wine! Not only did we enjoy the dance demonstrations, but we were able to participate in various dances that we knew, all the while whetting our appetite for our dance seminar starting tomorrow.

DAN

Here we sit at the Wine Festival with two carafes of wine and four bags of fabulous, crisp fried potatoes. After the children have finished reciting poems and the magician has left the stage, the Cretan dancers start. Red, blue, black and gold swim before our still sober eyes as they float past with small kicks and steps, hands held high. The women spin; now the men jump high and slap their heels. Then a slight pause and they all look toward their partners to see if they are ready to proceed to the escalated next step. Ahh! Three instruments make the music: two large string fiddles and an upright lyra. Leads change and solos are done like good jazz. The girls sit following every move, swaying with the music.

I went up closer to get photos of the dancers and sat in a chair next to an old woman (old as God). I made the mistake of saying in Greek, "Ti kanis?" (How are you?) As quick as you can say, "Kalla!" (Fine!), she rambled off this great smiling conversation opener and pointed to the dancers. My turn: "Neh" (yes). Then she went on again and I said *neh* again with more emphasis myself, pointing to the dancers, then, spreading my hands to encompass the whole festival. She nodded enthusiastically and I soon snuck off before she asked me to marry her.

ELIZABETH

After the dancers finished their first set, they invited the onlookers to come up and dance. Georgia and I couldn't resist the music and found ourselves in the middle of the crowd, dancing in delight!

"And the dancing young men were whirling around and among them flutes and lyres were sounding...

"Young girls and youths followed the music with dancing feet...

"And a great delighted company stood around the lovely dance..."

–Homer

FLOYD

Got a cab to Roustika, arriving after a steep and winding ride, and were delighted by the surroundings and setup for the seminar. It is a resort area called Mountain Vista being developed by a Greek-American, Manoli, or "Mike," who spent fifteen years running a supermarket in Chicago. He made enough money to come back to his father's land on Crete to begin to develop his mountaintop resort outside the center of the village.

We ate lunch with the dance group and met some of the participants from all over the world; twenty-seven people for the seminar and fifteen others who signed up but backed out because of the fear surrounding the Kosovo Civil War. The setup is excellent, nice bedrooms and all marble floors inside and outside under the trellised patio. A gorgeous large pool, which Dan and I used for most of the afternoon, swimming, drinking homemade ice-cold raki kept in a small fridge below the poolside bar.

DAN

We listened to Mike's philosophy of raising children by showing them how to work. Of course, taxation, government and all else has already been discussed.

ELIZABETH

It's exciting to be sitting down to our first meal with this new group of friends. The salad and huge chunks of olive bread are delicious, but the best part was the heaping platters of steaming orzo, or kritharaki, as it's called in Greece, glistening with brown butter and sprinkled with Mizithra cheese. This is the original comfort food to us, but also an ancient traditional meal, elegant in its simplicity.

Toasted Orzo with Brown Butter and Cheese
Kritharaki me Voutiro ke Tiri
Serves 6–8

Kritharaki is a tiny pasta that looks like flat grains of wheat. We learned that remnants of this pasta were found in the ancient amphorae of the Minoan Palace at Knossos.

2 c orzo
6 c broth
8 T butter
Juice of 1 lemon
1 c grated Kasseri or Parmesan cheese

½ cup chopped fresh herbs of
choice, such as parsley,
oregano, and/or scallions
Salt and pepper to taste

In a large saucepan melt one tablespoon butter and toast the orzo until it starts to color, stirring constantly. Bring the broth to a boil in a saucepan and add orzo, simmering until it is tender, about 10 minutes. Drain. Meanwhile, heat the remaining butter in a saucepan over very low heat until it's golden brown. Return the orzo to the large saucepan and add the brown butter, the cheese, the lemon juice, salt and pepper. Stir just to mix, heat to warm if needed. Add fresh herbs.

Olive Batter Bread
Eliopita
Serves 6–8

The Minoans were the first to bake olives into their bread.

1 c black Kalamata olives pitted and chopped
3 T dried mint or ½ c fresh chopped
1 large onion finely chopped
3½ c flour

3 t baking powder
1 c olive oil
2 c warm water

In a bowl mix olives, mint and onion. In another bowl mix flour, baking powder and oil. Stir in the water slowly and mix until batter is smooth. Stir in the olive mixture. In a greased 9- by 13-inch baking pan, spread the batter and bake in a preheated oven at 350 degrees F. for one hour, until browned. This is best served hot. It is also good toasted the next day.

ELIZABETH

Once we finished lunch we went to our room to unpack and then to the main hall to register. There we met the dance teachers and musicians from various regions of Greece and the participants, who were from all over the world. In the cool of the evening we gathered early for dinner. Tonight the cook chose pheasant for the meat, cooked in wine, the taste of which reminds us of our Papou trapping pheasants in our backyard for this very dish, which our mother prepared with Papou's home-made Retsina wine. We also had Briam, which is a savory blend of vegetables layered in a roasting pan steeped in olive oil, tomato sauce and herbs.

Chicken in Wine
Kotopoulo Krassato
Serves 4–6

Since pheasant is not usually available, chicken works just fine in this tasty dish.

¼ c butter
¼ c olive oil
3 medium onions
1 clove garlic, chopped
6 portions chicken
Salt and pepper

1 c white wine
1 14-oz can diced tomatoes
1 bay leaf
1 T fresh parsley chopped
1 c fresh mushrooms rinsed and sliced

Heat the butter and oil in a large frying pan. Sauté the onions and garlic until golden and remove to an oblong casserole dish. Sauté the chicken until golden. Sprinkle generously with salt and pepper and place over the onions in the casserole. Pour wine into frying pan and boil for about five minutes. Add the canned tomatoes, bay leaf, parsley, and mushrooms. Simmer for a few minutes and add to the chicken. Cover and bake for one hour in a preheated oven at 350 degrees F.

Baked Vegetables
Briam
Serves 10–12

A wonderful combination of vegetables layered in a roasting pan steeped in olive oil and tomato sauce, similar to ratatouille.

3 medium potatoes peeled and
    sliced into 1/4-inch rounds
1 large eggplant sliced into
    rounds 1/4-inch thick
3 medium zucchini cut into
    rounds ½-inch thick
2 bell peppers, chopped (1 green, 1 yellow)
2 c onions chopped

1 c Italian flat-leaf parsley chopped
2 c diced tomatoes
½ c olive oil
4 garlic cloves, minced
2 t each salt, pepper and oregano
½ c white wine
1 c grated hard Greek Kefalotiri
    or Parmesan

Brush bottom of a large 10- by 15-inch roasting pan with oil, sprinkle salt and pepper over entire pan. Layer vegetables in the order listed, starting with potatoes ending with tomatoes. Sprinkle each layer lightly with salt and pepper. Mix olive oil, minced garlic, oregano, and wine in a large measuring cup and pour over the top of the vegetables. Cover lightly with foil and bake in a preheated oven at 400 degrees F. for about half an hour and check for liquid. If more liquid is needed add some broth or hot water. Remove foil and put back in oven for another half hour or until vegetables are tender. Sprinkle grated cheese over the top while still hot and serve.

DAN

Floyd and I get a ride to a new pension near the village of Roustika. On the way we hear a shepherd singing to his sheep.

FLOYD

We walked back to the resort to have breakfast with Georgia and Elizabeth. At ten o'clock sharp in the morning Mike drove us down the mountain to Rethymnon in his fast and scary BMW! We're about to start our own adventure of hiking the Samarian Gorge.

GEORGIA

The nearby monastery bells wake us for breakfast—but wait, maybe it's the smell of fresh brewed coffee and cinnamon-laced paximathia, a twice-baked biscotti-like cookie. We rise slowly but eagerly, happy to be roommates. Out in the main room of the resort on the buffet table our eyes are filled with the sight of baskets of fresh baked goods, silver bowls of hard-boiled eggs, blue porcelain platters of meats and cheeses, amber jars of honey, ceramic containers of the famous creamy, full-fat Greek yogurt cooled on ice, colors of fruits and juices, shining urns of coffees and samovars of water for teas. Something for everyone! We eat on the front terrace that's high on the cliff side of the room, where the views are breathtaking. The evergreen mountains are surrounded in heavy mist. By the time we finished breakfast with our husbands and hugged them a "kalo taxithi," a Greek bon voyage for their hike, the sun has cleared away the mist outside and someone has cleared away tables and crumbs inside so that now the shiny marble floors are ready for dancing. The entire space is embraced by vast windows looking out at mountains, flowered patios and the shimmering pool.

ELIZABETH

The teachers, musician, and dancers were a varied group of interesting people who came from all over the world. Vasso, our dance teacher, and her brother, Penteli, a musician, both from northern Greece, even shared some of their regional recipes with us. We learned there are great numbers of people who travel far and wide to attend dance seminars to learn the dances of different countries. Some of those people were here. It was fascinating to find out where all these attendees had come from.

There was a mother and daughter from Amsterdam; four lovely ladies from Tokyo who had learned to speak Greek, with a Japanese accent, since this was their fourth Greek dance seminar, but didn't speak English; a married couple from the Midwest, who always videotaped the lessons so as not to forget any steps once home; two friends from Oahu; a ballerina from Redondo Beach, California; four friends from Washington D.C.; three sisters from Santa Barbara; a Spanish lady from Vancouver; a lady from Oceanside, California, who kept us laughing; one man who kept us enthralled at dinner with his Indiana Jones–type stories of his adventures around the world; one man who was an ethnomusicologist from Athens; and ourselves, the only Greek-Americans in the group.

After breakfast it was a delight to meet the owner's daughter, eleven-year-old Irini, who so wanted to be part of the group. When she discovered we were the only Greek-Americans there she wanted to practice her English with us and helped us practice our Greek. Her brother Stelio quietly observed us all. At 9 a.m. we were called to the dance floor and listened to our teacher describe the traditional folk-music instruments from the various regions: the gaida, which is the Greek bagpipe; the tambouri, a classical drum that is beaten hard and makes a muffled sound; and two stringed instruments; modeled on the ancient lyra, as seen on ancient pottery designs, and the bouzouki, considered the most Greek of all the instruments.

We danced until 1 p.m. and had lunch at 2 p.m. I was so exhausted I actually had toyed with the idea of napping rather than eating, but quickly came back to my senses when the aromas of lunch cooking reached me in our room. I found the patio tables strewn with bowls of salad; platters of bread; squash fritters (kolokithokeftethes) fried crispy on the outside and soft and creamy on the inside; green bean and potato casserole bathed in a tomato sauce; burgundy beets with oil, vinegar and fresh oregano; and cabbage stuffed with a savory blend of meat, rice and herbs. There were also carafes of ice water and cool Retsina wine.

Stuffed Cabbage with Egg-Lemon Sauce
Lahano Dolmathes Avgolemono
Serves 8

Beef, rice and herbs wrapped in cabbage leaves and simmered in egg-lemon sauce.

1 white cabbage (about 2 lb)
1½ lb ground beef
½ c long-grain rice
1 onion grated
½ c chopped flat-leaf parsley
½ c chopped fresh dill

½ c fresh chopped mint or 3 T dried
1 c olive oil
1 t each salt and pepper
3 c broth or to cover cabbage rolls
2 eggs
2 lemons

Wash cabbage and place whole head in a pan of water. Add 1 teaspoon salt and boil for ten minutes. Remove and separate leaves cutting out the thick stocks in center. Place ground meat in a bowl and mix with rice, onions, parsley, dill, mint, oil, salt and pepper. Place about a tablespoon of mixture on a cabbage leaf, tuck in sides and roll up firmly. Place rolls in saucepan, tightly packed together. Put an upturned plate on top of the rolls to keep them in place. Fill pot with broth to cover, and simmer over low heat for about 50 minutes until cabbage is very soft and meat and rice are cooked. Carefully remove the liquid to a bowl and reserve while keeping rolls warm in the pot.

In a separate bowl beat eggs until frothy, then slowly add lemon juice, beating constantly. Slowly add a cup of the reserved liquid to the egg-lemon mixture until well combined. Pour this sauce over the cabbage rolls and heat on very low fire until sauce slightly thickens. Do not boil or it will curdle. Serve hot.

Squash Fritters
Kolokithokeftethes
Serves 6–8

Crispy on the outside, soft on the inside.

2 lb zucchini, grated
1 t course salt
½ c thinly sliced scallions
3 T chopped fresh dill
3 T chopped fresh mint
2 garlic cloves, minced

½ t pepper
1 c fresh breadcrumbs
1 c crumbled feta cheese
1 large egg, beaten
1 c flour
1½ c canola oil for frying

Grate zucchini on large holes of a grater onto a cloth towel and sprinkle with coarse salt. Let stand for thirty minutes. Line a baking sheet with foil or parchment paper. Wrap zucchini in the towel and squeeze out the liquid. Place the zucchini in a medium bowl and mix in scallions, dill, mint, garlic and pepper. Stir in breadcrumbs, egg and feta. With a large spoon, scoop out about two tablespoon of mixture, form into balls, roll in flour and flatten into about a two-inch patty and place on baking sheet. Chill at least one hour. Heat the oil in a skillet until hot but not smoking and fry zucchini patties in batches over medium heat until golden and crisp, five to ten minutes. Remove and drain on paper towels. Serve immediately. Makes about twelve patties. Delicious with tzadziki (yogurt dip) or skordthalia (garlic dip).

Yogurt Cucumber Garlic Dip
Tzadziki
Serves 6–8

The most famous Greek dip of all.

1 16-oz container plain yogurt
1 large cucumber
4 garlic cloves minced
2 T finely chopped fresh dill

4 T olive oil
2 T red wine vinegar
Salt and pepper to taste

Strain yogurt in a strainer lined with paper towel for about two hours. Peel and grate cucumber. Squeeze cuke between palms of hands a little at a time, until water is removed. Place strained yogurt in a bowl with cucumbers and mix in garlic, dill, olive oil, vinegar, salt and pepper. Combine well and refrigerate for at least one hour before serving.

GEORGIA

We were so surprised at the abundance of food at lunchtime (little did we know this would be the norm at every meal). We linger longer at the table under the grapevine to chat with Bert and Rita, mother and daughter from Amsterdam. "Siga! Siga!" *Take it slow.* Though siesta calls and my knees are already aching from morning dancing, I stroll over to the poolside to watch the swallows swing down to the shimmering water, their breasts flashing the turquoise of reflection. It reminds me of the same playful activity captured in the swallow frescoes we'd seen in Akrotiri, the Minoan site excavated on Santorini. Finally all's quiet for a long restful siesta until a bell chimes a couple of hours later, announcing dance time before dinner. At about 6 p.m. we gather on the terrace under the red bougainvillea to practice for two hours the dances we'd learned this morning. Then there's time for a quick shower and change before dinner

120

at nine. A warm breeze and the scent of jasmine hover over the arbor as we feast for the second time today! Later the musicians play, inviting a few townspeople to help us master the dance! A new circle of friends dancing until dreamtime. This is heaven. And so goes the rhythm of our dance seminar days.

As the days and dancing progress our heads are filled with the Pontic beat of Asia Minor, a new rhythm to us. Our feet move on their own by now, but why are our knees killing us? Probably because we are dancing five to six hours a day! The last time Elizabeth and I were roommates was in college. Alas, we are roommates once again but this time we share a tube of Ben Gay for rubbing on our painful knees. Earlier today, Nan, a waiter from D.C., commented, "I've discovered the secret to Pontic dancing: if it's simple enough to do it, it's boring as hell! Otherwise you'll never figure out the rhythm!"

Today we skipped siesta in favor of a grand adventure. Irini invited us to go with her to visit her Yiayia in the next village, Moutras. Before leaving she called her mother on her cell phone to ask permission. As she waved her hand good-bye, we turned and saw her mother on the sun-drenched roof top of the resort hanging sheets to dry in the wind. As she was talking on her cell phone, she waved us on with snowy white sheets flapping all around her. "Over the river and through the woods to grandmother's house we go!" We would have sung this walking with Irini to her grandmother's house, but instead she quizzed us on our Greek vocabulary. She counts in English as we march along following her orders. "Close eyes now!" We complain so she asks us instead to "Look therrre"—with a long rolling *R*—"and walk! Okay, surprise now!" The beginning of the village appears down low in a winding hollow. "S-s-s!" she says, instead of "sh," a sound that does not occur in the Greek language. "Leesten, the river! You can hear?"

We're right in the midst of lovely peaks that seem to sink here and there with the weight of silvery olive groves. The village alleys wind down and up the center of the town. We pass an ancient watering trough with a wooden pipe and faucet over a carved marble sill. The Yiayia's house is two stories of stone topped with a tile roof. A Greek-blue wrought iron gate sits locked in the walls around the courtyard. We've told Irini that we hoped we wouldn't be disturbing Yiayia's siesta and she assures us Yiayia only rests watching her soap opera. Now we wait in the narrow street for Irini to go in and announce she's brought her "two very old girlfriends" for a visit. Within three minutes she's back, carefully closing the gate, saying without further explanation, "And now! We go to the jail!" But not before we get a peek inside the gate. The courtyard is immaculate black and white marble flooring, bright red geraniums bursting out of their pots, the color a lyrical contrast to the gray stone walls: a quiet, reserved, cool gray everywhere warmed only by the occasional golden orange blooms of the trumpet vine. The look is so different from the energetic quiet of the whitewashed island houses. Here it seems as if the people chose to keep only the six village churches whitewashed. We are led farther into the grayness up the hill to the glowing white church of her grandmother's neighborhood.

"You want to see?" our little guide asks. We say, "Parakalo!" *Please!* Irini opens the door into the church and her voice drops to a whisper as she scolds us for being too loud getting our cameras ready. "No pictures!" she says. About ten plain chairs flank each side of the aisle to the altar. The three doors of the iconostasis are covered with white curtains edged in a linen crocheted border. The center doorway, through which only the priest may enter, has carved marble peacocks in the upper corners. Two carved marble doves serve as holders for the red glass oil lamps hanging on silver chains on either side. Only these two flecks of light offer signs of activity in the tiny basilica. We leave still whispering. Its sanctity is contagious. Outside, cousin Christina, a little black-braided beauty, meets us. "Now, jail!" which must be the scary wonder to show us. Irini's glad her cousin's with us. Walking up farther still, the girls point to an open dark doorway in another wall of gray. This is an old abandoned jail, about which Irini has heard many stories, and she dares us to go in. We decline and in five or six more steps she and Christina are arguing about which road to take, the left or the right. "Not therrre!" she says, pointing to the left: "Therrre!" pointing to the right. We think the left looks more intriguing, but Irini is insistent that "It's not goood therrre. Something BAD!" Elizabeth and I honor our first guide's wishes to go right. The one village store, a room with an ice-cream freezer, a drinks refrigerator and two shelves of food items, beckons us. A short, not-happy-looking man dressed in Cretan black shirt, pants and boots, greets us and sells us cool peach apricot juices. Perfect! The elderly couple sitting outside in the street by their doorway, legs propped up on bright blue chairs, decline to have their photo taken. We wonder if they've ever been asked by strangers to be photographed. I remember the ladies in Anoya, a town nearby known for its handicrafts, relishing the Kodak moment! It helped sell tablecloths, scarves, rugs and crocheted delicates. They depended on tourism. This village, Moutras, is not far away in distance, only far away in attitude. After our refreshment, Irini tells us we'll be taking a new short way home. We're so glad. She only forgot to say it was not a road but very rough and very steep, and our knees were very achy all the way back to Roustika, but an afternoon rich with moments to remember.

ELIZABETH

Another missed siesta we spent in the kitchen with Katina, and her mother, Audrika, who were kitchen queens and responsible for all the delicious meals. We helped them prep green beans and zucchini for stuffing. We also tasted stuffed zucchini flowers, a new variation for us, as they toasted us: "Kali orexi." *Bon appétit*. They showed us how to fill these bright yellow-orange blossoms delicately with rice, herbs and shredded vegetables. We lament the fact that where we live, these blossoms are not often found in our markets. Both the green beans and stuffed zucchini recipes are familiar to us because we grew up enjoying them. It is known that the Greeks eat the least amount of meat though they are not vegetarians. Both of the following recipes are examples of hearty vegetarian entrées of the healthy Mediterranean diet.

Braised Green Beans and Potatoes
Fasolakia Yianni me Patates
Serves 4–5

This combination of vegetables makes a lovely vegetarian entrée.

1½ lb fresh green beans or
1-lb pkg frozen whole string beans
¼ c olive oil
2 large onions chopped
3 medium potatoes, peeled
   and quartered

1 garlic clove, chopped
½ t sugar
1 large can (28 oz) diced tomatoes
¼ c water
Salt and pepper to taste
1 c feta cheese, crumbled

Wash and trim beans. Heat olive oil in a large pot and sauté onions until translucent. Add beans and potatoes and stir with a wooden spoon for 3 minutes. Add garlic, sugar and stir. Add tomatoes and ¼ cup water. Season with salt and pepper. Cover pot and simmer for 1 hour. Add more water if necessary, and cook until beans are very soft and tender and potatoes are cooked completely. Serve hot or at room temperature with crumbled feta.

This dish is also very good without potatoes.

Stuffed Zucchini
Kolokithakia Yemista
Serves 5–6

Another dish that can stand alone.

2 medium zucchini about 4 inches long, per person

Filling:

1 T each of oil and butter	**1 t dry mint**
1 onion chopped	**1 t Greek oregano**
4 garlic cloves chopped	**1½ c water**
1 c tomato juice	**Juice of 1 lemon**
1 c rice, long grain	**1½ c fresh bread crumbs**
1 t salt	**½ c grated cheese (Kefalotiri or Parmesan)**
½ t pepper	**for topping**
2 T fresh chopped parsley	

Cut zucchinis in half the long way and scoop out enough pulp to leave a half-inch shell. Heat oil and butter in skillet. Sauté onions and garlic for 5 minutes. Add remaining ingredients for filling, including pulp of zucchini, and cook 10 minutes, stirring once or twice. Fill shells. Arrange stuffed vegetables in a baking pan, placing them close together. Add hot water and lemon juice to the pan. Cover with foil and bake for 45 minutes. Remove foil, sprinkle with cheese, drizzle with olive oil and continue to bake for another 10 minutes to brown topping.

At dinner tonight we heard the very sad news of John Kennedy Jr.'s plane crash. Tragically his wife and her sister perished with him ... echoes of a Greek tragedy.

"For lamentation they have remembrance."

—Simonides

ELIZABETH

Today is Sunday and we have no dance classes but they take us on a field trip. We all boarded a large bus and headed for Kournas Lake, Crete's only lake, set deep in a bowl of hills. We stopped at a small taverna for coffee and a snack. One of the things we had was a sweet cheese pie with honey. That was new to us and very good.

After our snack we explored this tiny village and its little shops full of avocado oils, soaps, lotions and handmade linens. The name of this village was Argyroupoli, but the ancient section of this 2,000-year-old town was Lappa. Not far from here were the famous waterfalls ("taheppa") spilling over terraced stones.

We were taken to a taverna under the trees with a table set for a banquet. We all sat down excitedly and were served a banquet-sized meal of warm, fluffy breads, colorful salad, buttery, crisp pita filled with warm melted cheese, garlicky roasted lamb and lemony, herbed potatoes and a wonderful aromatic baked fish. The trays of pastries made us groan with delight!

Baked Fish
Psari Plaki
Serves 4

A delicious baked fish with aromatic herbs and vegetables that make it impossible to forget.

2 lb fresh white fish fillets
3 T fresh lemon juice
Salt and pepper to taste
1/3 c olive oil
2 large onions sliced
1 celery rib cut into thin rounds

2 cloves garlic chopped
3 T fresh chopped flat-leaf parsley
3–4 tomatoes sliced into rounds or 1
  14-oz can diced tomatoes
½ can tomato paste
½ c dry white wine

125

Sprinkle fish with lemon juice, salt and pepper. In a heavy skillet, heat 2 tablespoons olive oil and sauté onion and celery until translucent. Remove pot from heat, let mixture cool, then stir in garlic, parsley, tomatoes and tomato paste. Spread 2 tablespoons olive oil in glass or clay baking dish and place fish in it. Top with onion, celery and tomatoes. Season with salt and pepper. Mix wine and remaining olive oil and pour over top. Bake uncovered until fish is fork-tender, 25 to 30 minutes in a preheated oven at 350 degrees (less time if fillets are thin). Add water if necessary to keep pan moist during baking. Serve on platter, garnish with more parsley.

ELIZABETH

The days fly by and our week of lessons comes to an end. Our last night at dinner, we were called to the phone. Our husbands were on their way back from their week-long hiking adventures and will arrive tomorrow, the day we are scheduled to leave.

DAN

We called the girls from Frangokasteli's bus stop, where it was very windy. They said their knees hurt. I guess that makes us even, with the aching muscles we experienced (and still feel) after hiking the Samarian Gorge.

FLOYD

We took the bus back to Roustika and a reunion with our happy dancers and we were welcomed by all.

GEORGIA

Besides our memories of fun with new friends, we take the new recipes they gave us, looking forward to trying them in our own kitchens. We are preparing to leave just two days earlier than the rest of the class. We will miss the music and fun we all had mastering the complicated dance steps.

Our new friends, Vasso and Penteli, musicians from Macedonia, tell us that peppers are abundant in many different varieties. And so they gave us some of their favorite pepper recipes.

Fried Sweet Red Peppers
Piperies Tiganites
Serves 6

After learning from Vasso and Pendeli that peppers are abundant in Macedonia, we read "peppers are to Macedonia what corn is to Kansas."

6 red peppers (or long green Italian peppers)
1 c plain yogurt
½ c olive oil
Salt to taste

Hot sauce to taste
2 cloves garlic minced
Generous sprinkling of
   red wine vinegar

Wash and pat dry the peppers. Core and slice into strips and fry over medium heat in hot oil until softened. Serve doused with vinegar and salt. Mix yogurt, garlic and a dash of hot sauce for dipping pepper slices.

Pendeli's Feta-Stuffed Peppers
Piperies me Feta
Serves 7–8

This makes a great appetizer with soft pita bread.

7 or 8 long Italian peppers
   (or Anaheim chiles)
1 c crumbled feta cheese

3 T olive oil
½ t hot pepper flakes
1 T dried Greek oregano

Cut off top of peppers and remove seeds. Mix together the rest of the ingredients. Carefully slit the peppers open from top to bottom (do not cut through to other side). Stuff each pepper with cheese filling. Place on foil-lined cookie sheet. Drizzle more olive oil over the top. Bake in a preheated oven at 350 degrees F. until peppers are very soft.

Vasso's Green Pepper Pie
Pita me Piperia
Serves 8–10

1-lb package of filo
½ lb butter, melted
½ c olive oil
4 cloves garlic minced
7 long green Italian peppers
   (about 5 c chopped)

1 c chopped fresh flat-leaf
   parsley
1½ lb feta crumbled
1 c cream cheese
4 eggs lightly beaten
Salt and pepper to taste

Line a 9- by 13-inch baking pan with half the filo sheets, brushing each sheet with melted butter mixed with olive oil. Mix together peppers, parsley, feta and cream cheese, garlic, eggs, salt and pepper. Spread mixture over the filo. Cover with remaining sheets, again brushing each with melted butter and oil mixture. Fold filo edges over onto top of pie and brush with melted butter-oil mix so they lie flat. Before baking, make several slits with a sharp knife through top layers of filo sheets for steam to escape. Bake 1 hour until golden brown in a preheated oven at 350 degrees F., cool slightly and cut into squares to serve.

Chicken with Red Peppers and Kalamata Olives
Kotopoulo me Piperies ke Kalamata Elies
Serves 4–6

2 onions sliced
1 small (3 lb or so) roasting chicken
Salt and pepper to taste
3 red bell peppers cut in large pieces
1 c pitted and chopped Kalamata olives

3 ripe tomatoes, diced (or
   14-oz can diced tomatoes)
1 c dry red wine
A pinch of thyme
¾ c olive oil

Oil a baking dish or pan and line bottom with sliced onions. Place chicken on top. Salt and pepper generously inside and out. Surround the chicken with the chopped peppers and olives. Combine tomatoes, wine, thyme, and olive oil and pour over the chicken and vegetables. Cover with foil and bake about 2 hours in a preheated oven at 325 degrees F., until veggies are soft and chicken is very tender. Baste at least once during roasting.

DAN

We have made it without incident and are all happy to see each other. We are having some cold beer and lamb, since we are starving. The girls are dancing now while swallows drink loudly from the pool, dipping in mid flight. I see that they are bathing actually. The girls have had a presentation of diplomas and a CD of the dance music to take home. Everyone says to Floyd and me, "Why are you taking our best dancers? They are so much fun to have here."

ELIZABETH

Tonight is bittersweet as often is the case when a group comes together for one purpose and must finally part. What could be better or more bonding than learning ancient dances with the haunting melodies in the background surrounding us, filling our ears and every pore with sounds, some familiar and some new. We are connecting to the music and sharing completely. So when the time comes to say good-bye there are tears mixed with laughter and promises to try to keep in touch.

DAN

Woke up to the ungodly bleating of goats outside our window. Sounded like a broken machine, loud and horrible. Walked over to the resort and had coffee and breakfast with the girls. We are now on the patio with a clear blue sky. The girls' knees are sore from dancing; it may actually be good we are leaving early. Last night with our new shot glasses filled with Metaxa, Floyd and I showed the girls the cool moves of our own special dance! They applauded and laughed with us. Fun. Today is the name day for all Greeks named Elias, like their Papou. Down the road about two kilometers is the Prophet Elias Monastery. So now the bells are ringing. Earlier, as Floyd and I walked up to the resort, we could hear the monks' chanting floating across the valley.

ELIZABETH

The rest of our stay on Crete includes stops in the village of Anoya, the city of Iraklion, and the Minoan Palace of Knossos, a famous archaeological site, and the beach town of Agios Nicholaos. On the bus to Anoya, we read our husbands' journals describing their days and nights without us.

GEORGIA

I'm eager to share with Floyd, Elizabeth, and Dan some adventures I had in Anoya, the village where I attended my first Greek dance seminar in 1994. The bus drops us off in front of the church in upper town. This is the very spot in which I saw my first Cretan dance.

Since a wedding was to take place the day after our seminar began, the whole group of 15 along with the entire village were invited to the festivities. I remembered looking out from the dorm's balcony the afternoon before the wedding day and watching the bride's family as they strolled to the upper town with baskets of gifts for the groom's family. Aunts, uncles, cousins, brothers, sisters, all carried something. A while later the groom's family walked down the hill through the platia, the square, with their treasures for the bride's family. That night sharp gunshots pierced the silent sky as the men and boys drove around in their shiny red Toyota pickups announcing the groom's last night as a single man. In the morning the church bells called the village to the churchyard, where all solemnly stood in their fancy finery. The older Cretan men were in their traditional jodhpurs, tall black boots and crocheted headscarves; the young men sharp in their tight shirts and jeans and Italian leather shoes; the older women staid and elegant in their ubiquitous black or navy outfits, mourning for someone from years gone by. But it was the young women who were dazzling with shining long black hair in tight waves and ringlets, and their classic profiles. All colorful fashionistas, looking as if they had just stepped out of the Minoan frescoes of dancers pictured in the throne room at Knossos Palace.

We could all hear the faint chanting of the Byzantine marriage ritual, priest singing the man and woman together and leading them in their ceremonial dance three times around the altar. Finally the couple emerges, radiant with love. In the churchyard a famous group of Cretan musicians strikes up the music for the couple's real first dance of their marriage. Everyone claps and whistles! Soon we all promenade to the lower town for the feast. Two hundred fifty lambs had been slaughtered for the village's festivities. The men in the platia were slicing fragrant racks of lamb from the sizzling roasts on the spits.

Women were passing out warm fresh bread, and bowls of white, crumbly feta cheese and deep purple Kalamata olives. The Retsina wine flowed freely. When the band set up on the makeshift stage and people were fortified with the first round of feasting, the circles of dancers grew so long and tight there was hardly room for the designated hosts to pass jiggers of Dewar's Scotch to the lead man in every dance line, the libations serving as an aid to the high jumps and famous leaps of Cretan dancers as they sharply slapped their heels. Our seminar group left en masse in the wee small hours of the morning, carefully stepping like a new dance over the lamb bones and watermelon rinds of the feast.

The bride and groom, still dancing, are applauded often by family and townspeople as if they were just limbering up. The next morning a few of us doing our morning walk before dance class were amazed that the platia was already swept clean. Every chair and table of the surrounding tavernas was upright and back in its place ready for another day's work. Not a trace of the festivities except for the wedding flowers festooning the tables in great abundance.

GEORGIA

Now I'm recounting another memorable story about the night a few dance seminar participants sat around a taverna table until 4 a.m., listening to a parea (group of friends) singing Cretan mantinathes, little songs of rhyming couplets. All night long, every half hour or so another man and his mandolin or lyra joined us, which meant another round of drinks and mezethes. This is the first time I tasted the famous Cretan crostini called Dakos, a dry round bread soaked in olive oil, smothered with grated tomatoes, feta crumbled, and Kalamata olives. The platter also held eggplant salad (melitzana salata), and hard-boiled eggs with oil, vinegar and oregano. What a lovely way to spend an evening.

I led Floyd, Dan, and Elizabeth down the hill past the Estia, the dormitory, where the dance seminar had been held. It's near the central square and we stop at a familiar place in the circle of cafés for a drink. An ancient man in black jodhpurs and headscarf, a welcoming smile and twinkling eyes, seats us at his café table and breaks out

131

into a personal mantinatha. He tells us that he sang this to his wife on their wedding night. She was behind the counter making our drinks, nodding her head and smiling, though bent over with age and clad in black.

Cretan Toasts with Savory Topping
Dakos
Serves 4–8

A dry round bread soaked in olive oil, smothered with grated tomatoes, feta crumbled, and Kalamata olives.

5 oz olive oil
3 garlic cloves chopped
¼ c fresh Greek oregano, chopped
2 lb ripe tomatoes
4 oz olive oil

Salt and pepper to taste
8 toasts (made by slow baking 8 thick slices French bread until crisp)
Feta and chopped olives for top

Put 5 ounces of olive oil, garlic and oregano in a saucepan and place over very low heat with the lid on for 10 minutes to infuse the oil, checking often so garlic does not burn but just softens. Grate the tomatoes on a coarse grater into a colander set in a bowl, saving the juice after draining for about 20 minutes. Place the drained pulp and 4 ounces of olive oil in a bowl; season well with salt and pepper. Dip the toasts on one side in the tomato juices for a few seconds to soften them. Place each toast on a small plate, spread with some of the softened garlic, and drizzle with the infused oil. Spoon the tomato mixture equally over the toasts. Sprinkle with the feta, olives, salt and pepper and drizzle with the remaining infused oil. Let them sit for a few minutes before serving.

Eggplant Dip
Melitzana Salata
Serves 6–8

A creamy, flavorful dip perfect with pita bread.

2 large eggplants (about 2½ lb)
2 garlic cloves slivered
¼ c olive oil
2 T fresh lemon juice

2 t dried Greek oregano
1 t ground cumin
Salt and pepper to taste

Cut slits in eggplants with tip of knife. Insert garlic sliver into each slit. Place eggplants in baking pan and bake for 1 hour in a preheated oven at 450 degreesF., or until very tender. Cut each eggplant in half. Cool slightly. Scrape eggplant pulp from skin into colander and drain. Place pulp in food processor; add olive oil, lemon juice, oregano and cumin. Puree until smooth. Season with salt and pepper, cool completely. Serve with pita bread. May be made a day ahead. Cover and refrigerate. Makes about three cups.

GEORGIA

As we leave this setting, Elizabeth and I hear faint strains of music calling our feet to find which of the Cretan dances we have just learned matches this rhythm. Is it left, two, three, hop, right touch? Or step left, back right, two, three? We try a couple more dance patterns; none would fit! Frustrated with ourselves for not finding the new rhythms, we looked up as the music got louder and saw a herd of goats "dancing" across the road, their brass bells jauntily ringing with the new dance rhythms we were sure we heard, good students that we were! We continue to stroll through the village as I tell about two unforgettable characters I met here at that first dance seminar. The first one is a woman named Eleni, with the emerald green eyes. She had told me she was the acclaimed beauty of the town. Her dyed black hair still shining, she describes how so many men wanted her she couldn't choose! Now, in her sixties, at least, she is a favorite aunt and doesn't leave the house on the square without her makeup on and her hair perfect. Still in mourning black for some member of her extended family, her black dress is short and fitted, her black hose is sheer and slinky and her black shoes high-heeled and sling-backed, not the typical Cretan matron but a modern Bouboulina. One day she ran into where we were dancing shouting, "Ta psomakia, Kyria Yioryia!" *The little breads, Madame Georgia!* She takes me to her friend's bakery around a few corners. Entering the doorway, we are engulfed in that unmistakable aroma of bread dough rising and bread dough baking. The focus of the room is round! The baker/sculptress is Stella, round with her black scarves and shawls. She sits in the center of the room in front of a round table, holding a large wreath of bread dough, half covered by now with tiny, perfectly formed dough roses, lilies, feathers of dove-wings, ferns and leaves. Introductions are made and I ordered three little wreaths from Stella. She never stopped sculpting the soft dough which falls from her flour-dusty fingers in perfect readiness, and deftly places each flower on a bread wreath like filigree on a gold brocade. The rounds of bread are baked to a golden hue and stacked on the counter, ready to be distributed to city bakeries as decorative loaves. Later, back in Iraklion, I buy a tiny wreath for Elizabeth in remembrance of Anoya.

The village of Anoya suffered greatly in WWII at the hands of the Germans in the Battle of Crete. It is still very fresh in the peoples' memories. Part of the recovery was the establishment of a Women's Cooperative for Arts and Crafts. Visitors are still tempted by these ladies, who stand in front of their doorways inviting people in with "Allo, allo, come look, look!" at the gorgeous embroideries and weavings hanging outside, festooning walls and windows and doors! One of the times Elizabeth and I succumbed to the invitation of Kyria Skoula. It was so hard to choose from her textiles and handiwork everywhere. In a dark corner of the room, lying on a couch, was her ancient mother. When I asked if I could take her picture the ancient one said, "Agoraseh katee?" *Did she buy something?* My proof of purchase gave me permission to capture the image of these two classic Anoyian ladies!

This experience with the embroideries brings me back to a memory of my grandmother, Nona, and her trunk full of embroidered dowry treasures!

Now I ask what that delicious aroma is wafting through the room and she insists we taste it to find out. Leading us to a tiny table she brings us a plate of warm bread, a

134

bottle of wine and two bowls of steaming lentil soup! We once again enjoy that natural Greek hospitality shown to both stranger and friend.

Lentil Soup
Soupa Fakes
Serves 6–8

A substantial soup is best with the saltiness of olives and/or anchovies to make a complete meal.

1 lb lentils (pick over the lentils
   and wash well)
¼ c olive oil
3 medium white onions coarsely chopped
2 medium carrots chopped
2 or 3 stalks celery chopped
2 garlic cloves chopped

1 14-oz can diced tomatoes
¼ c chopped fresh parsley
1 large bay leaf
8 c chicken broth
Salt and pepper to taste
¼ c red wine vinegar
Dash red pepper flakes (optional)

In a large pot, heat ¼ cup olive oil and sauté onions until translucent. Add carrots and celery and sauté 3 minutes, stirring constantly with a wooden spoon. Add garlic, tomatoes, parsley, bay leaf, and lentils, broth or water, and hot pepper flakes if desired. Cover and bring to a boil. Reduce heat to low, simmer for 1½ hours until lentils and vegetables are very tender. Add more water during cooking if too much gets absorbed. Before serving, salt and pepper to taste and pour in vinegar. Stir and serve.

ELIZABETH
We catch the next bus from Anoya to Iraklion, the seaside capital and largest town on Crete. We are stuck in many traffic jams trying to get into the city. Our large Mercedes bus has quite a time getting through these very narrow streets and the double-parked vehicles, an accepted and practiced art. Today Dan and I plan to visit the Palace of Knossos, a short ride out of the city, but first we all need a quick snack. We walked to the main platia, which was shaded by trees and lined with tavernas and sweet pastry shops called zacharoplastias. As we approached we could see small tables shaded by colorful umbrellas, which match the awnings of the restaurants they belong to, placed

randomly over the cobblestones. Floating on the breeze were the warm aromas of sugar and cinnamon beckoning to us. There behind the glass of a small stall we saw squares of custard pastries being warmed on the grill. Having never seen this before we're told it is called Bougatsa, made with the flaky filo and filled with a heavenly, pale yellow custard. The cook dusted it with sugar and cinnamon and brought it to our table with two tiny cups of steaming Greek coffee. The taste of the silky smooth vanilla custard and crispy buttery filo was a combination that reminded us of our mom's galactoboureko, the custard pie drenched in honey syrup, made for special occasions. Sighing with contentment, we asked the cook if he would share his recipe. When we told him we were unfamiliar with this lovely treat, he told us that in northern Greece, in the city of Thessaloniki, there are coffee shops devoted exclusively to making and serving bougatsas. We looked forward to having it again soon.

Hellenic Custard Pie
Bougatsa
Serves 8

Silky smooth vanilla custard surrounded by crisp, buttery filo, dusted with sugar and cinnamon. This is a popular street food in many regions of Greece.

4 c milk	3 eggs beaten
½ c sugar	12 12- by 17-inch filo leaves thawed
1 T butter	1 c melted butter for filo
½ c farina	1 c confectioners sugar
1 t vanilla	1 T cinnamon for dusting
1 T orange zest	

In a large saucepan, heat milk and sugar. Add one tablespoon of butter and the farina, mixing slowly. Cook on medium heat for 10 minutes *stirring constantly* until thick and creamy. Remove from heat and add flavorings first, then eggs, mixing quickly with a wooden spoon. When well blended, simmer again on very low heat until it thickens a bit more. Remove from heat. It will continue to thicken as it cools. Butter a 9- by 13-

inch pan and layer six filo leaves, buttering each one liberally. Make sure the filo leaves come up the sides of the pan so they will enclose the custard. Spread the cooled custard mixture over the filo, fold down the sides and butter them. Finally cover with the remaining six filo leaves, each buttered liberally and fitted into the pan. Bake in a preheated oven at 350 degrees F., until golden brown, 50 to 60 minutes. Let cool for 20 minutes or so, then sift together powdered sugar and cinnamon and dust the top.

DAN

Because Georgia and Floyd have already visited Knossos, Elizabeth and I decided to go on our own. We were stuck in traffic as we left the city. We went on the guided tour at Knossos. It was really very good. The palace demonstrated how smart and advanced the Minoans were. Had they not used wood as part of their stone walls, they would have lasted longer. The reconstruction in 1905 is badly aged as well. Concrete mingles with stone, but we could still get a feel for the past shape.

ELIZABETH

The palace at Knossos was quite amazing. I had read a lot about the history of the palace and how it had existed for years only in mythology. It was the court of Minos, the king of the Minoan civilization on Crete, whose wife, Pasiphae, bore the minotaur, half man, half bull. So the labyrinth was constructed here to contain the monster. Among the most amazing tales of archeology was the discovery of the palace and the interplay of these legends with fact. We become part of the group with a guide to hear even more. I was especially struck by the Queen's bathroom. She had a clay bathtub and a toilet with an actual flushing system! Imagine . . . they had figured out how to pipe water from the distant mountain streams all the way to the palace. There were many surprising "conveniences" that showed they were way beyond their time, considering the palace was built in 1,900 BCE.

The day was very hot, so we were happy to finally sit down in the café for a cool drink, only to find they had no ice! That was fairly common in many tavernas and cafés. You really had to ask specifically for ice if you wanted it, but there were no assurances that they would have it. We are so spoiled! By the time we finished the tour and lunch we decided to walk to the museum. Although we were sweating and exhausted we loved the frescoes, artifacts and gold jewels. We walked back to the bus stop for a bus to Agios Nicholaos. We were ecstatic to be sitting down in the cool comfort of the bus. We planned to meet Georgia and Floyd in this seaside town.

After a short search for a hotel, the four of us were charmed by Julia, the owner of the Hotel Domenico. This hotel is located on the south side of town near the bus station and on the edge of the best beach. Agios Nicholaos is very popular with British tourists, in particular. We were lucky once again to get rooms without reservations. Once we settled into our rooms with balconies facing the beach, we leave to explore the town center, which is on the Voulismeni Lake, ringed with tavernas and cafés. A bridge separates the man-made lake from the natural harbor called Mirabello Bay. Hungry as we are, we stop at the first taverna we see with the help of a persuasive waiter. Seated at a waterfront table we relax, sipping cool glasses of Retsina. Trying not to order everything on the menu, we finally decide on the beet greens, calamari with tzadziki, our favorite salad and a savory meat pie, kreotopita. This buttery filo crust is filled with tender, shredded beef, fragrant herbs and tangy feta. The perfect thing to satisfy our ravenous hunger.

Savory Meat Pie
Kreotopita
Serves 8

Buttery filo crust is filled with tender, shredded beef, fragrant herbs and tangy feta.

Filling:
2 T oil and 2 T butter
1 onion chopped
2 c cooked beef pot roast, shredded
2 T dried mint
2 T dried Greek oregano
½ c chopped parsley
1 t salt

Pepper to taste
1 c chopped green onions
1 c crumbled feta
2 eggs slightly beaten
Pastry:
½ lb filo
2 T melted butter
½ c olive oil

Heat oil and butter and fry onion until soft. In a large bowl, mix with cooked meat, mint, oregano, parsley, salt, pepper, green onions, feta and eggs. For pastry, melt butter and oil in a small pan. Oil a rectangular 9- by 13-inch baking pan. Lay half of the sheets of filo in the pan, brushing each sheet with butter-oil mixture. Spread meat filling on filo. Lay remaining filo sheets, oiling-each lightly. Score the top with a sharp knife for steam to escape. Bake in a preheated oven at 350 degrees F. for one hour, until golden brown.

ELIZABETH

We were surprised to see it was sprinkling. Then the wind came up and it got cool. When we got back to our rooms, fully expecting to need a blanket, we were shocked to find our rooms felt like 100 degrees! We opened the sliding door but the breeze stopped at some invisible barrier out on the balcony. We could hear beds scraping across floors as people dragged them closer to their door. Floyd put his mattress out on the balcony and slept there. We put our beds near the door, hoping a breeze would come in. Eventually it did and by morning it was cool again. At breakfast we tried to decide where to go next. Mochlos was discussed. It's a small fishing village recommended by a teacher friend of Georgia's. I said I didn't like riding on a bus all day only to get to a place, have dinner, sleep and leave the next day, never getting the flavor of it. We decided to find out if Julia had fans, which would allow us to stay here longer and make a day trip to Mochlos. She did, so we stayed. It's comforting to know we will be staying here for five more nights. We are tired but so happy!

DAN

We took a cab ride of about an hour east of here and were dropped off in this tiny fishing village, Mochlos. We sit at the taverna, Lemnenaria, down the road from the village. Rather than the sleepy calm water expected we have strong winds from the north and actual surf of two or three feet. There is an islet near the village called Psira. On it is a small church and excavations of a Minoan site. The islet is separated from the village by a narrow channel.

FLOYD

Dan swam across a very rough choppy current to reach Psira and look around. The girls sat on the beach watching him nervously.

139

ELIZABETH

The wind is strong and the surf is huge. Sitting on the rocks here I feel like I'm surrounded by the sea. I love to feel the wind and see and hear the crashing waves. Worriedly, I watch Dan exploring the ruins. I can see the little rock walls climbing the hillside. There appears to be a cross current between here and there with waves going in two or three directions. There are small boats moored out at sea, bobbing and rocking in the wind and surf. They are wonderful to look at. The sunlight makes the scene look as though it is coated in silver and molten gold. But still I sit here, worried.

FLOYD

Georgia and I leave Elizabeth on the beach and walk to the top of the hill to find a great little taverna for a cold Amstel and an interesting Greek bread salad. Georgia inquired about its origin and was told it was named after the breadcrumbs usually swept off the table for the dogs. Not a very charming image but a fabulous simple salad. A great day of strolling, eating and enjoying the beauty of the sea and the setting. We decide to go get Dan and Elizabeth and bring them up here for tasting and sharing this surprising treat.

Breadcrumb Salad
Skilopsihola Salata
Serves 2–4

The few and simple ingredients of this salad make it a delicious surprise.

½ c olive oil
¼ c wine vinegar
Salt and pepper to taste
2 c rusks (slices of French bread toasted
  until crisp) broken into chunks

½ c thinly sliced red onion
½ c crumbled feta cheese
¼ c Kalamata olives pitted and
  chopped

Whisk together oil, vinegar, salt and pepper. Place the rusk chunks in a shallow bowl and pour dressing over all. Toss gently and let sit for 2 or 3 minutes to absorb. Add feta, onions and olives and toss again.

DAN

What pure open air, breathing sweet wind! The site itself was not excavated enough to be exciting—a few square pillars, pottery shards—the best thing was a huge amphora, a wine or oil jar like what we saw at Knossos Palace. It is ceramic, of course, and still half buried. When fully uncovered, it will be about six feet high. A rough swim back, but very buoyant water! Now we all sit at the hilltop taverna, "Amstelling" and eating.

GEORGIA

We check the hour and find it is time to go down the hill and meet our cab driver, who will return us to Agios Nicholaos. We wait at his cousin's taverna eating wonderful mezethes—our first tasting of a small fried fish eaten whole called Atherina. They were golden brown and crispy, flavorful, and sprinkled with fresh lemon juice and thyme, which, we learned, is the small sculpted shrub that covers the hillsides all over and perfumes the air.

Tiny Fried Fish
Atherina
Serves 6–8

These are eaten whole as a crispy, lemony snack.

1 lb white bait fish (smelts)
½ c flour
1 t black pepper
¾ c olive oil

¼ c lemon juice
2 T chopped flat-leaf parsley
2 T fresh thyme chopped

Add black pepper to the flour and dust the fish with it. Heat the oil on medium high and fry the floured fish until golden brown (in two batches). Tumble onto paper towels to drain. Douse with lemon juice and sprinkle with parsley and thyme. Serve hot.

DAN

Back in Agios Nicholaos, Floyd and I decide we need a swim around the jetties. On the way to the blowhole we had seen there, we watched the spectacle of the swimming priest. He was all in black robes which he slowly stripped down to . . . yes, black underwear! Just below us was a cemetery with a small church right on the water. After crossing himself and pausing a moment, he finally dived in. We had a good laugh, putting the scenario immediately into our memory book. After our refreshing swim, we got a quick snack, a pizza from the corner place and decided two things: one, it isn't very good, and two, we don't need anything else. We've eaten enough. We almost never reached that conclusion before!

GEORGIA

Back at the hotel, Julia meets us in the lobby and with a sad face says, "Eho megalo provlema," *I have a big problem.* She has promised the fans to someone else for tonight so she has to take them from our room. We're not happy about this, but "Tee na kanoome?" *What are we gonna do?* Little did we know that would be her refrain during our stay here. As our mother would say, "God love her."

FLOYD

Right now I'm on our balcony at the Domenico where we've spent two nights already. At Dan's request, Julia is used to cooking our breakfast of fried eggs with fresh slices of succulent, summer tomatoes instead of the usual buffet of hard-boiled eggs. We're the envy of other guests, who wonder how we got this version of morning eggs.

Dan and I want the girls to see the Libyan Sea so we're taking a bus to the south coast and will arrive at the city of Ieraptera, which faces Africa. From this point we will be closer to Africa than mainland Greece. It's Europe's southernmost town, with a mild climate and year-round fresh fruits and vegetables.

DAN

At the suggestion of a Belgian couple we have met on the bus, we've gone west to the village of Myrtos, about 15 minutes away. A very nice spot of dark sand and gravel, not the soft beach of Agios Nicholaos, but the water is just as warm. Again a wind has pursued us, blowing from the southwest this time—not smooth swimming.

ELIZABETH

For lunch we go to the taverna Manos, the best food yet! First we all shared Cretan cheese pies called Kaltsounakia. It was feta cheese and dried mint inside dough-like turnovers. We savored every bite of this regional treat. Dan had spaghetti with meat sauce perfectly spiced and Floyd had souvlaki with fries that were out of this world! Georgia and I had stewed green beans and pastitsio, a favorite dish of baked pasta layered with a seasoned meat, tomato and cheese filling, and topped with a béchamel cream sauce. This béchamel sauce was high and light as a cloud. We asked the cook for her recipe and discovered that baking powder was her secret ingredient for this béchamel. We loved it all.

Baked Pasta Crowned with Béchamel
Pastitsio
Serves 8

A rich and elegant pasta casserole famous in Greek cuisine.

1 lb thick spaghetti or ziti
2 T olive oil
2 large onions chopped
1 c celery chopped
3 cloves garlic chopped
2 lb ground beef
½ of a 6-oz can tomato paste
1 c red wine

1 large (28-oz) can diced tomatoes
3 t salt
1 t ground black pepper
1 t ground cinnamon
2 c grated Romano cheese
1 stick of butter melted
1 T oregano
Béchamel sauce (see recipe below)

Boil pasta as package directs. Drain but do not rinse. Meanwhile, in a large saucepan heat oil and sauté onions, celery and garlic until soft, then add ground beef and sprinkle with oregano. Cook until pink color is gone, then add tomato paste mixed with wine, diced tomatoes, salt, pepper, cinnamon. Reduce heat and simmer about 20 minutes. Stir in ½ cup grated cheese. In a deep 9- by 13-inch baking pan, brush well with melted butter and add half the pasta, covering pan evenly. Drizzle with half the melted butter and sprinkle with ½ cup grated cheese. Spread meat mixture evenly over pasta layer. Sprinkle meat with another ½ cup grated cheese. Top with remaining pasta. Drizzle second half of melted butter and ½ cup grated cheese. Pour béchamel sauce over all. Bake in a preheated oven at 350 degrees F. for 1 hour until golden. Let sit at least 10 minutes, then cut into large squares to serve.

Béchamel Cream Sauce

6 T butter
½ c flour
2 t baking powder
4 c milk
½ c grated Romano cheese

3 eggs lightly beaten
1 t salt
¼ t pepper
Dash of nutmeg

Melt the butter in a heavy large pan. Add flour and baking powder to make a roux, stirring constantly for 3 minutes. While whisking, slowly add milk and continue cooking on very low heat, whisking constantly, until mixture bubbles and becomes thick. Remove pan from heat, and stir in grated cheese, eggs, salt, pepper, and nutmeg. Set aside, covered, until ready to assemble (see above).

Little Cheese Pies
Kaltsounakia
Serves 10

The mint in these small cheese turnovers makes it a regional specialty.

Pastry:

1 c butter at room temperature
1 c plain yogurt
1 t baking soda

1 c flour
1 egg, lightly beaten
Toasted sesame seeds

Filling:

1 lb feta cheese
1 lb cottage cheese

4 eggs
3 T dried mint

Beat butter with yogurt. Add soda to flour then add to butter mixture. Add more flour as needed to make a soft dough. Turn out onto a floured surface and knead well. Wrap in waxed paper and let stand at room temperature about half an hour. Break off a small piece and roll out dough. Dough should be ¼-inch thick. Roll dough and cut into rounds using an upside-down three-inch-wide glass as cutter. Place 1 teaspoon filling at one end, fold over and seal by pressing tines of fork around crescent. Place on greased cookie sheet and brush tops with lightly beaten egg. Sprinkle with toasted sesame seeds. Bake for 25 minutes in a preheated oven at 350 degrees F.

DAN

Now that we are pleasantly full, we plan to go back to the beach to sleep but first confirm with the waiter that there is a bus coming soon to take us back to Agios Nicholaos. He assured us—"Yes, yes!"—that there was a bus, so we decided to walk through town to the bus stop to wait.

ELIZABETH

Walking towards us in the middle of town was a group of finely dressed families. The men wore black and gray designer suits, crisp white shirts, lovely ties and shiny black shoes. The women were breathtaking in their bright red satin and crinkling blue taffeta dresses. They all wore beautiful gold jewelry, which we have heard is the traditional and expected gift in Greece for every celebration and holiday like name days, baptisms, engagements, marriages, Christmas, and anniversaries. Everyone gives everyone gold! The little boys were in tiny suits and starched shirts like their dads, and the little girls, in pinks and peach silk and satin dresses, were replicas of their moms.

At the corner we see another group of well-dressed men carrying musical instruments and walking into a barbershop, where they surround a young man in a barber chair. Enchanted by all this activity, we asked a young lady, who was just catching up with the group, what was happening. She wore a dream of lemon satin, rustling as she walked with flowers tangled in her flowing black curls. She smiled brightly as she told us it was a wedding. The custom is that the groom is serenaded as he gets shaved and dressed for the ceremony. The bride's family is in another part of the village going through their ritual of preparation for her wedding day.

We are so mesmerized we've almost forgotten the bus and its scheduled time of arrival. The minutes become an hour, the hour an hour and a half, when we finally go into a nearby taverna to inquire if anyone knows when the bus will arrive. It is then we are told that since it is Saturday there is no bus! Now we repeat the words of that Scottish couple on another bus we almost missed, "Never take yes for an answer." We were laughing at the time, and even now, though slightly annoyed, we all started laughing. The waiter, with a quizzical look, was kind enough to call us a cab. We waited for the cab in their lovely patio area covered by a lush green grapevine and surrounded by fragrant jasmine. We sip cold fruit drinks and plan our next day trip.

We read about a boat excursion to the island of Spinalonga that became a leper colony at the end of the nineteen-hundreds. It leaves from Agios Nicolaos and includes a midday barbecue lunch and a swim by this deserted islet. We loved the sound of this tour and unanimously agreed to take it!

DAN

We are on a beautiful small boat headed to Spinalonga Island. Blue sky, blue water, blue rail on boat. It's our last day in Agios Nicholaos and this tour promised us a barbecue lunch in a secluded cove. The cove was, in fact, secluded though there were two boats already there. The water was pristine and clear as glass.

ELIZABETH

The water was so inviting that Georgia and I couldn't resist going in. It was calm and warm. As we stood waist-deep, we commented on how clear the water was and I suddenly became aware of little pinches on my thighs. I asked if she felt anything and as she said yes we both looked down into the clear water and saw the tiniest of fishes nipping at our skin.

Soon there were so many it felt like little electric shocks, at which point we decided to curtail our almost blissful dip in the bay.

The ship's bell calling us back to the boat sounded and we were more than thrilled to find that the barbecue lunch held to its brochure-promise.

The buffet included succulent, thick, and juicy grilled pork chops, Greek potato salad made with oil and vinegar and oregano (so different from the usual potato salad made with mayonnaise), Village Salad, and buckets of icy, cold shrimp with the ever-present fresh Greek bread. We were offered both chilled Retsina wine and sweet, quenching lemonada. Though we were stuffed, we couldn't resist a few pieces off the huge platters of fresh, cold crimson watermelon, karpouzi.

As we sailed out of our "secluded" cove, five more boats full of people like us were fast approaching.

Greek Grilled Pork Chops
Hirinehs Brizolehs
Serves 4

With the traditional Greek marinade, these chops are juicy and succulent.

½ c olive oil
½ c fresh lemon juice
1 T dried Greek oregano

2 cloves minced garlic
½ t each salt and pepper
4 thick center-cut pork chops

Mix together first five ingredients in a ziplock plastic bag. Add the 4 pork chops and marinate at least two hours. Grill, broil or pan fry till done.

Greek Potato Salad
Patata Salata
Serves 4

Warm potatoes tossed with oil, vinegar and oregano make this a delectable version of potato salad.

8 medium potatoes cut in 1½-inch chunks
½ c olive oil
1 onion finely chopped
½ c green onions finely chopped

2 T chopped parsley
1 T dried Greek oregano
Salt and pepper to taste
4 T red wine vinegar

Boil potatoes till tender; drain. Mix remaining ingredients in a bowl and pour over hot potatoes and immediately cover with aluminum foil. Toss again before serving.

148

FLOYD

Once back in town we went back to the Seagull Taverna on the lake, where our favorite waiter, Yiorgo, remembered each of our names when he saw us. We were celebrating Dan's birthday.

DAN

Before leaving for dinner, Georgia and Floyd invited us to have wine on their balcony. They gave me a nice T-shirt with Apollo on it and a leather case for my glasses for my birthday—a nice surprise.

ELIZABETH

We are dining leisurely tonight to celebrate Dan's birthday and our last night on Crete. Yiorgo recommends the chef's special: roast chicken with Kalamata olives and red peppers, basted in wine and olive oil. It sounded similar to what we first tasted in Roustika! We indulged ourselves and ordered two bottles of Cretan wine—Kourtaki Retsina and Koutari, dry red country wine. The waiter surprised us with a birthday cake of karithopita, a moist cake filled with walnuts and soaked in honey, bedecked in candles. On his tray were four sparkling small glasses of raki. We toast the fact that so many people respond to us generously with small glasses of raki here, a special dessert there, always with warmth and in the spirit of giving, Greek kefi.

Greek Walnut Cake
Karithopita
Serves 8–10

A moist exotic cake filled with walnuts and soaked in honey.

1 c walnuts	½ t ground cloves
2 c flour	1 c (2 sticks) softened butter
1½ t baking powder	1 c sugar
½ t baking soda	6 large eggs
½ t salt	1 T grated orange zest
½ t ground cinnamon	1 8-oz container plain low-fat yogurt

Spread nuts on a baking sheet and toast until golden, about 15 minutes. Cool slightly and finely chop. In large bowl stir together flour, baking soda, baking powder, salt, cloves and cinnamon. In another large bowl beat butter and sugar at medium speed until light and fluffy. Add eggs one at a time, beating well after each addition. Add orange zest, reduce speed to low; add flour mixture alternately with yogurt, beginning and ending with flour mixture. Fold in chopped nuts. Grease a 9- by 13-inch baking pan and spoon in batter, smoothing top with spatula. Bake in a preheated oven at 350 degrees F. until a toothpick inserted in center comes out clean, 35 to 40 minutes. Cool in pan on a wire rack.

Syrup: **1 c sugar, ½ c honey, ¾ c water**

Stir together sugar, honey and water in a quart saucepan. Bring to a boil over medium heat, stirring often. Simmer 5 minutes. Remove from heat and cool down. Spoon lukewarm syrup over cake. Cool. Cut into squares or diamonds.

150

ELIZABETH

The next morning we say good-bye to Julia and go back to Iraklion to catch the ferry. When we got to the ferry and our cabin, we showered with wonderful HOT water then went to dinner with the encouragement of the loudspeaker saying, "Kali orexi!" (bon appétit). It was like a floating taverna. The food was wonderful. Hopefully we are in for a good sleep and early disembarking.

FLOYD

We sadly leave Crete to return to mainland Greece. It's an overnight ferry ride and our boat, the Preveli, is huge and filled to the gills. Our four-bunk room seemed pleasant but proved very stuffy during the night. No one slept very well.

DAN

Our room was a nice-sized oven that the girls sweltered in and Floyd and I fled from around one o'clock in the morning.

Mani

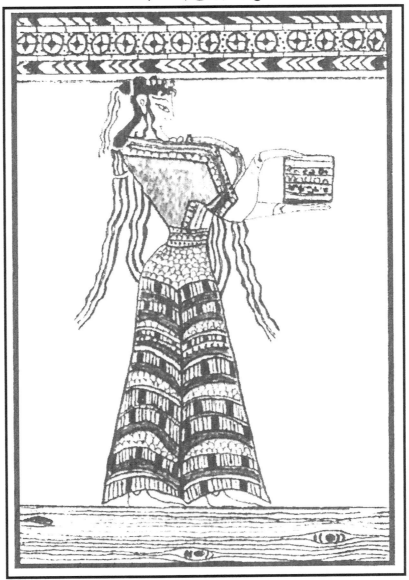

"Olives have a taste older than meat, older than wine. A taste as old as cold water."

— Lawrence Durrell

GEORGIA

Last night after our ferry ride from Crete, we arrived in Neapoli on the mainland. This is a village on the southern tip of the Peloponnese.

ELIZABETH

We stayed at the hotel Limira Mare, which was very new and modern. The glistening lobby and marble-tiled bedroom with the huge sink and bathtub in the bathrooms were incredible. We appreciated the plush comfort of this hotel with pure ocean views and air-conditioning. We had a long, leisurely breakfast buffet on the patio. This was a far more sumptuous breakfast than most places. Along with the usual hard-boiled eggs, there were avga matia (literally "egg eyes"), sunny-side-up eggs, and omelets. The sausages, loukanika, with their wonderful orange zest flavoring, were reminiscent of our favorite childhood loukanika from Liamos Market in Nashua, where we bought them after church every Sunday. Not only did they serve the fresh Greek bread that we have become accustomed to, but also had soft, fluffy pita bread, paximathia (cinnamon biscotti-type toasts) and sweet breads, tsoureki, along with baked ham slices, feta cheese, fruit salad and full-bodied, freshly ground coffee. We especially liked the surprise of fresh-off-the-trees orange juice. It was all lovely and memorable.

Greek Sausages
Loukanika
Serves 6–8

This sausage is flavored with orange zest, making it unique.

4 oz ground beef
12 oz ground pork
1 garlic clove crushed
½ t ground cinnamon

¼ t dried thyme
Grated zest of one small orange
1 t black pepper
Lemon wedges

Put all ingredients in a bowl and mix well. Cover and let marinate overnight in the refrigerator. Preheat broiler or grill. Stir the mixture and then with damp hands form about 24 sausage shapes 2 inches long. Broil or grill sausages for 15 minutes, turning several times until brown on all sides. Serve hot with lemon wedges.

GEORGIA

Mid-afternoon, we walked across the street to look at the ferry dock and discovered a tiny roadside taverna. We decided to get a traditional snack of ice-cold ouzo and chunks of juicy, lemony, charbroiled octopus. What a meze! Just then we saw a magnificent sight; a shiny red Toyota pickup, stuffed to overflowing with braids of garlic, gleaming white in the afternoon sunlight. We await our bus to Gythio. I am remembering our first trip to Greece when one day at lunch we were chatting with a young man from Athens who told me I looked like I came from the Peloponnese, the southern part of Greece. I never knew there was a recognizable look! Both sides of our family had their roots there: Dad's parents near Patras on the north; Mother's near Sparta in the south. In particular, the middle of the three peninsulas that points directly south to Crete and Africa is the Mani, renowned for its wild landscape, fiercely independent people, and strong sense of hospitality.

Gythio was the port for ancient Sparta, and connected to it is the tiny islet of Marothonisi. According to Greek mythology this is the place where Paris, Prince of Troy, and Helen, wife of Menelaus of Greece, consummated their affair, leading to the Trojan War. The eighteenth-century tower there once belonged to the family of the Mavromichalis, who were responsible for the assassination of Greece's first president in the town of Nafplion right after independence.

DAN

We have arrived in Gythio. We stopped for a sunset Retsina. Our hotel overlooks a twinkling harbor of moderate size and exquisite beauty. The lighthouse on the Marathonisi Islet flickers. The water is the color of pewter with overtones of mauve, orange, and greens. Georgia said, "I love that little purple puddle over there." The light wind skips over the water, causing textures that mix with the various currents. Quite a sight from the balcony we share. We are going now for calamari and cold beer. Later we will have souvlaki and more Retsina.

FLOYD

We have a long bus ride from Neapoli to Gythio. This seaside town is always a delightful surprise. It is most certainly of the picture postcard variety. We looked for and found the pink pension we had stayed at before and got a room on the second floor with a marvelous oceanfront view. It's a tourist spot, lots of action, very busy. The older business section of the town is a bit away from the water and more for the locals, quieter and actually more interesting. We're waiting now to take a taxi to Neohori to introduce Dan and Elizabeth to the family homestead and our cousin Angeliki.

GEORGIA

I called Angeliki to tell her we were all coming and she said, "Ellate! Tha tsimbisoume ligo." *Come along and we will have a bite to eat.* While we wait for the cab, I tell Dan and Elizabeth about our first trip to the family's hilltop village and how it unfolded.

We looked forward to the meeting of Mother's cousin, who had inherited and restored the family homestead in the southern Peloponnese. Armed with telephone numbers and addresses we began the search by calling her at her home in suburban Athens. No luck; no answer. The next step was to make our way to the homestead itself in Neohori, a village outside of Gythio, the port for ancient Sparta. As the bus descended to sea level we get our first wide view of the Greek waterfront town, the harbor beating with the rhythmic bobbing of fishing boats in all the bright colors of the rainbow and houses stacked up the hillside in soft pastel variations. We find lodging on the second floor of a pink pension. The owner lives on the third floor, her son and daughter-in-law have a jewelry business on the first floor. He also drives a cab, so after inquiring about the family name, which they don't recognize, we hire him to drive us to the village, which they do recognize. At the top of the hill we are dropped off in front of the tiny taverna with only one table outside. Gregory, the cab driver, agrees to pick us up in one hour. I practice again my Greek words to introduce myself when I suddenly find myself saying them out loud to the taverna keeper. I'm from America but my grandfather was born here in this village and I'm looking for my cousin. He twists his head aside and asks suspiciously What's the family name? I say, "Angeliki Kakakos." His eyes widen, his arms stretch to the sky, and he shouts in a very loud voice, "Angeliki? She's right up the street. Come in! Come in! I'll call her right away! Sit down! Have a coffee or do you want ouzo and keftethes [meatballs]?" As he escorts us in and runs to the telephone he's still shouting, "Eat! Drink! Relax! Welcome!" Floyd is laughing and shaking his head at this first encounter with a Greek stranger's welcome. In two minutes I see shuffling towards us an older woman in a flowered house dress, her hair decorated in big pink rollers wrapped in an orange hairnet, smiling and waving. I stand up and introduce myself as her cousin Poppy's daughter whose arrival was totally unexpected. She looks at me with eyes like my mother's, smiles and says, "And now, I will take you home!" I'm crying now and she is chattering away, asking a million questions but not waiting for answers as we walk arm in arm to the gates of the courtyard and I entered the enchanted world of one of my dreams, to be in the garden where the roots of our family tree were planted and still grow. We meet Yianni, her husband, who immediately poured Stavro a Dewar's scotch and talked to him in Greek as if he were the long-lost relative. She insists we cancel our hotel reservation and stay here with them because, after all, it was home! We spend the afternoon laughing with her as she tells us stories about life with her father who left for America with our grandfather and two more brothers, but soon returned feeling the pace of life there was not to his liking. Angeliki married and moved to Athens but over the years lovingly restored the primitive tower house, characteristic of the Mani peninsula. Now it glowed with marble floors and wooden shutters that open to the view of the olive groves shimmering down to the sea. From Athens, where they live half of the year, she had brought every seed, tree, and cutting to plant in the sandy, arid yard of her youth and created this paradise of roses and geraniums, grape arbors and lemon trees, amphorae filled with basil and marigolds for blessings. In the garden shines a palette of purple eggplants for frying, deep green zucchini tipped with golden blossoms for stuffing; the veranda was steeped in aromas of carnations and oranges and hung with bunches of her hand-picked oregano for seasonings. I recognize the familiar family love of cooking expressed over and over again. In the corner of this resplendent garden are her plump chickens which she affectionately called "the girls" (*ee kopelles*), one of whom she was eager to sacrifice for our roasted dinner that evening. We decline this invitation for now since Gregory will be returning for us soon, but agree to come back. After thanking her profusely we leave with the gift of a bag of fragrant oregano, and promise that we'll see her tomorrow and stay for a few days to be overwhelmed with her filoxenia, the hospitality that is as natural and ancient in Greece as the olive itself.

since we were "special" family, she baked a galatoboureko, a heavenly custard, filo and honey confection which is usually reserved for holidays. We could barely move when we were done. This lovely house with its marble floors is a far cry from what it was when our mother visited here 30 years ago. She would have been very surprised to see it now. Seeing Angeliki's chicken coop full of hens and chicks took me back to my Papou's own chicken coop.

One of the things I most looked forward to every year, as Easter approached, was Papou coming home with a box full of fluffy, yellow chicks, peeping all at once, in a symphony of chaos. They were softer than almost anything I had touched before and we were allowed to pick them up and hold them to our heart's content, knowing they were going into the chicken coop where they would be fed and fattened until they were just right for many of our Sunday dinners. Even knowing that, I was more happy than sad for the short time that we could cuddle them, because I was able to separate that knowledge from this moment of joy.

GEORGIA

During this time with Mother's cousin I recognize so many tastes and smells of Angeliki's cooking, the same ingredients and manner of preparation as Mom's and all the aunts and uncles. We read later that tomatoes and lemon are not usual companions in other regions of Greece but we grew up with that combination.

Artichoke Stew
Anginares a la Polita
Serves 6–8

The easiest way to enjoy artichokes is in this savory stew.

¼ c olive oil
1½ c chopped onion
1 c chopped scallions
2 c diced potatoes
2 c diced carrots

1 can (14 oz) artichoke hearts or bottoms (not marinated)
¼ c chopped fresh dill
Salt and pepper to taste
½ c lemon juice
2 c water or broth

In a large pot, heat olive oil and sauté onions and scallions until translucent. Add potatoes, sauté 5 minutes. Add carrots, stir, add artichokes, dill, salt and pepper and continue to stir. Add water or broth and lemon juice. Cover and simmer for 25 minutes or until potatoes and carrots are very tender. Serve hot or at room temperature.

White Bean Salad
Fasoulakia Salata
Serves 6–8

Greeks have honored the simple bean since ancient times. This is a casual summer salad.

1 15-oz can of cannellini beans drained
½ c fresh chopped flat-leaf parsley
1/3 c fresh lemon juice
3 T capers rinsed and drained

1 medium red onion finely chopped
½ t cayenne pepper
¼ t salt
½ c olive oil

Rinse beans with cold water and drain. In a medium bowl, add all ingredients and mix well. Let it sit for at least an hour before serving.

Leek Pie
Prasopita
Serves 8–10

A pita that features green: green leeks, green onions, fresh dill and fresh parsley.

7– 8 leeks
4 T butter
8 whole green onions chopped
½ c fresh dill chopped
½ t black pepper
1 t salt
½ c flat-leaf parsley chopped
1 c crumbled feta

½ c grated Romano cheese
¼ c dry white wine
1 12-oz container small-curd cottage cheese
1 lb filo at room temperature
4 eggs beaten
1 16-oz can diced tomatoes drained
1 to 1¼ cups butter melted

Wash leeks in a bowl of cold water then drain well in a colander and chop finely. In a large skillet melt 4 tablespoons butter and sauté leeks, onions, dill, salt and pepper until tender. Add wine and tomatoes and simmer until liquid is absorbed. Cool. Combine eggs and all cheeses in a large bowl and add the cooled leek mixture. Set aside.

Assemble pita as follows: Remove filo from plastic bag and unfold. Line buttered 11- by 14-inch pan with half of the filo (10 sheets), brushing each sheet with melted butter. Overlap and drape filo over sides of pan to prevent filling from leaking. Spread filling evenly over filo. Fold overhanging filo over filling and brush with butter. Top with remaining 10 sheets of filo, buttering each sheet and tucking them down the sides of pan with the edge of the pastry brush to seal. Score through top layers of filo with a sharp knife in five equal rows lengthwise to let steam escape.

Bake in a preheated oven at 350 degrees F. for 50 to 60 minutes until golden brown. Remove from oven; let stand 15 minutes before cutting into squares. Makes about 30 pieces. Serve warm for best flavor. Refrigerate leftovers. To reheat, place in a 300-degree oven for 15 minutes uncovered.

FLOYD

Last night we were entertained by Yianni and Angeliki, chief cook, gardener, chicken keeper. She showed us all around the walled gardens and house and pointed out the breath-taking view over the olive groves to the sea.

GEORGIA

One of our first adventures in Mani was a visit to the Dirou caves, the entrance to the underworld! We take the bus to Areopolis and find a room in the Mani Tower guesthouse. We are served a wonderful breakfast by Popi, daughter of Kyrios Bazbakos, with the bright blue Mani eyes! After showing us his display case lit up with Mani guns, swords, knives, and pistols, he excuses his daughter to go sing in the church choir next door. She's probably in her thirties, seems to be past her prime according to Greek standards, and she lives at home with her father helping with the B&B and museum. Later I walked over to the church and sat on the steps listening to the familiar sounds of the Greek liturgy and the melodious voices of the few women in the choir. I was sure I could tell Popi's voice, and she was still humming when she came out.

ELIZABETH

This trip, Dan and I went to the Dirou caves on the west side of the Mani peninsula. The landscape is incredible, resembling northern Baja California with the eucalyptus trees gracefully hanging over the road we travel. The Mani family fortresses dot the tops of hills and ridge-lines with their rock towers, 25 feet square and walls over three feet thick. This style of building was necessary back in the days when the Mani held out as the stronghold of independence, as well as protection for family against family vendettas! Lunch at the café in this archaeological site was wonderful. We had the best baked chicken and orzo. The chicken was golden with a delicious seasoned skin. The orzo was infused with the pan gravies of wine, tomatoes, lemon and herbs.

Baked Chicken and Orzo
Kotopoulo me Manestra
Serves 4

This chicken is golden with a delicious seasoned skin. The orzo is infused with the pan gravies of wine, tomatoes, lemon and herbs.

1 3-lb chicken cut in pieces
¼ lb butter
2 T olive oil
¼ c lemon juice
1 t salt
½ t pepper
1 28-oz can diced tomatoes

1 onion thinly sliced
1 T Greek oregano
1 t marjoram
1 bay leaf
½ c red wine
1 c orzo
2 c hot water

Wash chicken well with cold water and place in roasting pan. Combine butter and oil and heat, then pour half of it over the chicken pieces. Mix lemon juice in remaining oil mixture and baste chicken. Sprinkle with salt and pepper. Bake in a preheated oven at 400 degrees F. for 30 minutes. Remove pan from oven. Mix tomatoes, onion, herbs and wine together and pour over chicken. Reduce oven heat to 350 degrees and continue baking for 45 more minutes.

Meanwhile, bring 4 to 6 quarts of water to a rolling boil. Add salt and orzo, stir gently and return to a boil for 10 minutes and drain. Remove baked chicken from pan to a covered dish. Add 2 cups hot water to remaining juices in roasting pan, then add drained pasta and stir well. Bake 15 minutes at 400 degrees.

DAN

Elizabeth and I now sit by a turquoise bay of bobbing boats and swimming families, sharing an Amstel and a Greek salad, reflecting on the caves we've just left. They are known in Greek mythology as one of the entrances to Hades, the underworld. The lighting allowed us to see various formations, stalactites and stalagmites, as we were pushed along in a small boat by the guide maneuvering with a long stick. He spoke only Greek to describe the interior except when he addressed me,"Mister, problem, mister!" or "Mister, duck, mister, duck head, please!" The water-filled caves tasted only slightly salty. The caves had no single impressive feature, but rather a collection of delicate, feathery, almost coral-like shapes of salmon and tan. The reflections in the water added another eerie dimension entirely. The quiet gliding was interrupted only by our guide's quick speech.

ELIZABETH

Our cab driver in Gythio, Gregory, found out we wanted to go to a beach and told us about his parents' small apartment resort on the beach in Vathi, a few miles from town. He drove us there to take a look at it. We told him it was perfect so he accepted our reservation.

DAN

Sand, sun, salt, sea and an ever-present taverna on this small beach. We sit in filtered shade provided by a cane patio cover, drinking Amstel beers at $1.60 each (it's 300 drachmas). We are staying here for a few days, sharing a room with kitchenette to make our morning coffee. Ten thousand drachmas a night equals twenty dollars! It's so nice to see the sisters talking and laughing, as is the nature of sisters. Thinking they think alike even when they don't. Outside our room, every morning, we see an old man and his small grandson weaving intricate baskets for sale.

GEORGIA

We're psyched about this little apartment in Vathi we rented for three days. It's tiny but the price is right and we can walk to the beach and go in the water! Elizabeth and I have our own style of enjoying the Aegean: sitting on the edge of the surf and inviting the warm turquoise waves to lap over our legs! An occasional cool Amstel when the guys are ordering under the bamboo of the beach cabana is just the perfect liquid refreshment for slow beaching. The variety of Aegean aquas is infinite, pale to deep with colors on the horizon often blurring sky and sea. Elizabeth and I go to the market in Gythio for essential food items before moving in with plastic bags full of feta, bread, tomatoes, olives, oregano, lemons, greens, chicken, coffee, milk, wine. We replenish our traveling bottles of extra virgin olive oil and vinegar. Now we are ready to create our own daily feasts in the three- by three-foot space of kitchen devoted to the tiniest fridge and stove and sink. Next to this area is a small bathroom and the front room with couch, cot and double bed. Once we flipped a coin for the bed, we set up our bags each in our own territory and quickly slipped into a rhythmic routine of morning coffee, bread and cheese, walk to the beach, stroll the blue crescent gathering our ocean jewels: sea glass and shells. It's a quiet meditative activity until we sit to refresh ourselves on the water's edge to "ooh and aah" over each others' findings. Watching the men swim and dive and vigorously play like happy porpoises was just as delightful for us as it was for them. We often remark on how lucky we are that these two men who have married sisters are such good friends and traveling companions, just as we are. Another Greek thavma!

An indelible memory of this place, Vathi, even more poignant than the beauty of the sky and sea, was the daily site of a dignified, fine-looking older man and a little boy who came daily to the tree in the front yard of our apartment and spread a blanket and supplies. All day they sat weaving thin reed baskets of all sizes. We learned later he was a gypsy from the north who traveled this far south in the summer to make and sell baskets to the beach tourists. He was raising his grandson himself and teaching him his ancient craft. He tenderly bathed the boy with the hose borrowed from the apartment manager every morning and shared some bread and melons for breakfast on the blanket. They took their afternoon siesta there under the tree, but where they slept for the night was a mystery. Occasionally we heard the clicking, tapping of the old man's fine leather shoes as he walked away from his station down the road to gather more reeds and grasses for the baskets, returning with flashing knife still in hand. He'd sit next to the boy very close and show him how to prepare the reeds for weaving, silver knife blade glinting in the sun. Once I overheard a few phrases of a conversation he had with the manager. The gypsy sadly remembered when on this same land, before the apartment units, he sat with his own grandfather, who proudly had several family blankets spread out here. "This was our land," he almost shouted. The apartment manager took his own boy in the truck to the town market and when they returned his son ran to the blanket and gave the little gypsy boy a snack from his grocery bag. "Yiasou!" we heard the proud grandfather say as he waved to the gift giver. We wondered if we could give him a parting gift as well though we'd never exchanged anything more than Yiasous as we passed them on the way to the beach. How I wanted to buy one of their baskets, but they were all too large for our travels.

"For as you go, all the pebbles sing, spinning off your shoes."
—Theocritus

ELIZABETH

Today's excursion from Gythio will be north to Nafplion. When we arrive in Nafplion we begin our search for a hotel, since we have no reservations. The Tirins Hotel seems to be perfectly located near the square, so we walk in and get our rooms. We all took showers and discovered there was absolutely no hot water. In fact, it was ice cold! The desk clerk assured us it was because they had not turned on the correct switch. The rooms seemed to shrink once we opened our suitcases and finally we noticed our balconies overlooked the back doors of all the tavernas, so we decided we would look for another hotel tomorrow. We left to explore.

DAN

We began our visit of the town by strolling the waterfront then walking to the Syntagma Square, where I have jotted down the name of a taverna recommended in one of our travel books. We found it easily and sat at a table under a Lefca tree watching children play, hearing the invisible cicadas, and feeling the breeze as the light softens over the cobbled square.

ELIZABETH

This Hellas Taverna had very good food, but the waiter was very pushy. The minute he came to our table he told us what we would have, rather than asking us. We then decided on stuffed tomatoes that we've often had and stewed cauliflower that we've never had. When the bill came, Floyd said, "That's impossible!" Looking closer we found that he had charged us 4,500 drachma for a bottle of wine that was 450 drachma. His overly confident attitude changed to a very apologetic one when we pointed it out to him.

Stuffed Tomatoes
Domates Yemistes
Serves 5

Using the best tomatoes is key to these rice-herb stuffed tomatoes.

10 large tomatoes
1 c rice
1 onion chopped
¼ c tomato paste stirred into ½ c water
½ c olive oil
1 T sugar

5 cloves garlic minced
½ c fresh dill chopped
½ c fresh parsley chopped
2 t each salt and pepper
2 c chopped pulp and juice
    scooped from tomatoes

Slice tops from tomatoes and scoop out centers. Put tomato shells in a large 9- by 13-inch baking pan. Stir tomato paste into water, then mix all ingredients together and spoon into tomato shells. Replace tops, pour in enough water to cover bottom of pan (about a half-inch). Cover and bake in a preheated oven at 350 degrees F. for about 45 minutes, then uncover and continue to bake until rice is done. Drizzle with olive oil before serving.

Stewed Cauliflower
Kounoupithi Kapama
Serves 4–6

Kapama usually refers to stewing with tomatoes and onions.

1/3 c olive oil
2 large red onions chopped
2 celery stalks chopped
2 cloves garlic chopped
1 large cauliflower cut into small florets

1 T tomato paste dissolved in ¼ c water
½ c dry red or white wine
1 bay leaf
2 T red or white wine vinegar

Heat 3 teaspoons oil in a stewing pot and cook the onions, stirring over medium-low heat until soft (10 to 12 minutes). Add the celery and garlic and stir a few minutes. Toss in the cauliflower. Add the dissolved tomato paste, bay leaf, wine and vinegar. Add enough water to come about two-thirds of the way up the pot. Season with salt and pepper and simmer, covered, until the sauce is thick and the cauliflower and celery are tender. Just before removing from heat, add remaining olive oil and adjust seasoning.

DAN

Nafplion is a busy place on Saturday. We have adjoining rooms that overlook the alley filled with restaurants. We got back to our hotel late and worried that we might not sleep since the windows are right on the sidewalk. All sounds seem to come up from the street, despite the noise of the air-conditioning and windows being closed. In spite of that, I slept pretty well until around 7 a.m., when the trash trucks chose right outside our window to park and grind up the trash for half an hour. Then the dog started barking and right now at 9:50 he is still barking. We're outta here!

FLOYD

Finally we're settled in our new room in the Hotel Victoria. We rinsed out a few things and hung them on the balcony, where the hot winds finally served a purpose!

DAN

The rooms here were pricey since this very day the high season prices went into effect. We didn't care, however, after our experience last night. Nafplion has been a major port since the Bronze Age. The elegant Venetian houses and mansions are dwarfed by the towering Palamidi Fortress. I got up at seven and climbed a thousand steps to the huge complex maze of forts, walls, and artillery placements covering the harbor. Looking at the roofs from here—the old, tired, perhaps brittle tile roof—could take a year's examination: the orange lichen, the almost brown tiles with so many interplays of light and dark, the mortar grays and blacks, often with flowers growing in their seams.

We typically have breakfast at this café called To Sokaki outside our hotel behind the church. The morning bells and the monks' chanting draw us out of our morning sleep and over to the table under the ancient grapevine that climbs to the top of the three-story building and has a tree-trunk thickness at its base. Reading the breakfast menu, we run across this translation again for sunny-side-up eggs: avga matia, which literally means "egg eyes." Part of the charm of this city is the Venetian pink stucco buildings surrounding the platia (the square) in the old town. It is tiled completely in marble.

In the late afternoon on into evening we watched families gathered here for frappes, ice cream, or pastries. The adults sit at tables in front of every shop watching their children of all ages playing on tricycles, bicycles and skateboards, or just running gleefully around on the ancient marble tiles of the square. We sit in the shade and finally a different wind has come to this warm town, cooling us slightly.

GEORGIA
Greek families usually have platters of fruit in season with nuts and cheeses for dessert, but enjoy pastry and sweets in the late afternoon at the zacharoplastia, a sweet shop, where we are now doing the same. We choose a few different ones to share, like the irresistible filo custard pie drenched in honey syrup, galatoboureko; the buttery, shortbread cookies, dusted in confectioners sugar, kourambiethes; and the most famous of Greek pastries, baklava. Perhaps its universal appeal is in the perfect blending of crushed nuts, cinnamon, cloves, crisp buttery filo and honey.

At home, we make it ourselves using our family recipe, so we are anxious to try it here with our cool frappes.

Nut Pastry
Baklava
About 25 pieces

One of the most well-known Greek desserts. Baklava can be made with your choice of walnuts, almonds, or pistachios. The most common is made with walnuts.

Prepare the syrup before assembling the baklava. To make the syrup, mix the following ingredients in a medium saucepan and heat gently until the sugar has dissolved completely. Increase the heat and boil rapidly for about 10 minutes without stirring. Set aside to cool. Discard the cinnamon stick and lemon or orange peel.

Syrup:

2½ c water

2 c sugar

1 c honey

1 cinnamon stick

1 strip of lemon or orange peel

Mix the first four ingredients of the filling before you start working with the filo.

1 lb shelled walnuts coarsely chopped

¼ c sugar

2 heaping T ground cinnamon

2 T ground cloves

1 lb filo pastry thawed
to room temperature

1 lb unsalted butter, melted

Butter a 9- by 13-inch baking pan. Place the first sheet of filo in the buttered pan and brush evenly with melted butter. Lay another sheet of filo on top and brush again with melted butter. Repeat this process until you've used twelve sheets of filo layered on the bottom of the pan.

Sprinkle a handful of nut mixture over the filo, covering it, lay two or three sheets of filo on top, brushing each with melted butter. Repeat the nut mixture, then the filo process until you have used all the nuts. Put the remaining sheets of filo, each one brushed with melted butter, on the top. Brush the top with melted butter and cut into two-inch diamond shapes. Bake for one hour in a preheated oven at 350 degrees F., until crisp and golden. Remove from the oven, set on a wire rack and pour cooled syrup evenly over hot pastry. Ideally, the baklava should stand at room temperature overnight before serving.

Iced Coffee
Kafes Frappe
Serves 1

This is a favorite afternoon drink enjoyed with a Greek sweet snack.

1 t instant coffee
1 t sugar
1 t fresh cream or canned evaporated milk

Ice cubes
16-oz glass tumbler full of water

Place the coffee, sugar and ¼ glass of cold water in a shaker and shake vigorously till all liquid has turned to foam. The firmer the consistency of the foam, the better the frappe will be. Pour the mixture into a tall tumbler, add a few ice cubes and top off with cold water. Add a dash of fresh cream or milk and stir with a straw. Adjust sweetness to taste.

ELIZABETH
As evening approaches we follow the sounds of the bouzouki and find a narrow alley arched in brilliant bougainvillea. There is a tiny taverna on the first floor of an old Venetian mansion. Because of the three musicians who were playing with such enjoyment, we sit at the first small available table near them. A limited menu, but we found some of our favorites, like spanakorizo me kotopoulo—spinach and rice with chicken—while the bouzouki, guitars and vocals serenaded us.

Spinach and Rice Casserole with Chicken
Spanakorizo me Kotopoulo
Serves 4–6

This is a spinach dish that even children love. It is also delicious without the chicken.

4 chicken breast halves or 4
   chicken leg quarters
1 medium onion chopped
3 cloves of garlic sliced
½ c fresh chopped flat-leaf parsley
1 c crushed canned tomatoes

¼ c olive oil
½ c dry white wine
1 c long grain rice
Salt and pepper to taste
3 cans chicken broth (14-oz size)
1 lb fresh spinach or 2 packages frozen

Wash chicken pieces and pat dry. Sprinkle generously with salt and pepper and brown in hot oil on both sides. Remove from skillet and place in large pot. Sauté garlic, onion, and parsley in skillet. Add tomatoes and wine, salt and pepper and simmer for about 10 minutes. Add to chicken along with three cans of broth. Simmer for about 25 minutes. Remove chicken and keep warm. Add rice to pot and cook for about 15 minutes. Add chopped spinach and cook another 5 minutes, mixing well. Return chicken to pot, placing carefully on top. Simmer for another 10–15 minutes or until rice is cooked. Let sit for about 10 minutes.

ELIZABETH

Once we have placed our orders and give full attention to the musicians, we hear soft applause coming down from above the bougainvillea. There on a tiny ornate Venetian balcony sits an elegant elderly lady draped in a shawl with her eyes closed and swaying to the music. How lucky she was to have such a personal performance every night. She had a timelessness about her in the midst of the deep purple flowers that surround her.

DAN

On our last day in Nafplion, under our favorite plane tree we decide where to go for lunch. Before we decide where to be, we comment on the wonderful lady sitting on the balcony last night and that she reminded us of Kazantzakis's endearing character

174

past a farmhouse with a pen full of chickens and goats, on up to a large house with a tiny church sitting next to it. He explains this was once his uncle's house and thinks it might have been the house our Yiayia lived in as well. The church is locked but he thinks he remembers where they keep the key for that once-a-year visit from the priest who celebrates the Holy Liturgy on the name day of the church. He starts his key search, feeling above the door frame, patting the tops of the window frames, but to no avail. Then, tall as he is, he bumps his head on one of the rafters over the door and the key falls to the floor in front of him! We all scream, "Thavma!" *A miracle!* He unlocks the small wooden door and we squeeze inside, where there is a small room with about ten old wooden chairs facing the altar. There are ancient, fading icons on the walls and small incense burners on either side of the nave. There is a bare lightbulb overhead, hanging on a wire, where once there was probably nothing but candles. It definitely feels as though we have stepped back in time. It is peaceful here, inside and out. After a few minutes of whispered conversation and explanations from Yiorgo, we walk back outside amidst the many olive trees before getting into the car again. On the way back to Gythio, Yiorgo waves at an elderly woman, who comes out to the car to talk to him. He explains who we are and she thinks she remembers our Yiayia's family those many years ago. I wish I could get every detail of what she remembers, but we drive on, back to Yiorgo's boat. We thank him profusely for taking the time to drive us out to the village, for giving us a sense of where some of our roots are still buried deep in that soil beneath the olive trees.

DAN

We were all crowded into Yiorgo's little car. The sun was slanted a bit and Yiorgo wound his way back down the mountain from the almost-abandoned hill town and did not slow down until we got to the main road into Gythio. The capers were in bloom, growing in the crevices of rocks!

FLOYD

After more discussion about travel plans, we ended up renting a car and spent a great day at Mavrovouni Beach. Set up our towels under a tree and Dan and I went for a swim while the girls went to search for coffee. They found that the café near us on the beach was not quite open for business this morning and the two matronly ladies did

179

not know how to work the filter coffee pot. Elizabeth ended up behind the counter, making coffee! We've decided to go south and tour the entire Mani Peninsula. We've discovered the delights of having a car and feel as though we've improved our travel experience immensely. It's a great sense of freedom, having our own transportation.

GEORGIA

We have found Skoutari! The most exquisite beach so far. The small blue- hued crescent is empty except for three rowboats, a yellow, a blue, and a red, resting with noses toward the few buildings here on the sand. The first is a fish taverna, tidy with new blue painted trim and white stucco walls. Next to it is another tidy building in blue and white; we later learned that it had been restored to a tiny three-unit rental. On the other side of the taverna is a long, low one-story fishing shack. It has not been white-washed recently. The pink, purple and mauve stones from the beach show through the crumbling old gray stucco. To one side is the doorway, very old blue, protected by a bit of old bamboo ceiling whose edges have been repaired with newer reeds, the feathery tops creating a charming ruffle to this roof. Under this were one pale blue table and two chairs and two bursting bags of fishing nets. The hulk of a sad old boat leans against the corner post supporting the reed roof. We wonder if the strings of lights are waiting to be snapped on one night soon for calamari fishing. The sweetest building on this tiny strand is the little chapel of St. Barbara, buried in bushes of pink oleander. I immediately walk towards it to try to peek inside and am greeted by the brightness of a single red poppy guarding the doorway.

DAN

Well, we have found another paradise! Petro recommended this beach as one of the best around. We are here now and he is right. The taverna we are sitting at, T'Akroti-ali, is a fish taverna. We drove down a narrow road winding through the town to a beautiful bay. The sand is a mix of rock, fine shell and sand. After going into the water we saw a man who walked out onto a big rock in the water with a plastic bag. Then he took out some good-sized octopus and began the methodical whacking of it on the rock to tenderize it. I got out of the water and took a picture of him several times, only to find out later that the setting was wrong. Finally the taverna opens and we find out its specialty is fish. We share two plates of village salad and a couple of Amstel beers. The lady who runs it is a young widow with a bad attitude. Too bad this paradise, with its one and only tavern, is one with a somewhat sour disposition.

FLOYD
We decided to keep the car a third day and found the great beach of Skoutari, a beautiful secluded spot with one taverna, not too far from Vathi, the place we had recently stayed. We spent the day talking, swimming, exploring, napping, and swimming again. Reluctantly we made our way back to Gythio.

GEORGIA
While exploring this new area for us, we tell Dan and Elizabeth about our incredible experience on another peninsula nearby, several trips ago. A friend of ours, Christina, who now lives in Thessaloniki, had told us while we were visiting her that we were welcome to stay at the tiny house she had bought twenty years ago, not too far from Monemvasia and gave us the key in case we decided to check it out. It sounds adventurous to us, so after visiting Monemvasia, we take a bus south to the seaside town of Neapoli and then a taxi to this tiny mountain village of Velanithia. Actually we shared the cab with a young seminary student who was going home for a visit near our destination. We got off in the center of Velanithia at siesta time. All is quiet with warm, beautiful views of the sea down the mountain to the left. We go into the one and only taverna, the Monte Carlo, and introduce ourselves as friends of Christina, who bought the little house on the hillside a long time ago. The owners, Maria and Antoni, are jubilant to hear news of Christina and point out that this house is behind the little white church far across the village on the hillside. We can't see the house but know it's up there. We tell them our plans to stay overnight and they're skeptical. "You're not taking your suitcase are you?" A warning! We are escorted to the market next door and Maria wakes the owner, who helps us pick out peaches, tomatoes, cheese, bread, water and oil and wicks for the oil lamps. We're ready for our romantic overnight in the little house. First, the woman at the Monte Carlo says she'll make us a little food for the hike. She fries fish in vinegar sauce, serving it with bread and fries. Delicious. Then we're off. A cab drives us up to the church pointing in the direction of Christina's house. None of us can see it still. After he leaves us with our one bag of goodies we start wandering around the hillside searching. How hard could it be to find a house?

Much harder than we thought! My sandals find every pebble on the path and my gauzy dress catches on all the bramble bushes as Floyd leads the way. Excited at finally seeing footprints, we discover we had walked around in a large dusty circle back to where we started. I sat down for a rest while he went on alone and finally came back to lead me to the house. The key would hardly go in the rusty lock. Finally the door opened and we were in. One shabby room, two broken chairs, a tiny hearth, the trunk of moth-eaten blankets and sheets, and the dust of a couple of decades. No table or bed or lamps. Floyd tries to make a bed of the two saw horses. Then he says we can sleep on the roof under the stars! As romantic as that sounds in theory, we surprised ourselves by deciding not to stay at all. We sat out front eating our juicy peaches, gazing at the sea and laughing about what we found. We swept the stone steps of this lonely shepherd's hut and could see its potential just as Christina had decades ago, when she worked for a whole summer with her brother "fixing it up." But time and neglect had taken its toll. We found an actual path from the house to the little white church and soon were on the road back to the village. Arriving at the Monte Carlo before sunset, thank God, we asked Maria if we could rent a room in town for the night. She said, "Aha, you came back early!" She and Antoni confessed smilingly that they had been watching us with binoculars as we crisscrossed the hillside looking for Christina's spitaki, her little house. There are no rooms to let here, she told us. We couldn't even sleep on the floor of their taverna! Maria tells us her cousin has a hotel in Neapoli. She'll call ahead and make the arrangements. While she's on the phone Antoni proudly introduces us to his grandchildren, saying, "Then malono ta pethia, mono t'agapo." *I never scold the children, I just love them.* The one and only cab, its driver a young mother on the dole, takes us back down the mountain to Neapoli. The driver's little daughter falls asleep in the front seat as we wind our way down the pitch-black road. Finally we arrive in the metropolis of this town and are welcomed at the Hotel Limara Mare as if we were long-lost family. The glittering lobby and marble tiled bedroom were heaven compared to the rustic charm of Velanithia and we sat on the balcony eating the tomatoes, bread, cheese and local wine intended for Christina's spitaki, but appreciated hugely in the plush comfort of the Limara Mare.

Savory Fried Fish
Psari Savoro
Serves 4

The savory pan juices of this fish make it even more delicious the next day.

1½ lb small white fish fillets
Flour for dredging
Salt and pepper to taste
½ c olive oil
½ c white wine vinegar

1 large red onion chopped
2 garlic cloves minced
2 bay leaves
3 T fresh chopped flat-leaf parsley

Dredge fish with flour and salt and pepper. Heat olive oil in a large skillet. Fry fish until golden on both sides, about 8–10 minutes. Remove with a slotted spoon and keep hot on a glass plate. In the pan drippings, add a little more flour to make a roux, stirring well. Add the wine vinegar, the onions, the cloves of minced garlic, and bay leaves. Stir on low until thickened. Remove bay leaves and pour sauce over the fish. Sprinkle with fresh parsley.

GEORGIA

We've reached the western coast of Mani. Dan, as usual, has his camera arm out the window all the way, trying to capture the beauty passing us by. It's siesta time and we drive into the stillness of a small, empty fishing village with an aquamarine inlet. Floyd and Dan can't wait to swim in it!

DAN

Floyd and I loved having a swim at the tiny Maniot village of Agios Yiorgos. What a spot! I only hope the photos reflect a fraction of the real magic in the colors of the water.

FLOYD

This is the most magnificent swimming place I've seen! One man in a fishing boat, moored at the edge of this deep water, is the only human we see around the place. It looks like he's winding his nets in slow motion.

DAN

We are now at the southernmost tip of the peninsula at Gerolimenos. We drive out onto a dirt road, and I decide it is to be avoided, so I back up and hit a small boulder with the tire. I hear that *hiss!* Anyway I pull it up to a nearby taverna and instead of a simple valve stem being broken it is a sidewall puncture. Oh boy. Does a cheap Greek rental car really have a spare? Does it have a jack? It does! We change the tire and go into the eating place. We ordered beers from two grumpy men with comb-overs, and I take another quick swim. The guy does not have souvlaki so we head elsewhere while enjoying the beautiful view. I hope the pictures turn out!

GEORGIA

We can't stop exclaiming about the spectacular eerie beauty of this landscape. The tower houses of every hill puncture the blue Mani sky like soldiers standing guard. The history here speaks of the tradition of wild independence of the inhabitants, who protected the area from the occupying Ottoman Empire centuries ago. Even our family has a story, of our great-great-grandfather Kyrios Stratiatakos, the name suggesting a brave soldier. Mother's cousin told us when he heard of an approaching fierce Turk he galloped down the hill from Neohori in pursuit. Later he returned wielding a Turkish sword and dressed in the Turk's military regalia. He told the townspeople how he'd massacred the Turkish invader and then hid in the hollow of an ancient tree until it was safe to emerge. He then exchanged clothing and returned home. The villagers, in honor of his bravery and success, awed and grateful for his saving the village, started calling him Kyrie Kakakos, suggesting "the one who killed the bad guy!"

That's how the story goes! Back to the rising and falling and curving of the road around the Mani Peninsula.

DAN

We're back in Gythio and it's time for dinner again. After our long drive we opt for a taverna next door that we can walk to. The waiter sings the praises of the rooster and pasta, and so Georgia and I order that. Floyd gets pasta Bolognese and Elizabeth gets pasta with cheese, her favorite, Mizithra!

Braised Rooster with Noodles
Kokoras me Hylopites
Serves 4–6

Substituting chicken for the rooster works equally well.

1½ lb rooster or chicken cut in pieces
¼ c each butter and olive oil
1 large onion coarsely chopped
Salt and pepper to taste
1 can (28-oz) diced tomatoes

1 T dried Greek oregano
1 c water
4 c chicken broth
1 lb large flat egg noodles

Heat the butter and oil in a pot and sauté the onions for about 5 minutes. Generously salt and pepper the chicken or rooster portions and add to the pot, browning on all sides, and cook for about 5 minutes. Add the tomatoes and oregano. Add 1 cup water and cook gently for another 45 minutes. Finally, add the chicken broth, bring it to a boil, then add the noodles and continue cooking for another 15 minutes until noodles are done. Check for seasoning. Noodles will probably need more salt.

DAN

I just mentioned to Costa, at the hotel, that we have a flat tire and he said, "No problem. Ten minutes new tire." I said thanks. We will see. It worked. We went to Pirelli and after much bickering the guy fixed it. It's probably good for a spare.

Finishing the flat-tire story, in short, the girl at the place was going to charge us for a new tire even though I followed Costa's advice and said it happened here and that it was already damaged. She seemed really unconvinced. She's heard it all before. Anyway, Costa comes in and starts talking to her in Greek back-and-forth. She slowly lets him assert himself and she finally says to me, "Okay, okay!" I should mention that there has been some heat! Thirty degrees centigrade is nineties for us and so we include as much water fun as possible, taking dips at inviting spots.

We read in our guide book that Monemvasia is known as the Gibraltar of Greece, looming over the village at the edge of the sea. The name comes from the Greek term for a single entrance, *mone embasis*. Off the eastern coast of the Peloponnese in 583 CE, nearby residents from the mainland tried to escape Slavic invaders. Years later its growing wealth attracted Arabian pirates. But the residents put up a valiant defense against them, as well as the Normans and Franks, until their stock of provisions was used up and they surrendered. It became a prosperous and important seaport of the Byzantine Empire. At the end of the Ottoman occupation, this sacred rock was the first fortification that the Turks had to surrender. By 1911, the few last residents moved off the plateau of the rock. Recently, Greeks from Athens and many foreigners rebuilt the area, and its alluring beauty continues to be a magnet for visitors.

GEORGIA

En route to Monemvasia, we pass through the beautifully named town of Glykovrissi, Sweet Fountain. It seems like miles of green groves of figs. Suddenly a flash of another color catches my eye: a tiny chapel, its courtyard fringed with tall walls of gold marigolds gleaming in all their splendor!

For the first time we're driving our rented car to one of our favorite spots, Monemvasia. Before we hike up the rocky hill to the citadel Elizabeth and I have a splendid, creamy cappuccino at the foot of the hill. The white ceramic cups were big as soup bowls and full to the brim with foamy cream sprinkled with fresh-grated nutmeg. Each sip we took filled our mouths with the rich coffee flavor, which lingered luxuriously on our tongues and in our memories long after. The winding road along the sea is hot and steep. We stopped to rest at the cemetery and walking through its marble tombstones, we see the grave, all flower-strewn, of the famous Greek poet, Yiannis Ritsos, on which his words are carved:

"Scanning the frenzied sea where the broken mast of the moon had sunk."

ELIZABETH

As we walk the sharp ascent to the fortress we stopped again for Dan and Floyd to swim in a place we remember right outside the old city walls. I took a picture of Georgia and Floyd and then Floyd said, "Look at this strange rock formation." Georgia said, "It looks like pumice," and I said, "Like hummus?" Then we laughed hysterically. There is a word for that-when you hear something different from what is said (not deaf)! We strolled around the town and found the shaded and flowered walkway down to the swimming place off the rocks where Dan and Floyd swam. They swim every chance they get. After this, we're all dying of thirst. It's been so hot! So we went into a cool and inviting café called Kenoni and asked for lemonatha! They only had portokalatha, fresh-squeezed orange juice, which we find everywhere as a popular, refreshing drink.

GEORGIA

Finally into the city walls and the magical world from the past. The narrow streets and shop fronts restored to their original façades and beautiful arts and crafts in the windows; tantalizing aromas wafting through the doorways of cafés tucked under grapevines and the spreading umbrellas of plane trees, flowers growing up stone walls and cascading from the balconies. On our left are archways leading from the merchants' level where we walked, inviting one to climb higher still to the castle and church ruins at the top where the aristocrats held out, protected against the pirates who could only gain entry to the lower cliff level where the traders lived. The waves eternally crashing on the right. The colors are all the blue-greens of the sea and the sepia tones of tile, stone and stucco.

ELIZABETH

After we walked through the tunnel entrance we are aware of much work being done. They are using horses to carry in the building supplies, since no vehicles and very few other machines are allowed. We found one of our favorite spots for lunch, a well-known taverna called Matoula's. We had cool wine, luscious stuffed grape leaves in creamy avgolemono sauce, warm bread, village salad and beet root salad, a perfect early lunch. The beet salad was gorgeous in a pure white ceramic bowl—burgundy beets with deep green leaves glistening in olive oil. A waiter came by with our bill and

Dan said, "Your eyes are very blue," and he said to Dan, "Like yours." Georgia asked where his family was from and he said Corfu. Then she asked, "Where are you from?" and he said, "I am from here but my eyes are from Corfu!"

Beet Root Salad
Patsaria Salata
Serves 3

Burgundy beets with deep green leaves glisten in olive oil.

12 young beets with green tops
1 T salt
1 T Greek oregano

½ c olive oil
3 T wine vinegar

Cut off the leaves and wash well in cold running water. Scrub beets well under running water to remove dirt. In a large pot place beets and cover with cold water and salt. Bring to a boil. Reduce heat and cover. Boil 45 minutes. Add leaves and boil until tender. Drain all. Remove beet skin with fingers. Slice beets into a bowl and add leaves. Toss with olive oil, vinegar and oregano. Serve hot or cold.

Stuffed Grape Leaves
Dolmathakia
Serves 4–8

There is a certain tanginess in the grape leaves that makes these appetizers irresistible.

1 lb jar of grape leaves (drained, rinsed in
    cool water, then drained again)
1½ c long grain rice
4 medium onions chopped
½ c fresh dill chopped

½ t salt
½ t pepper
1 c olive oil
1 bay leaf
3 c chicken broth or water
½ c lemon juice

Set aside grape leaves, then in a large bowl, mix all ingredients except bay leaf, broth and lemon juice. Rinse grape leaves, setting aside the largest six or seven leaves. Lay each leaf shiny side down, cut out tough stem. One at a time, place about 1 tablespoon of rice mixture at the bottom of each leaf. Fold sides in and roll firmly toward the point. Line a heavy pot with the larger leaves and place each rolled little package tightly against each other. If there are any leaves left lay them across the top of the rolls. Drizzle all with a little more olive oil and add enough broth or water plus the lemon juice to reach the top of the dolmathes. Before covering, place a heavy plate over all to keep them from shifting. Bring to a gentle boil, then immediately reduce heat and simmer for about one hour. There should always be some liquid in the pot. If necessary, add more water. Serve at room temperature with lemon wedges.

To prepare as an entrée, add one pound of ground beef or ground lamb, uncooked, to the rice mixture and proceed as above, stuffing and cooking. Serve with egg-lemon sauce.

Sauce:
3 eggs
½ c lemon juice
1 c hot broth from pot

Beat eggs and lemon until thickened. Gradually beat in broth from pot, then pour slowly back into pot over dolmathes after removing plate. Simmer over very low heat until ready to serve.

ELIZABETH

Niko and Stavro explored the top of Monemvasia earlier and along the way, met a couple who invited them into their home and gardens. They are lawyers from Athens. They have restored this ancient home here in the Castro. The furniture, art, antique guns and views from every window were spectacular. As they toasted with Amstel beers, they agreed that moments like these are what make a trip unforgettable! (We were just a little envious.)

Georgia and I went into a jewelry store with gorgeous bronze cuff bracelets and other jewelry. We talked to a young woman who said she and her father design and make all the jewelry. Some of the designs are from the ancient doors and architecture of buildings and churches in the city, very beautiful.

We decided to go back to Matoula's Restaurant for a fabulous dinner of fried zucchini, baked briam, bourekakia, and the most succulent chicken with the appropriate amount of Retsina and ice cold beer. We relax under a grape arbor and we're wrapped in geraniums of all colors! The Aegean stretches before us.

Fried Zucchini
Kolokithakia Tiganita
Serves 4–6

It is traditional to sprinkle vinegar over these fried zucchini slices.

2 lb medium zucchini (4 to 6 inches long and 1 to 2 inches thick)
Salt
1½ c flour
Vegetable oil for frying

Trim ends from zucchini and wash and dry well. Cut into quarter-inch slices. Sprinkle with salt. Let stand in fridge for 30 minutes. Rinse in very cold water, pat dry in paper towels. Dredge zucchini slices in flour. Shake off excess flour. Fry slices in hot oil on both sides until golden brown. Drain on paper towels. Serve hot with garlic sauce or tzadziki, or sprinkle with vinegar and serve. These can be served as an appetizer or a side dish.

Filo Pastry Appetizers
Bourekakia
Serves 10

Bourekakia are small and flaky cigar-shaped appetizers filled with any of several combinations of cheese, vegetables, meat or seafood. You can put them in the freezer and remove as needed, ready to put in a hot oven (425 degrees F.) directly from freezer for something quick.

6 bunches scallions, chopped to make 3 cups
¼ c each olive oil and melted butter
¾ c fresh dill chopped
1 t dried mint

½ t salt or to taste
Ground black pepper to taste
8 sheets filo pastry
2 T sesame seeds

In a medium bowl, mix the scallions, 1 tablespoon of the olive oil–butter mixture, chopped dill, mint, and salt and pepper. Set aside.

Meanwhile take out eight sheets of filo, thawed from the package, reseal and refrigerate the rest of the package. Lay the first sheet of filo on your work surface and brush with oil-butter mixture. Put a second sheet over the first and brush with mixture. On the short side of the filo leave a one-inch margin and then sprinkle a quarter of the scallion mixture in a strip and roll up from that same side, making a long tube. Make sure the filling is spread all the way to the ends before rolling. Place on a greased baking sheet. Continue this procedure three more times, dividing the filling evenly over each filo stack.

Brush each with the butter-oil mixture. Sprinkle sesame seeds over each roll and bake in a preheated oven at 350 degrees F. for about 30 minutes. Tops should be golden. Cool a few minutes then cut each roll into one- to two-inch pieces. Serve these cold or hot.

DAN

Leaving Monemvasia and heading to Gythio, we're prepared for a long ride back. Along the way we find a very nice taverna called Ta Teegania, the frying pans, where we stopped for a snack. We sampled fried calamari and fresh fried potato patties. It's on the opposite side of the Laconic Peninsula from Monemvasia, near Elia. What a location, and to think that you can camp there for free and swim in lovely water! Just magical! Very undeveloped, and the sun slides a bit closer to the horizon as the sea glints!

Fried Calamari
Kalamarakia Tiganita
Serves 4–6

These have become very popular in every restaurant today.

2 lb baby squid
Salt and pepper
1 c flour

1 c vegetable oil
Juice of one lemon

Wash squid. Drain well on paper towels. Cut squid into rings and tentacles into pieces. Season with salt and pepper. Place squid and flour in a plastic bag. Shake bag to flour evenly. Heat oil in a deep skillet and fry squid for seven to ten minutes, until golden brown. Drain on paper towels, place on platter and sprinkle with lemon juice. Serve hot.

Potato Patties
Patatokeftethes
Serves 8

Simple to prepare and luscious to eat. A splendid side dish.

3 lb cooked potatoes, mashed
1 c grated Parmesan cheese
1 T minced fresh flat-leaf parsley
Salt and pepper to taste

2 scallions or 2 T chopped onion
4 large eggs, lightly beaten
1 c flour
Vegetable oil for frying

In a mixing bowl, combine all ingredients except flour and oil and mix thoroughly. Cover and chill for at least one hour. Shape into round patties, rather thick. Pat in flour, shake off excess and flatten. Heat oil to medium high in a large skillet and fry patties until golden brown on each side. Drain on paper towels before serving.

DAN

Our last night in Gythio and we're having our favorite souvlaki at Takis and Eva Kelepouri, the youthful proprietors, along with Uncle Sederis, who was the original owner of the butcher shop, which also sold wonderful grilled meats. Tonight we have ten souvlaki skewers with fries and a liter of white wine. We are done! We have already bought a box of very nice sweets and dropped it by Yiorgo's boat to give him as a thank-you.

He was all greasy working on his engine and accepted hugs and kisses from the girls. Are they related? After the visit to the Stelianakos homestead it is very possible but without going into records, who knows for sure? He will get his boat ready for his island tours to Kythera. We stopped at the same sweet shop and each got a chocolate mousse then went up to the balcony to have a sip of Metaxa. "Poli orea!" *Very nice!*

GEORGIA

Looking ahead to Olympia, we are so happy we rented a car for our travels on Mani. Driving was a new adventure for us. It was our first car rental and it gave us much more freedom to go anywhere we wanted. We will do it again!

FLOYD

We're up and ready for our bus ride to Olympia. Caught the bus right on time, saw Gregory, our friend the cab driver, and said our good-byes. The bus went to Tripoli. We changed stations and buses and then began a mere five-hour ride through some beautiful, sometimes scary mountainous terrain. Finally arrived in the serene town of Olympia, found the lovely Hotel Pelops, and settled in for our visit to the sanctuary of Olympia.

Olympia

"I fling red poppies down, may the world burst into flames."

        — Nikos Kazantzakis

GEORGIA

We returned our rental car and go to the bus station. Leaving Gythio we're so excited to visit Olympia, one of the last major archaeological sites we'll see. The bus from Sparta to Olympia, west and north across the Peloponnese, is a new adventure.

This one sign at the bus station makes us laugh. "Apogorevete pites!" No cheese pies allowed on the bus! A short way out of the city, I spy a freshly mowed hay field with a big patch of scarlet poppies left standing for beauty! It reminds me of the Robert Frost poem "A Tuft of Flowers." This road crosses the middle of the Peloponnese from Tripoli to Olympia and the Ionian Sea. The first stretch travels along the narrow plain between forested hills. Out of the bus window we can see a patchwork of greens, almost like the greens of Ireland, a spring landscape punctuated by poppies. This is the sight I've waited to behold on our trip at this time of the year in mid-June. The village of Levidi is on a high ridge with the valley down on the right. Brown fields dance through the greens and a scattering of white beehives dot the hillsides. The next village, on Oros Mainalon, is Vlahinia. All the stone houses between the turns and curves of the steep mountainside are guarded by walls of evergreens skirting the highway. We've left the olive groves far behind, only some ancient terraces, long unattended, lie still. Now we start to see mountain ash, walnut and pecan trees as we continue to climb. In the distance we see a village whose rooftops look like red-capped toadstools scattered on the thousand meter–high slope. After risky curves, we arrived there. The bus seems to be breaking its wide way through these needle-thin streets. Floyd pretends he has the tour guide microphone and whispers, "Please don't talk to the bus driver while the coach is in motion!" I feel like I went to what I imagine Tibet is like as we crawl out of the jeweled village of Langathia's all-stone houses. The village of Leufkohori appears on the next curve, bright yellow and full of flowers. The bus stops and lets out an old man with bent legs and a cane, who had shouted to the bus driver "Vasili, don't forget me!" The driver tells us he's walking all the way down to the church in the village of Stavrothromi, low and flat, at the bottom of this valley. We continue to climb to the next town, Tropia, which is buried in bushes of roses and geraniums that hang out into the street. The bus brushes through, close enough to be kissed on both cheeks by these blossoms. The rest of the road to Olympia calms down as we descend from this wildly beautiful Mainalon mountain range.

DAN

We have survived another minor scam at the small Tripoli bus station, where we were told, in no uncertain terms, that this was Tripoli and we had to get off here. So we walked into a small bus station café where various cab drivers tried to hawk their services to Olympia. Of course, we are going to ride the bus, so we say, "Ohee, ohee, efharisto!" No thank you. But then we find out there is no bus to Olympia from this little station. Then the guy behind the bus counter tries to convince us to take a taxi to Olympia. What kind of kickback would he be getting? Anyway we finally found out how far the real bus station is and perhaps we're going to walk there, but finally we get a cab for four euros to take us down the road to the real bus station. We have a sandwich, lemonade with ice, and oregano potato chips. Now we are on the bus, which seats sixteen. We'll see if the air conditioning works. I think not. Nope. No A/C but the scenery coming over the mountains is really impressive with towns tucked away. The bus makes frequent stops and slight detours and towards what we think is the end of a very long bus ride, Georgia says, "I think I could ride any roller coaster now," and Floyd says, "This is worse than the turbulence on the flight over!"

ELIZABETH

I'm watching Dan take what seems like hundreds of pictures as we ride through these incredible landscapes. This is not unusual for him, since he is a real "plant hound." He has studied and knows all about plants, especially our California natives, his specialty. Back home, he manages a California native plant garden at Golden West College, where he works. These are the wonderful drought-tolerant plants that can thrive in our California climate, which is so similar to the climate here in Greece. Everywhere we go he is comparing different plant species to those that are similar or actually the same as some of those at home. There are many sketches of these plants in his journal, which he calls his "Bus Botany." (In fact, when we returned home he wrote about his "Bus Botany" in a newsletter of the California Native Plant Society.)

DAN

Although bus rides in Greece can be especially frustrating for the amateur naturalist, the compensations once you arrive are immense. What a beautiful country! And having a chance to ride along with its people from all walks of life makes the long trips worth it. After getting to the various regions, I did actually have time to hike around (sometimes at a trot on short visits), checking out the local flora.

DAN

Olympia! We have arrived and take our luggage up the street. At Floyd's suggestion we employ our old method of arrival by having a drink at a café, so we ordered dio (two) Amstel. The owner is a Greek who spent much time in Melbourne, Australia. His recommendation for a hotel was the same as my guide book said, the Hotel Pelops, at 100 euros with what is supposed to be a really good breakfast included. That's a 24-euro value right there. The owner's son, Christopher, showed us around and we took the four-bed suite. The owner had run the torch procession of two separate Olympics and his oldest son Alex ran in Athens 2004! A lot of history and a very comfortable environment. After our long bus ride, showers felt great. We then head out to the Museum of Olympia. So nice! Great presentation and displays. Olympia is a lovely tree-shaded site with the scattered remains of the gymnasium, the locker, the oil rooms, and various temples. Everything was destroyed by an earthquake. What statues there were left had been deliberately broken and defaced by zealots of that era. An expert could stay for weeks and not even see it all. We enjoyed leisurely walking and reading inscriptions from the tombstones, in the Gallery of the Olympic Games.

"Agathos Daimon Carmelos of Alexandria, boxer, winner in the Nemian Games, died here in the stadium while he was boxing after he prayed to Zeus to give him either the crown or death."

❊ ❊ ❊

Inscription on the circular base of a statue: "Kings of Sparta were my forefathers and my brothers."

199

Victorious Kynska with her chariot (drawn by) swift-footed horses erected this statue. "I assert that I am the only woman in all of Greece who has won this crown." Made by Apelles, son of Kallikles, 390–380 BCE

❋ ❋ ❋

Inscription on a bronze statuette of a runner in starting position (on his thigh): "I belong to Zeus..."

FLOYD

After a shower and rest, we headed for the Olympia Museum. We lucked out with senior discounts, five euros instead of nine euros to visit one of the most beautiful and impressive museums in Greece, full of art and artifacts associated with this marvelous historic spot. The Hermes of Phidias is the supreme piece, on a par with Michelangelo's Pieta and the Charioteer of Delphi. The area itself is, in my mind, equal to the Parthenon and the ruins of Knossos, for after all, it's the site of the first Olympics. There is serenity about the place that befits its function as a sanctuary. The model of it in the museum gives a sense of completeness. I'm glad we came here, the one major archaeological spot we missed so far. On to Zakynthos.

DAN

Café Zeus. Dinner is at the place we originally stopped for a beer. The menu is nice. What they actually have is a bit more limited. Georgia and I both order Stifatho, a beef and onion stew. But there is only one order left so I had Kotopoulo Riganato, chicken roasted with oregano. Elizabeth had little meatballs studded with rice in an egg-lemon sauce called Yiouvarlakia. The tzadziki is very good and the fries were fresh. All our dishes were above average and Georgia's was outstanding. We knew they took credit cards but when we asked him to split the bill into two for us he looked a little stunned and said okay. His eyes were saying no. Floyd throws him a ten-dollar tip after the largest Greek eye-roll ever seen. As I walked a few steps away and turned towards the coffee bar where the register and girl were, he gave such an eye roll again, I could see it from behind; he almost got whiplash. He's good at it. He was a good waiter though. After Floyd's "tenner" he did not hold it against us, funny.

200

P.S. We were given four little slices of a chocolate cake. Nice gesture. Our waiter turns out to have lived on the island of Zakynthos for ten years waiting on tables at a Chinese restaurant. Anyway, he gives us some good tips since that is our next stop. Back to the hotel for some early bed. I have a shot of Metaxa and I dream about tomorrow.

Rice Studded Meatballs in Egg Lemon Sauce
Yiouvarlakia
24 meatballs

These little meatballs swim in the picante flavor of lemon sauce.

1 lb ground pork
¾ c long-grain rice
1 onion chopped
2 garlic cloves minced
2 T fresh chopped mint
5 T fresh chopped parsley
1 T dried Greek oregano

1 egg yolk
Salt and pepper to taste
Flour for dredging
3 T olive oil
3 eggs beaten
½ c fresh lemon juice
Chopped parsley for garnish

Combine pork, rice, onion, garlic and herbs in a large mixing bowl. Add the egg yolk, salt and pepper. Mix thoroughly. Using damp hands, shape the meat mixture into two-inch balls and dredge with flour, flattening them slightly. Place them in a large skillet, add the olive oil and enough boiling water to just cover the meatballs. Cover pan and simmer for 40 minutes until meatballs are cooked. Add a little extra water to keep meatballs covered during cooking. Remove skillet from the heat.

To make the lemon sauce: beat together the eggs and lemon juice in a bowl until very frothy. Add the cooking liquid from the skillet to the bowl, beating vigorously. Pour the egg mixture over the meatballs and return the skillet to the heat, stirring continuously until thickened. Do not allow the sauce to boil or it will curdle. Transfer the meatballs and sauce to a serving dish and garnish with parsley.

Zakynthos

"Let us drink gently with beautiful songs."

—Anacreon

FLOYD

We got a bus in Olympia to Pyrgos and then to Kilini to catch the ferry to Zakynthos. The ferry ride was about an hour and we arrived in the hot, bustling town of Zakynthos itself. Struggled our way with luggage along its waterfront street until finally taking a rest for drinks and ice cream. Finally Dan and I went in search of lodging and found the beautiful Hotel Diana and friendly and helpful Rita. We booked two beautiful rooms for forty euros each and breakfast for two nights and headed back to collect much luggage and two wives, who were wonderfully surprised at the comfort and luxury of our rooms. Settled in and rested for our first night's adventure in this spot.

DAN

We sit upon the still-docked ferry of orange and white, the *Dionysus Solomos*, which is bound for Zakynthos, the flower of the Ionian, and we are aboard. Had a scare as we were having our leisurely, light lunch of meatballs, and a Greek olive spread with fresh pita bread at the café nearby. We noticed only a Zakynthos ferry was there at departure time and not our Ionian Line ferry as noted on our tickets. Eli looked up the boat names and discovered that was actually ours! So, let's go! "Logoriasmo, parakalo!" The bill, please. The girls made a head start and we paid our bill, thirty-one euros! Comfortably on board now, we think, "Never take yes for an answer" is our motto, to which we should add "Always question the obvious." I took a quick photo of Eli in orange and white by the ramp.

Pita Bread
Serves 6

Making your own fresh pita bread is easier than you think.

1 c plus 2 T warm water
1 T sugar
1¼-oz package active dry yeast

3–3¼ c flour
1 t salt
2 T olive oil

In a small bowl, combine water, a pinch of the sugar and the yeast. Let stand 5 minutes or until bubbles form. In a large bowl, combine 3 c flour, remaining sugar and salt.

205

Add yeast mixture and oil; mix until soft dough forms, adding more flour if necessary. Turn dough onto lightly floured surface; knead 5 to 6 minutes or until dough is smooth and very elastic. Cover, let rest. Knead an additional 5 minutes. Place in a large greased bowl, cover and let rise in warm place until double in size, about 30 minutes. Meanwhile, place oven rack in lowest rack position. Put heavy-duty baking sheet in a preheated oven at 350 degrees F. and let heat for 15 minutes. Gently punch down dough to deflate. Divide into six pieces. On lightly floured surface, roll each piece into a seven-inch round, about ¼-inch thick. With fingers, tuck ¼-inch of dough under edge and press flat to form a narrow edge (this will help pita puff up in oven). Place pitas on hot baking sheet and bake 5–7 minutes, or just until bottoms are lightly brown. Place pitas on wire rack and cover with clean towel to keep them soft. Cool completely. If necessary, bake pitas in batches, letting baking sheet reheat 5–10 minutes between baking.

Greek Olive Spread
Chaviari tou Ftohou
Makes about 1 cup

The olives and capers blend together into a pungent, flavorful spread.

½ lb pitted Kalamata olives
½ lb pitted green olives
5 garlic cloves
1 c capers (preferably salt- packed)
6 T fresh lemon juice

½ c flat-leaf parsley
4 T olive oil
1 t dried Greek oregano
1 t white pepper
3 t breadcrumbs (optional)

Rinse olives and capers in cold water. Drain on paper towels. In food processor, combine olives, capers, lemon juice and garlic. Process into smooth paste. Add parsley and process until incorporated. Add 3 tablespoons olive oil, oregano and pepper, and process until blended. Taste and adjust seasonings with lemon and pepper. If mix is too dry, add more oil. If too moist, stir in breadcrumbs. Cover, and refrigerate three hours or more. Serve on pita as appetizer.

Greek Fried Meatballs
Keftethakia
Makes about 4 dozen

The dried mint is what makes these meatballs unique.

2–3 slices of bread
1 lb ground beef
2 T olive oil
1 c finely chopped onion
1 garlic clove minced
2 eggs lightly beaten
¼ c chopped flat-leaf parsley

3 T dried mint
1 T dried Greek oregano
Salt and pepper
Juice of 1 lemon
Flour for dredging
Oil for frying

Dampen each slice of bread under tap, and squeeze out some of the water. In a large bowl combine bread, meat, oil, onions, garlic, eggs, parsley, mint, salt, pepper and oregano. Knead until ingredients are blended. If mixture seems dry add another egg. Shape one heaping teaspoon at a time of meat mixture into small meatballs about one inch in diameter. Dredge in flour. Fill a large, heavy skillet with about an inch of vegetable oil and heat almost to smoking point. Fry keftethakia a few at a time, turn once until golden brown on each side. Remove to serving dish and squeeze fresh lemon over all. Serve hot or cold.

FLOYD

With the help of the very friendly concierge, Rita, we discovered a music taverna that she said was very close by, but felt more like a two-mile walk away. It was a great recommendation in the end. The food was good and the musicians better. The highlight of the evening was a strolling rendition of "Ta Matia," the old love song Georgia and Elizabeth's parents used to sing. Though it was requested so that they could sing along, emotion overcame them as the memories flooded forth and all they could do was smile and cry. Later we sent four "Scotias" (scotches) to the musicians' table in appreciation and were roundly thanked and toasted in return.

DAN

The Alivisos Taverna that Rita told us about was truly authentic. I have the local rabbit, stifatho, and the others have chicken, kotopoulo. We love the music, like Italian Cantadas in flavor, though the lyrics are in Greek. The girls shed some tears as we were serenaded at our table.

Rabbit Stew
Lagos Stifatho
Serves 6

Rabbit is a favorite meat in the mountains of Greece. The typical seasonings for stifatho go as well with rabbit as they do with beef.

1/3 c olive oil	5 garlic cloves
1 rabbit (4 lb) cut into serving pieces	5 whole cloves
Flour for dredging	1 cinnamon stick
1¾ c dry red wine	Salt to taste
3 T red wine vinegar	1 t black peppercorns
1 c tomato sauce	3 lb pearl onions or very
3 bay leaves	small white onions peeled

In a large pot heat the oil. Season the flour with salt and dredge each piece of rabbit, shaking off any excess. Put the pieces in hot oil without crowding. Sauté the pieces over medium heat until brown on all sides, 10–12 minutes. Mix the wine and vinegar and add to pot and turn the heat to high. Let the liquid boil 5–10 minutes until most of it has evaporated. Add the tomato sauce and enough hot water to cover the rabbit. Wrap the following in cheesecloth or tea-ball: bay leaves, garlic, cloves, cinnamon stick, peppercorns. Put it into the pot. Cover and simmer over medium-low heat for about 45 minutes or until half the liquid has evaporated. Then add the pearl onions, stirring into the sauce. Cover and simmer for another 30 minutes until onions are tender. Remove the herb packet and place rabbit pieces on serving dish with sauce. Serve with rice, pasta or potatoes.

FLOYD
We decided to rent a car for the day so we could see the island and maybe go on a small cruise. Ended up with a Hyundai Atos and made our way around part of the island. We had lunch at a taverna in Agios Nicholaos and rented a spot on a small boat to the blue caves and the beach famous for its huge shipwreck, half-buried in the sand. Beautiful scenery.

GEORGIA
Our small boat takes us into the blue of this famously beautiful harbor, whose white cliffs form a crescent reaching out like a shining, beckoning embrace! Elizabeth and I stand on the shore cooling our legs in the aqua waves and slowly sinking every few minutes into the pebbly sand. Again, we vicariously enjoy our husbands' exuberant swimming!

DAN
The water here is almost artificially blue. Petros was the deckhand and he drove the boat slowly through an arch carved by water into a rock formation. Although the boat was pretty large, it went through the arch into a cave, which I would not have thought it would fit. Petros backed out and we headed to Shipwreck Beach, passing huge cliffs of green vegetation and rather tall Aleppo pines mixed in. Shipwreck has water of the particular color blue that is famous around here. A luminous blue that is light in color. We swim, we walk around the shipwreck. I take a picture of stones in the sand that spell the Italian name for this island, Zante–2006. Lovely spot, though it's inaccessible except by boat. After the trip, we take the car and stop at a taverna on a little deep harbor. Again the lovely water! We got two lemonathes with no ice and two big frosty mugs of Amstels with fries. We continue to drive south and take a dip on the south end of the island at Porto Roma. I show Floyd how to squeeze out water from his suit, then get him to make balloons of his shorts. The girls are hysterical. We used the shower and WC without buying a single thing! Tourists!

DAN
It's Monday morning in Zakynthos town and we sit on the Main Street eating little fried donuts, Loukoumathes, as the morning evolves. A very nice man and his daugh-

209

er run the place, Yianni Vlochopoulos and Anna. Right now the girls are talking to the owner about the recipe while a shop behind us plays Eric Borden's "House of New Orleans" and little kids ride their tricycles. We decide to go for a walk later, the girls go one way, I go another. We meet back at Yianni's and Elizabeth remembers the dream she had last night. She and Georgia had a pension they owned and were living in and the doorway into it was a refrigerator door! The interior of the place had shelves like a fridge and they were empty! Talk about a nightmare!

ELIZABETH

We love Yianni's sign out front: "The Adonis Café—Loukoumathes Mania." Yianni told us these feathery light fried puffs that he specializes in were given as prizes to athletes who won in the ancient Olympic Games. We wonder if it is a real historical fact or just a good story. In any case, these would be a wonderful prize for anyone.

Sweet Honey Dumplings
Loukoumathes
Makes 35–40

Feathery light fried puffs soaked in honey.

1 package dry yeast
¼ c warm water
2 c flour
1 t sugar

A pinch of salt
1 c warm water
1 quart of vegetable oil for frying

Topping—mix together in a saucepan:
2 c honey
1 c water
Cinnamon

Dissolve yeast in ¼ cup warm water until it bubbles. Put dry ingredients in a bowl, add the 1 cup warm water and the yeast mixture. Mix well with spoon. Soft dough will form and batter should plop from the spoon. Set aside in a warm place to rise 2–3

210

hours. Gently stir down and let rise again for an hour then stir down again. Heat oil in a large frying pan to 375 degrees F. Drop a teaspoon of the batter into hot oil, using two spoons, one to assist you to push the dough off the other. Fry about four minutes, turning each one in the oil until golden all over. With a slotted spoon, remove from oil to paper towels. Heat the honey and water and dip each dumpling completely into the syrup quickly. Stack on a large plate and sprinkle with cinnamon. Serve immediately while warm.

GEORGIA

Before we leave our hotel, I take a last look at the square below over the wrought-iron ornament crowning the bell tower of the Catholic church next to our balcony. Thanking both concierges, Vasso and Merci, we ask about certain recipes and we are surprised to be turned down. It seems that the women of Zakynthos are very reluctant to share, fearing that the traditional recipe might become adulterated, no longer the pure island way of cooking. Of course, we could respect that, though now we'll have to approximate some of these island recipes. Here they feel that Greek cuisine is best in its purity; blending the Italian and French influences with the Greek is not the same. One of the island's specialties is Mandilato Zante, a nougat which requires special equipment to make the concoction of egg whites, walnuts and sugar. Another tasty new sweet treat for us was called Frygania, something like a bread pudding of rusks, syrup, light custard and whipped cream, a specialty of the island. But no recipes to be had!

FLOYD

One coffee and more loukoumathes at the Adonis Café. The owner took our picture and then went to serve two German ladies sitting next to us. It was ten o'clock in the morning but they wanted hors d'oeuvres and a small bottle of wine. He said if they could wait two minutes he would try to find a bottle of wine. Off he goes on his scooter to look and came back apologizing. "I cannot find a small bottle," he said. "Drink as much as you want from this big one!" We said our thanks and farewells.

ELIZABETH

We had an early breakfast in the hotel and later asked Mercedes, the other girl at the desk, about the ferry and the bus schedules. She told us we could buy a ticket combination to Patras, which thrilled us. Any time we can shorten the time or need to drag suitcases behind us the better we like it. They let us leave our luggage in the reception while we went out to the square to have lunch. We went back to the grill place from last night for chicken souvlaki because they were good and fast. As a final treat, we decided to try the almond cakes Zakynthos is famous for. Found a recipe when we got home.

Garlic Chicken on A Stick
Kota me Skortho
Serves 6

Lots of garlic in this marinade flavors and tenderizes the chunks of chicken.

6 skinless, boneless chicken breasts　　　½ c lemon juice
6 garlic cloves crushed　　　　　　　　　¼ c olive oil
Salt and pepper to taste　　　　　　　　　6 T finely chopped flat-leaf parsley

Cut the chicken into one-inch pieces and place in a shallow dish. In a large plastic bag mix together the garlic, salt, pepper, lemon juice and olive oil.

Add the chicken pieces, seal and marinate 2–4 hours in the fridge, turning occasionally. Spread the chopped parsley out on a plate. Divide the chicken pieces into six equal portions and thread onto six wooden skewers previously soaked in lemon juice for 30 minutes. Roll each skewer of meat in the chopped parsley to coat evenly. Arrange the skewers on an oiled grill and cook for 5–10 minutes or until chicken is golden and cooked through. Turn and rearrange the skewers, basting them with marinade during grilling.

Almond Cakes
Amygthalota
50–60 cookies

These almond cakes are chewy like meringues but not as light.

2½ c blanched almonds
1 heaping cup of sugar
1 t vanilla extract
3 egg whites

2½ c fresh white breadcrumbs
Butter for greasing
1¼ c water with ¼ t orange extract
Sugar for dredging

Place the almonds and 2 tablespoons of sugar in a food processor and blend until very fine. Add the remaining sugar with the vanilla. In a cold bowl, lightly beat the egg whites and add to the food processor with the breadcrumbs. Blend until a soft dough is formed. Then turn the mixture out onto a work surface. Lightly butter two cookie sheets. With damp hands, shape the almond mixture into walnut-sized balls and arrange on cookie sheets. Bake for about 15 minutes or until golden and firm on the outside in a preheated oven at 350 degrees F. Allow the cakes to cool slightly, then transfer them to a wire rack to cool. Pour the orange-flavored water into a small bowl and dip each cake into the liquid, then return it to wire rack. Dredge with sugar and allow to dry before serving.

ELIZABETH
Said good-bye to Mercy and Rita and asked them to call us a cab for the dock. It appeared in an instant, it seemed, and we were off. We were there quite early so we boarded and settled on Deck 5 in quite a luxurious-looking room. We all got ice cream sticks. Dan decided to take a nap on one of the couches. Slowly but surely the room started to fill with people the closer we got to departure time until there were masses of people in there, all smoking! There was a couple across from us with two small boys who were quite rambunctious—whining, crying, and running from their parents, who never once said no or tried to stop the behavior. Finally they left, probably the pressure of hundreds of eyes staring at them and willing them to leave. Floyd noticed a camera that had been left on another chair. Georgia remembered the couple who'd been sitting there so

we went looking for them and found them right away on the upper deck. They were most grateful. We all decided to leave the smoke-filled Deck 5 for the fresh air, staying there for the rest of the trip. As we were told, but didn't completely believe, the bus was waiting for us at the dock! We rode it to the Patras bus station.

Kalavryta and Kertezi

Dimitrios Sardounis, known in Patras as
Mimaros, the famous nineteenth century
puppeteer.

FLOYD

We are now planning our strategy for getting to Kalavryta and ultimately to the village of Kertezi, home of the girls' paternal grandfather. The Patras bus station was such that we were not eager to stay there for the night. We decide to keep going to Egio by bus, where we found a great cabbie, who drove us to Diakopto, the place from which the train takes us up to the village of Papou Sardonis, a place no relatives had ever been.

DAN

We are at the Hotel Lemoni, in Diakopto, between the train station and the beach. We carry our luggage up the steepest staircase with the help of the kind concierge. He unlocks our rooms and clicks on the A/C. We head for a taverna near the water, where we have great calamari and share pork steaks. We head back, shower, repack a day pack's worth of clothes for the trip up the mountain, set the alarm for 5:30 a.m. and hit the sack in very modest but comfy rooms. The sound of the ouzeria below us fades as we drift immediately to sleep.

FLOYD

We're up early to catch the small train through the gorge and up to the Greek ski town of Kalavryta, which Georgia tells us translates to "beautiful springs." A slow, winding, relaxing ride up the mountains and some spectacular views. Checked in at the Hotel Maria.

DAN

The train ride up the gorge is just like the guidebooks say, spectacular! Too bad they don't mention a train driver who smokes and yells at you when you open the window to take a picture. I slip into the next car, but the best stuff has passed, vertical walls right next to the little train soaring upwards with big pines standing sentinel. Plane trees along the river, cascading falls and rapids, incredible views and nice cool, mountain air—very crisp! The next morning we marvel at our great breakfast of bacon omelets! Thirty-one euros for all of us. Po! Po! Now we are ready to explore the town and its surroundings. We don't linger because we are anxious to get to Kertezi, their grandfather's village.

GEORGIA

We were a bit reluctant to return to the group of cabdrivers lounging at the bus and taxi stop at the edge of the square in Kalavryta. They had had a good laugh about something we'd said when asking them earlier about the cost for the ride to the village. Anyway, this time a young cabbie agreed to take us there and wait thirty minutes for twenty-two euros. The twenty-minute drive is fast and furious. Fortunately the village is on the flats of the Kalavryta elevation and the driver careens around the curving road, passing fields of cows busy grazing, bales of hay resting in pale green flatness, squares of bright green grasses, and finally the unmistakable wide ribbons of red poppies! A few houses start to appear and now we are in the village, a place embraced by a circle of tall wooded mountains and capped by a round canopy of sky as blue as the church dome below it. We are dropped off in the square, the platia, empty of people now at this siesta hour. We did however notice a kafenion serving coffee to what looked like the village elders, who stared at the taxi full of people arriving.

FLOYD

Off to Kertezi. We got a cab for twenty-two euros round-trip even if we only stayed a half-hour. The young driver drove ninety to one hundred miles per hour in his late model Mercedes, but it was not scary, given the road and superb engineering of the car. Made our way into the village and stopped at what appeared to be the platia, or square. Told the cabbie we would meet him back there at noon and headed off to try to find anyone who remembered the name Sardounis, the Greek spelling with a *u*. The first few attempts were fruitless and we thought we were in for a short stay. Finally we came to a group of eight or nine older Greeks having coffee in front of a small shop and Georgia asked her question again. This time it paid off. A rustle of excitement and exclamation and recognition! All this response was spearheaded by a woman, now a Greek Australian, who with her husband returns to this home village every two years to stay for six months. Serving as a go-between, she coordinated a remarkable identification party! A number of people recognize the name Sardonis, as well as the family photo Georgia has brought along of her grandfather, his wife and two oldest sons. Tongues were loosened and flying and I had to go tell our cabbie to head back as we would be here for some time. Paid him fifteen euros and he headed out of town. Went back to the now clamorous group, all engaged in talk about Sardouni! The family name was well known, in fact, he was once "mayor" of this village, and the old house has a plaque inscribed on it with the name clearly visible. Georgia produced pictures of her Papou and Nona with two uncles at a young age, and another photo of them much older. Later we heard about the old woman who claimed to have the same family photo in this Sardonis home she now owned as a summer house with her brother from Patras.

ELIZABETH

Finally the cab gets us here. The song of the cicadas has followed us. We get out and see a sleepy little village. What are the chances anyone will know our family name, which was not very common? Our Papou died at the age of ninety-four and that was over fifty-five years ago. Who would be alive now with any memory of that family, especially when the young people of these remote villages typically move away as soon as they can? Who is left to remember or at least pass on the stories they heard as children?

Georgia asks the first person we see, who happens to be a workman busy raking under the trees. He shakes his head and calls to his co-worker, asks the same question and gets the same shaking of his head. There are not a lot of people around, so we start walking down the road and soon see a small taverna with six or seven elderly men sitting outside. This time when Georgia asks if anyone knows the name of Sardouni we see a nodding of heads. There is a buzz of excitement and conversation as my sister explains who we are and pulls out some old family photos. As we are offered chairs and drinks, someone calls the president of the village; he comes over and joins the conversation. There is a couple here from Australia who visit their home village here every other year and are wonderful at translating most of what is being rapidly spoken. We are given much information, drawn from their memories and then told they will take us over to the house. We are stunned to see a marble plaque on one wall with the family name and dates engraved there. Apparently the current owners found a chipped and broken plaque in the rubble when they were clearing the area on move-in day. Our new friends apologize for not being able to take us inside, since the owners are away right now. Georgia and I look in the window to the kitchen, drinking in the little we can see from this angle. We proceed to the ancient cemetery and church, all the while adding more villagers to our procession. I feel as though we are in our own parade. It is so sweet that everyone we pass wants to become part of whatever we are doing. Visitors, especially foreign visitors (xeni), are probably a rarity. We are invited by the Australian couple to stay into the evening for dinner, and sample the bean soup, fasolatha, that Kertezi is famous for. We were so worried about being able to get back to our hotel in Kalavryta that we declined but were given the recipe to take with us.

Bean Soup
Fasolatha
Serves 4–6

This hearty soup is the highlight of the Bean Festival in Kertezi. It is very nutritious.

2 c of great northern beans (soaked overnight or 4 hours in water to cover) or 2 c canned cannellini beans
1/3 c olive oil plus 3 T for garnish
2 cloves of garlic, minced
1 c celery, chopped
1½ c carrots, chopped
2 c onions, chopped
8 c of water or broth or mixture of both

2 T dried Greek oregano
1 c finely chopped parsley
3 bay leaves
1 14-ounce can diced tomatoes
2 T tomato paste diluted with 3 T water
Salt and pepper to taste
1 T lemon juice or vinegar for each bowl when serving

If soaking dried beans, drain and place in a large saucepan. Add cold water to cover by three inches, bring slowly to a boil, drain and rinse. Set aside. If using canned beans, just rinse and set aside. Rinse out stockpot, set over medium-low heat and add one-third cup olive oil. Heat oil and add onion, carrot and celery. Sauté 30 minutes until pale gold, stirring occasionally with a wooden spoon. Add garlic and oregano, half the parsley, the bay leaves, the great northern beans and the water. Bring to a boil. Cover and simmer for at least one hour until beans are soft and creamy, but not disintegrating. Stir tomato paste into canned tomatoes and pour into soup. Season with salt and pepper. If using canned beans, here is where you would add them to the above simmered ingredients. Simmer for 15 minutes more. Remove bay leaves. Stir in remaining parsley and three tablespoons of olive oil. Serve hot with lemon or vinegar for each bowl.

220

DAN

We are surrounded by people who know of the family, offering us chairs, coffee, conversation, even when we don't understand it and asked a million questions. We meet Costas, "Kon" (sounds like Cone!) Konstandinos, who is the president of the town. He offers to walk us through the village, giving us historical information all the way. He points out the old church where the icons are ancient, and where the Sardounis family of the very old generations would probably have worshipped. We learn about the new church as well as the water piping system of old and most important, we get to the old family house. Wow! Now, we did not get to go in but we walked into the courtyard and looked into the downstairs office area. I got pictures of the girls on the steps peeking in the windows. I got stinging nettles on the inside of one calf and on the left foot. The tingling of that remains, just as the memory of several coincidences and stories from the Grecian village, whose memory is long! One guy up on a balcony tells us he is the one who as a young child pounded the rocks individually into the asphalt of what is now the main drag, named Sardounis Boulevard! Another person leaning out the window remembers stepping on the stones leading to the Sardounis house. They tell of the woodland road that leads to the chestnut trees on the hillsides. We talked of the president's father's burial site, of the plans for the town's water system, and of how the houses that are falling into ruin are in limbo since so many family members have a piece of the pie and cannot agree to share it, sell it or whatever. Of course, when they found out we had a taxi waiting for us they had us send it away. The Aussies, Christo and Vasso, invited us to have a farewell cold drink while we wait for the bus to take us back to Kalavryta. We say thanks and good-bye to the mayor and his wife.

GEORGIA

Our parade is led by Kon, the president of the village, who points out many historical spots on our way to Kyria Dina's, the present owner of the Sardounis homestead. He stops at a house and shouts out her name a few times. A very old man who has been standing out front under a plane tree quietly says, "She's not here, Kon! I think she's at your house." The president takes us next door to quite a large and lovely whitewashed house almost buried in a tangle of trellises, grapevines, and flowers everywhere! I remark about them and he says, Neh, neh, ti na kanoume? Omodfiah!" *Yes, yes, what are we going to do? Such great beauty!* Under the grapevine two ladies are chattering to each

221

other all at the same time. It's Kyria Dina and Kyria Effie, the president's wife, who greet us and are a bit amazed at our mission, but more important to them, they're annoyed that the baker is late. "So where is he?" they ask. Kon's cell phone rings and he excuses himself as he mutters that everyone needs him to do one thing or another! The call from Patras is about doing a job for the town. He now asks Kyria Dina if she'll take us over to the homestead. "Of course, I'll be honored," she said but told us that since it was now a summer home her brother had the key and wouldn't be here for another week. Now the parade grows, with Effie and Dina added to the four xeni—the guests—the president, Vasso and Christo, and a few of the men who left their coffee to join the parade. We turned a corner, past the courtyard covered with the kiwi vines, and then the president points and exclaims, "Na to!" *There it is.* Behind a stone wall, covered with tumbling roses, a two-story house loomed above the faded aqua door, set into the wall. The number 23 in black iron is nailed into the old wood. The president tells us about the political career of this man, Panayiotis Sardounis, while Vasso translates to me and Elizabeth, Christo translates to Dan and Floyd, and Dina and Effie are still chattering about the baker, wondering why he is so late, all the while patting us on our backs as their part of this important conversation. "These folks from America came here looking for the house of their grandfather," they remind each other. Christo picks two big old-fashioned roses for me and Elizabeth and we climbed the stairs to peek in the window. The president tells us the original marble plaque was found here in the basement below where he leads us in for a look around.

Christo elaborates by adding that the plaque was replicated in Athens in the very same marble which is found all over the Acropolis. "Nowadays, though, the marble is not the same. It melts quicker," making it sound as if it's the marble and not the smog that causes the erosion. He also points out the higher level of the courtyard and remembers from his childhood that it used to be full of gardenias. What a fragrant image! At the foot of this garden was the house's water source piped up from the spring in the middle of town. Finally we leave the courtyard of the homestead, wondering if we'll ever really learn our connection to this house, this man. Back on the main drag, Sardounis Boulevard, we strolled over to one of the thirteen ancient Byzantine chapels in the village and wind our way through the radiance of white marble gravestones into the deep darkness of the inner church.

ELIZABETH

Going into this dark, ancient church, I hear our own footsteps echoing, but it is easy to imagine I'm hearing the ancient echoes of all the villagers who worshipped here with their families each Sunday and on Holy Days. Christo told us there are robbers around so they have to keep the old churches locked up. The church is Agios Haralambos. The president tells us the frescoes are the second oldest in all of Greece. As our eyes adjust to the shadows, we begin to see every inch of the walls is painted with saints and sacred images. They seem to be in remarkably good condition, though all along the edge of the floor we see crumbles of ancient frescoes. Kon is now behind the iconostasis searching for the new light switch, so we can better appreciate the paintings. We love and marvel at them more in the mystery of this darkness and feel the sense of sanctity shared by all these people who reverently point out the old wooden high-back chairs along the walls and the small round windows in the dome that light the painted ceilings.

GEORGIA

Our visit here is almost over. Walking back to the café for farewell drinks we're greeted by several people who by now have heard about the "xeni" in town. One man leaning out of his second-story window asks if we happen to know his cousin in New York. No, he doesn't remember his name, but he knows he opened the first ice-cream factory in America! Another person shouts from her balcony that she has the name and address of a doctor in Patras whose mother-in-law is part of a Sardounis clan. Christo picks another rose from a vine close to the street and an elderly lady up on her porch asks if he's stealing her flowers again. "If it's for me, it's okay," she smiles. I can imagine our Papou growing up in this lovely green village of flowers, vegetable gardens, small farms and family chapels and I think I understand how important it was for him to replicate in my very first home on Lovell street in Nashua, New Hampshire, the grapevines and flowers, fruit trees and gardens, chicken coop and wine cellar of his childhood home in Kertezi.

As we leave Kertezi and continue to search for Sardounis relatives, we learn that in the late nineteenth century in Patras, a man named Dimitrios Sardounis Hellenized the shadow puppet tradition, whose origins were in the Far East. Karagiozi became a comic character and the shows were popular for adults and children alike. "Mimaros" became the stage name for this Sardounis man, the founder of the Karagiozi Theater,

223

an entertainment venue for families in Greece and the new immigrants in America. We remember our grandfather taking us to these shows, appearing regularly on weekends at the hall of our Greek church in Nashua. We now wonder if he knew the fame of Dimitrios Sardounis in Greece and how they were related.

FLOYD

Being in this scenario I feel like we're in a Fellini movie! Back in Kalavryta now, we take a sad stroll through the cemetery where almost every gravestone is etched with the date December 13, 1943, commemorating the massacre of hundreds of local men by the Nazis. Every family lost a father, a brother, an uncle, a son. When the Germans invaded the city all the local children were sent to school in Kertezi.

ELIZABETH

Part of the story was about a teacher who was ordered to lock all the children in the schoolhouse then set it on fire. Amazingly, one soldier took pity and unlocked a back door for them to get out and run to safety.

DAN

For dinner tonight we stop at the taverna Stani, which means "sheep fold." And there, instead of lamb, we have roast pork off the rotisserie, very good. Ice cream for dessert and off to bed.

Roast Pork Loin
Hirino Psito
Serves 4–6

This delectable roast pork sizzles fresh out of the oven.

3–4 lb pork loin
2 cloves or more garlic sliced
2 T olive oil
Juice of a lemon

Salt and pepper to taste
2 T oregano
1 c chicken broth
1 c dry white wine

With a sharp knife, make slits all over the roast and insert slices of garlic. Rub all sides with olive oil and sprinkle with lemon juice, salt, pepper and oregano. Place a rack in a roasting pan and place the roast on the rack. Add chicken broth and wine to the pan. Roast for 1½ hours. Turn the roast and baste with pan juices and roast for 30 minutes longer or until roast is done. Add more broth to the pan if needed. Transfer the pork roast to a cutting board and let stand for 10 minutes. Carve the roast, arrange on a serving platter and spoon hot pan juices over all.

FLOYD
Up early for breakfast and a bus back down to the sea at Diakopto to retrieve our luggage then get a bus to Egio in hopes of catching the ferry across the Corinthian Gulf to Agios Nicholaos and the next leg of our journey.

GEORGIA
The bus ride leaving Kalavryta has a more quiet beauty than the dramatic train ride up through the gorge. The huge Mercedes diesel does the switchback dance on the cliffs and curves for two thousand feet down to sea level. The side trips to every little village on the way down were more amazing; every home's garden included a small orchard, each tree dripping with droplets of red ripe cherries. In exactly one hour we had arrived back in the seaside town of Diakopto. Our kind and helpful hotel-keeper greeted us with a smile and a genuine interest in our adventure to our grandfather's village. He calls us a cab for Egio Harbor and our ferry across the Gulf of Corinth.

ELIZABETH
The cypress trees are scattered through the wooded landscape like dark exclamation points among the pale, gray-green olive trees and bright neon-green plane trees.

DAN
On the south side of the Gulf of Corinth, we wait for the ferry. At the nearby bus stop, we nibble on various snacks and watch three scruffy dogs sleep under our seats. Anyway, after some tasty little meatballs called soudzoukakia and excellent, garlicky tzadziki, we walk back to the ferry landing and board, hoping, at best, to get a bus on the other side to Delphi. On the ferry the ropes are cast off as we begin our way across

the Corinthian Gulf. The last truck on carried a gigantic load of rough-cut wool. I walk over and grab a small tuft of very coarse brown, almost black wool for my journal. Spirits are high as we point our bow toward the mainland. The wind and very choppy sea buffets the long but narrow ferry.

ELIZABETH

For the first time, we ate dinner at a bus-stop taverna. That was one of our many surprising food discoveries—that bus stations serve taverna-style food. In fact, we had the best oven-roasted potatoes here, as well as wonderful spicy meatballs rich with cumin, butter and a garlicky tomato sauce.

Meatballs Smyrna-Style
Soudzoukakia a la Smirni
Serves 4–6

The cumin in this recipe creates a spicy, zestful meatball.

1½ lb ground beef
½ c dry unseasoned breadcrumbs
1 t cumin
1 t salt
¼ t pepper
Sauce (see below)

2 cloves garlic crushed
Dash of cinnamon
2 t minced fresh parsley
¼ c water
½ c butter

Combine all ingredients except butter in a large bowl. Knead thoroughly. Shape into oblong balls; brown on all sides in hot melted butter. Do not drain. Pour sauce over meatballs and pan drippings; simmer 30 minutes. Freezes well. Reheat in covered casserole at 350 degrees F. or place in microwave. Makes about 20 meatballs.

Sauce:
2 c tomato sauce
1 c water
2 bay leaves

1 clove minced garlic
½ t salt
3 T red wine

Combine all ingredients in a pan and bring to a boil. Reduce heat; simmer until thickened, about 15–20 minutes.

Oven-Roasted Lemon Potatoes
Patates Lemonates
Serves 4

These potatoes are sublime. They are extremely lemony but irresistible.

8 medium peeled potatoes
½ c olive oil
½ c fresh lemon juice
1 T salt

1 T pepper
1 T dried Greek oregano
½ c water as needed

Cut potatoes into quarters and place in large bowl. In a separate small bowl, mix together all ingredients except the water. Pour over potatoes and toss well until they are well coated. Pour all potatoes and marinade into a nine-by thirteen-inch roasting pan and spread potatoes into one layer. Put into preheated oven at 400 degrees F. and cook about half an hour. Pull out pan and baste. Add some of the water if necessary, pouring into one corner of the pan so as not to wash off the marinade, then shake pan to distribute evenly. Continue to bake for another half-hour or until potatoes are soft and cooked through.

Delphi

"And the Delphic woman, on the most holy tripod,
chanting for the Greeks the things Apollo sings."

—Euripides

there, which has a large collection of artifacts from Delphi and other spots. The famous bronze young man with the glass eyes, the Charioteer, standing tall and holding the flared-out reins of a vanished horse, reminds Georgia of all our three sons' profiles combined! We spent both nights at the Varonos Hotel, in air-conditioned rooms, plus a great breakfast of the ubiquitous hard-boiled egg with breads, including koulouria, cheeses, cold meats, yogurt, coffee and fruit at a very good price for this area. Tourism has declined in the last few years in Greece. Rooms are always available anywhere.

GEORGIA

I'm especially fascinated by the sacred spring at this historic site. It was at this spot that the Delphic Oracle, called a Pythia, an older woman of a blameless life, was chosen to be the voice of Apollo. While she was in a trance she would prophesy the future. Kings and princes from all over the ancient world would consult this oracle.

DAN

The ruins are quite wonderful, surrounded by cicadas, cypress, and mallows. Apollo's Temple is especially stunning with its famous inscriptions: "Pan Metreon Ariston" (Moderation in all things); "Gnothi S'auton" (Know thyself).

From the top of the theater, polite clapping from a group of four is very clear. Almond trees are in abundance, but also many annual grasses, which are a fire hazard. We saw the main section, then the museum. The charioteer was rather eerie, but great. My favorite item was a small bowl with a painting of Apollo.

Then two Amstel, lunch and a quick nap before seeing the lower sections, a one-mile walk from the hotel. When we returned to the hotel, the television was blaring: a soap opera in Italian with Greek subtitles!

ELIZABETH

We had lunch at the Gigantos Grill and shared two combo meals of salata, bread, moussaka, pasta, souvlaki, lamb chops, fries, fruit and, of course, Amstel. Whew! What a lot of food that was. My favorite was the grilled lamb chops. I especially love these on the charcoal grill, which lends a different flavor from a gas grill. The smoky aroma connects us to the fun we used to have as kids dancing at the summer picnics at our Greek festivals.

233

Charcoal-Grilled Lamb Chops
Arni sti Schara
Serves 6

Using a charcoal grill is preferable for the most authentic Greek flavor.

6 loin or shoulder lamb chops
½ c olive oil
Juice of one lemon

3 t dried Greek oregano
Salt and pepper to taste

Trim fat from chops, if desired. Rinse and pat them dry. Place into large plastic bag with oil, lemon juice, and one teaspoon of oregano. Seal the bag and coat all meat with marinade. Refrigerate three to four hours, turning bag over periodically. Prepare a charcoal grill. When the coals have burned down to medium heat, take the chops from the marinade and put them on the hot grill. Cook about five minutes on each side, basting with the marinade. Mix the remaining oregano and salt and pepper and sprinkle over the chops when they are done. Serve with lemon wedges.

ELIZABETH

Later at the Lekaria Taverna for dinner, we ordered as though we hadn't eaten for a week. We ordered kotopoulo (chicken), moscari (veal), horta (greens) and a classic Greek pilaf. As we ate, we experienced an unfamiliar flavor in the sauce over our rice pilaf. When we asked the waiter what was in it he would only say, "special recipe." We later found out it was flavored with the broth of simmered lamb brains and herbs. Special recipe, indeed!

234

Boiled Greens
Horta
Serves 6

Boiled and tossed with olive oil, these vitamin-rich greens make a great salad.

3 lb greens (spinach, escarole, chicory, or Swiss chard)
1/3 c olive oil

Juice of one lemon
Salt and pepper to taste

Wash greens extremely well. Fill a large pot with water and add a generous pinch of salt. Bring to a rolling boil. Add horta (greens). Keep the lid half on and cook until very soft, 30–40 minutes. Strain well and cool slightly. Mix oil, lemon juice, salt and pepper and pour over greens.

Note: Once boiled, horta are greatly reduced in volume. A half-pound per serving is needed.

Classic Greek Pilaf
Pilafi
Serves 4

A light and fluffy rice.

1 c long-grain converted rice
¼ c butter
Salt and pepper
2½ c chicken broth

In a medium saucepan, sauté rice in hot butter for three minutes, stirring constantly. Add salt, pepper and broth; bring to a boil. Cover and simmer 15–20 minutes, or until liquid is absorbed. Remove from heat; leave covered rice to stand 10 minutes. Fluff with fork and serve hot.

DAN

Just ate our first dinner at a taverna by the bus stop. The temperature is perfect now with a fingernail moon in the sky. Georgia said the word for the image of the moonlight on water is "moon-glade." The lower ruins were a bit of a letdown this afternoon. The Temple of Tholos (round) was the only upright feature and was very nice.

FLOYD

It's the end of the day and we're hungry and I decide to break from my pasta tradition I've been stuck in and go with yiouvarlakia, little rice-studded meatballs in a sauce of avgolemono. The zucchini pita has just arrived.

Savory Zucchini Pie
Kolokithopita
Serves 6–8

This pita has a subtle but fulfilling flavor.

2 T olive oil	5 T flat-leaf parsley chopped
3 bunches scallions thinly sliced	5 T fresh mint, chopped
1/3 c short-grain rice	3 eggs beaten
¾ c vegetable or chicken stock	½ c feta crumbled
2 lb zucchini, grated coarsely and drained 10 minutes in a colander; then squeeze remaining water out by hand	½ t each salt and pepper
	½ c butter melted
	7 oz filo (about half a package)

Heat oil in a saucepan and add scallions; fry five minutes. Add rice and cook one minute, stirring. Add broth to pan and simmer fifteen minutes till rice is tender. Remove from heat and add squeeze-dried zucchini. Mix and let cool. Add parsley, mint, and beaten eggs to cool mixture. Add crumbled feta with salt and pepper and mix. Butter nine- by thirteen-inch baking pan and line with one sheet of filo, brushing with melted butter. Continue the process with half of the filo sheets, buttering each one. Spread the zucchini mixture over the filo evenly. Cover with the rest of the filo sheets, buttering each one. Cut through only top layers of filo to let steam escape. Bake in a preheated oven at 375 degrees F. for about 40 minutes, until top is golden.

DAN

We all enjoyed our breakfast here at the hotel. It was punctuated by laughter beginning when Georgia mentioned they bought bracelets at a jewelry shop last night. Floyd says, "I can see the news now: 'Delphi economy picks up while the rest of nation remains depressed. Thanks to the Gourouni Sisters.' Then, 'Upturn in jewelry sales and restaurant sales attributed to this visit. Economic surge follows path of Gourouni Sisters.' Then, 'Meteora is promising free hotel and transportation for the upcoming stop of the 'Gourouni Sisters.' " We're still laughing as we leave Delphi.

ELIZABETH

We've been reading about the monasteries of Meteora, and all agree that should be our next stop.

Meteora

"Blurred by the kisses of a thousand years."

This is such a remarkable place of sky-piercing rock formations crowned with shimmering monasteries, so high you almost can't see them from the ground. We were so stunned that words escaped us.

It is fascinating to learn that the Greek word *meteora* means "suspended in the air"; seeing this geological enigma proves how accurate the name is.

Monks started inhabiting these high rock pillars in the nineteenth century, and eventually built six monasteries on their towering tops, as safe and peaceful retreats. All the monasteries have Byzantine frescoes and icons that seem to be "blurred by the kisses of a thousand years."

GEORGIA

In Kalambaka, the town at the foot of the Meteora rock spires, a church pillar sprouted from the rooftops and on top of the cross a sunset silhouette of a stork stood perfectly balanced on a stick leg. To the left, its bulging nest, copying the church dome shape, was filled with fledglings. We soon viewed the monasteries, aeries for monks for centuries. These hermit monks, living in caves in the cliffs, used to hoist up materials by rope and basket to build their monasteries. Now the tour buses twist their way around cliffs to reach the courtyards filled with gardens, frescoed chapels, convents, darkened kitchens and dining rooms, even rooms for the sacred skulls of the ancient elders. The awesome isolation of this spot gave us the gift of preserving the ancient manuscripts, frescoes and icons of the Byzantine legacy. Today visitors have to dress appropriately since the area is still a place of worship. One stubborn tourist while we were visiting, argued about going in with his shorts on instead of borrowing long pants hung on hooks for visitors to borrow for this kind of moment.

ELIZABETH

We ride the bus through Trikala to Kalambaka, where we will be staying while visiting Meteora. When the bus driver asked where we would be staying we told him we had no reservations. When we came to our stop in the middle of town he insisted we go with him to see his mother's rooms for rent. Our husbands got off the bus, trusting we'd be fine without them while we went to see the rooms. Looking back we wonder how we could have gone off with a stranger, but remember feeling perfectly comfortable going with him. Once there, we walked down a few steps into an immaculate, though dark, little kitchen and were shown two bedrooms down the hallway. We politely declined by saying our husbands insisted on air conditioning. When we returned to the town center, we found our guys drinking the ever-present cold Amstel and reporting great success in finding rooms at the Edelweiss Hotel. It was so very hot we spent a lazy afternoon at the hotel pool. We decided a light meal would be enough for dinner tonight.

The next morning we're surprised by this hotel breakfast. It isn't often we saw anything on the menu resembling our American breakfast. Instead the typical breakfast fare in hotels is hard-boiled eggs, fresh-baked bread, yogurt with honey, fruit, cheese, Nescafe and cookies. In general, eggs were more often considered a light meal, not breakfast. A few of our favorite omelets were on this menu, but the one we picked was one familiar to us because our mother often made this for a light supper.

Scrambled Omelette with Ground Meat
Omeleta me Kima
Serves 1 or 2

This filling omelette can be served for any meal.

1 onion diced
3 T ground meat
1 T butter
1 tomato diced
2 T milk

Salt and pepper to taste
2 T oil for frying
3 eggs
1 T grated cheese

In a hot pan brown the onion and meat together. When the liquid has evaporated, add the butter and stir with a wooden spoon. Add the diced tomato, the milk, salt and pepper, and a small amount of water. Let everything simmer until all the water is absorbed. In another frying pan, heat the oil well. Beat the eggs and pour them into this frying pan along with the grated cheese and more salt to taste. Add the meat mixture and scramble together until eggs are cooked. Serve hot.

Once again, as we read this menu, we are amused at the translations of the menu items. They are funny because the Greek is translated literally. We recognize this list as a perfect example of the saying, "Something is lost in the translation." These are a few:

Fried Greek Balls (meaning fried Greek meatballs)
Roast Kids (refers to roasted goat)
Rooster Drowned in Wine (the Greek version of coq au vin)
Creamed Fungus (for mushrooms with cream sauce)
Baked Giants (for the butter beans baked in tomato sauce)
Hothead Cheese with Egg Eyes (fried cheese with sunny-side eggs)
Boiled Grass Salad (boiled greens)
Baked Brains (the whole head of the lamb, baked)
Pregnant Tomatoes (for stuffed tomatoes)
Dried Bread Slices (for toast)
Fried Unmentionables (cooked pieces of offal)
Eggs Imprisoned in Potatoes (an egg cooked in a baked potato)
Eggs with Brain Rissoles (egg and brain meatballs)

ELIZABETH

Today we went to the Holy Monastery of the Great Meteoron. The towering rocks are everywhere and it feels eerie, especially at night. They are lit from below and throw strange shadows that make them look even scarier than they are. However, the monasteries are remarkable. To think everything in them was hoisted up in baskets from below. The icons and paintings on the ceilings are exquisite and it's hard to imagine how they were done. There is a sacred room with the skulls and bones of the monks who lived and died up here.

DAN

Yesterday during siesta, I walked around our part of the town and saw, among other things, a cemetery of veterans of the German occupation. The heat of the day is tremendous. Two rows of upright evergreen cypress trees reach for the towering rocks of Meteora. There is a walkway between the trees. Beside the trees are very modest marble sarcophagi about ten inches above the ground. Small chapel-like houses one foot tall (kandylakia) with an image of the person, long since gone, and offerings left by loved ones. The fields on each side have weeds of thistle and long grass with a few dried wildflowers baking in the heat—the dying thistles bend like plant corpses.

FLOYD

Leaving Meteora, we take the bus to Larisa, a long, hot, humid ride. After checking the bus schedule there, we decide to make a deal with the young cab driver for him to take us to Volos. First he had to pick up his daughter and take her to ballet lessons and asked if we would mind. We swung by his house, picked her up and she got in the back seat and sat on Georgia's lap. After an amusing drive, listening to his appraisal of life in Greece, cultural, economic, political, etc., we arrived at our destination. Very worth it! We got a room at a hotel right next to where he dropped us off. Rested for a while then hit the square to get our hydrofoil tickets to Skopelos and find a place for dinner.

On the waterfront is a huge bronze sculpture of Jason and the Argonauts. In the myth this is the site of their departure for their great journey in pursuit of the Golden Fleece. There are many menu items but I always fall back on my favorite and tonight everyone joined me in pasta with meat sauce after an appetizer of Greek-style tabbouleh. Tomorrow we head back to Skopelos.

244

Macaroni with Meat Sauce
Macaronia me Kima
Serves 6–8

This looks pretty standard, but the cinnamon stick changes everything.

3 lb ground beef
2 T butter
Salt and pepper to taste
1 28-oz can of diced tomatoes
1 T tomato paste dissolved in
    a cup of warm water

A pinch of sugar
½-inch cinnamon stick
1 lb macaroni
½ c butter for pasta
½ c grated Kefalotiri or Parmesan
    cheese

Brown the ground beef in two tablespoons butter in a pan with salt and pepper. When meat is browned add canned tomatoes, tomato paste dissolved in a cup of water, a pinch of sugar and the cinnamon stick. Stir well. Cover and cook slowly about 45 minutes until liquid is absorbed, stirring occasionally. Remove from heat and remove cinnamon stick. Meanwhile, boil a pound of macaroni according to directions and drain well. In a small pan, heat butter until sizzling brown, being careful not to burn. Place pasta in a baking pan. Pour sizzling brown butter over all. Sprinkle with cheese and spread meat sauce evenly on top. Bake in a 350-degree oven for 15 minutes and serve.

Cracked Wheat and Herb Salad Greek Style
Tabbouleh me Feta
Serves 4

This tabbouleh has an added Greek twist: the feta and kalamata olives.

1 c fine bulgur wheat, soaked in
   boiling water for 20 minutes
8 chopped scallions
1 c chopped tomatoes
¾ c chopped fresh flat-leaf parsley
½ c chopped fresh mint

½ c lemon juice
¾ c olive oil
½ t each salt and pepper
½ c feta crumbled
1 c chopped cucumber
½ c chopped Kalamata olives

Drain the bulgur wheat and squeeze dry with hands and place in a large bowl. Add the chopped scallions, tomatoes, herbs, cucumber, and gently mix with the wheat. In a small bowl beat together the lemon juice, olive oil, salt and pepper. Pour over the salad. Sprinkle with feta and olives and gently toss. Set aside for 30 minutes for the flavors to meld before serving.

DAN

Volos had a lovely church, which we visited this morning. We later got the girls a lemonatha, while Floyd and I had an Amstel each. I had to force it upon him. We also had a snackola in the form of pork souvlaki. Now on board the flying dolphin, back to Skopelos Town. Can't wait!

Skopelos Return

"The salty swell of the sea smiled."
—Homeric hymn

DAN

Skopelos! We have arrived in town and make our way over to the Molos Taverna where we have, in the past, especially enjoyed the fried zucchini. Now we feast on pork with prunes. This island is famous for its plums in every form. Floyd and I looked all over for the place to settle down for the next night or two. After several adventures, including a nice hotel where the price rose five euros from the time when Floyd asked about it until I did, I took a look into the Regina Hotel, and Vicki, the wonderful lady of the house was great! She showed us rooms and told me we could move upstairs into the big rooms tomorrow night. The hotel is intimately decorated with lovely lace curtains and even her Yiayia's furnishings. The price, Vicki promises, will include an extensive breakfast. While we are in Floyd and Georgia's room unpacking, Vicki stuck her head in to ask if she could make us coffee. Then about the rental car, she said to ask around and then she would have her son check around also for an even lower price. She's the type who takes over in a very nice way. I don't think she would become pushy. It is not in her nature. Back to the Aktaion Taverna for another Skopelos feast. Our waiter, Christo, is from Thessaloniki, and when he asked our names we told him Stavros and Niko, our Greek names, because there were no translations for Floyd or Daniel. He did not buy it right away, but was nice. When Georgia asked him his name he said, "Christo, but you can call me Al." Good guy! Big tip for this guy.

ELIZABETH

Our new concierge, Vicki, is full of information about her island of Skopelos. She said that there is a large number of plum trees on the island, but only a few plums are sold fresh while the rest are used for the island's specialties, plum brandy and prunes.

We told Vicki we were planning to write a cookbook and wondered if she would like to give us a few of her favorite recipes. She was thrilled and invited us to sit at the dining room table with her while she shared her recipes. She was very animated when she talked and always smiling. What a lovely lady. She gave us her own recipes for briam, keftethes, leg of lamb, moussaka, pastitisio, octopus stifatho, and pork with prunes.

All of these off the top of her head, demonstrating how much a part of her everyday life they are. She was a wonderful cook, judging from her special cheese pies that she had made us. Her willingness to share so many of her recipes with us was another example of her generous spirit, her kefi. She proceeded to tell us how to cook meat with prunes, since this is a new combination for us.

Pork with Prunes
Hirino me Damaskina
Serves 6–8

The rich taste of prunes adds a nice touch to this casserole.

3 lb boneless pork cut into chunks	2 bay leaves
½ c olive oil	¼ t cinnamon
½ c butter	½ t sugar
3 onions finely chopped	Salt and pepper to taste
1 c dry white wine	1 lb prunes

Heat the oil and butter in a large skillet and brown the meat on both sides. Add the onions and sauté quickly, adding white wine before the onions brown. Add bay leaves, cinnamon, sugar and season with salt and pepper. Pour in enough water to cover all the ingredients. Bring to a boil then reduce heat and simmer 30 minutes.

Line the base of a deep saucepan with the prunes and place the meat and stock on top. Simmer over moderate heat for 15–20 minutes. Serve hot with rice.

FLOYD

We're back to our cherished Skopelos Town, celebrating our forty-third anniversary (but who's counting?). Great dinner and special wine! Looking forward to Vicki's promised breakfast: tiropita, the island specialty cheese pie, another celebration for us!

DAN

We're lounging in the patio of the hotel courtyard while the coffee is brewing and Vicki is checking about something at a table in the dining room. I met Abraham and April, a Greek and American who met on Santorini a year ago and came back to Greece to have this vacation. The breakfast is great, hard-boiled eggs, toasted ham and cheese, filtered coffee and, yes, her special tiropita!

250

ELIZABETH

This cheese pie is the one we watched Fotini make in Agnonda. No doubt they each have their own "twist" as we all often do when we make a recipe over and over again. It's as delicious as the other one, so we have no complaints. To Vicki, the secret to this cheese pie is the island's hard goat cheese, which doesn't completely melt when the pita is fried. As we complimented her on this breakfast treat, she invited us to have dinner with her. She said she was making lamb fricassee and began telling us the recipe before we could blink.

We are full of breakfast but can hardly wait for dinner!

Lamb Fricassée
Arni Frikase
Serves 4–5

A light lamb stew made with fresh dill and romaine, bathed in egg-lemon sauce.

4 T olive oil
2 lb lamb shoulder chops
Salt and pepper to taste
10 scallions chopped
2 c chicken broth

2 lb greens (romaine or Swiss chard)
   rinsed, drained and chopped
½ c fresh chopped dill
3 eggs beaten at room temperature
½ c lemon juice

In a large casserole, heat oil and sauté chops until brown on both sides, seasoning liberally with salt and pepper. Add scallions and cook two minutes longer. Add chicken broth to cover meat and simmer, covered, for one hour until very tender. Add the greens and dill and cook 30 minutes more. Remove from heat. Make egg-lemon sauce as follows:

In a bowl beat eggs until frothy. Gradually beat in lemon juice. Slowly beat in one cup of hot lamb juice and pour egg-lemon sauce over meat and greens and simmer very gently until sauce slightly thickens, 5–6 minutes. Do not boil or sauce will curdle.

FLOYD

Spent the day roaming the town and we decided to rent a car from Spyro. We rented a Hyundai Atos at fifty-five euros for three days with the option to keep it longer if we chose. Headed for Agnonda with me at the wheel. The drive, so familiar, seemed much shorter than the bus trip of other times here.

DAN

Don't know what we'll find in Agnonda! It's been seven years since our last visit. Will Maria still be there? Fotini? Will the rooms be there? Will development have ruined the feel there? No! Yes! We park. The tavernas look the same. We walk towards Maria's and see that her little house has the gate open and there's a toolbox on the steps. We can hear work going on. Georgia calls, "Maria."

FLOYD

There are some obvious changes: a few more places behind Maria's and Fotini's, and some still being built. The dock has been enlarged, but overall it has the same look of old Agnonda. No sign of Maria immediately but as I walked toward the mini market, I heard the hoots and hollers of greetings. Maria and Tasso were there hugging and kissing the long-lost arrivals. I went over for my greetings and Maria excitedly wanted to know if we'd be staying today ("seemera"). But we told her no, tomorrow ("avrio"). She got the keys to show us the newly renovated rooms, number four and five. Our room had a kitchenette and was spiffed up considerably, new bathroom and windows and shutters. The look from the balcony brought back fond memories and we felt very much at home. Maria and Tasso were getting ready for a wedding in Volos so we told them we'd be back tomorrow to check in. Said hi to Evi and ran into Fotini coming out of the mini market. Greetings of hugs and kisses all over again, and a brief hello to Yiorgo at their taverna, where we learned the sad news that his sister from California, Vasso, who had known Jim and Poppy Sardonis, had died in September. We ate lunch there and headed back to town and the Hotel Regina with Vicki's promise of not one but two tiropitas for breakfast.

DAN

Floyd and I take a dip in our favorite bay before lunch at Fotini's. She talk, talk, talks as she pours Yiorgo's homemade wine from their vineyards in Larisa, a very nice rosé. It was like a homecoming. We remarked that she looks just the same, and the same pretty much goes for Maria and Tasso and especially for Evi. We drive over to Limnonari Beach and have another brief swim. Cooler than Agnonda but quite nice. Who's going to tell Vicki that our days at the Hotel Regina are over after tonight?

GEORGIA

Farewell to Vicki at the Regina Hotel. She has made us two delectable Skopelos tiropitas. Floyd has tried a Celtic twist and smeared cherry preserves, madmelatha kedasi, on top for the savory-sweet taste. We arrange to return a week from Sunday. She advises us to drive up to the monastery, Agios Ioannes, if we wind our way north. When she addresses all four of us her hands swing into sign language as she describes "ta keemata," the waves, and "fourdouna," loud surf. The steps up, up, many steep! But that road . . . Po! Po! Be careful. Look over only little, you could go bloop, bloop, down, down in water!" She has developed an excellent system of signing, embellished with facial expressions, swooping arm movements, meaningful giggles just in the right places and a few key English words, "Back toomoorrow?"

After Dan ingeniously stuffs our little Hyundai with our two suitcases, one huge duffel, one small suitcase, two knapsacks, and three small bags, we drive to the health clinic to get cough medicine for Elizabeth. We also stopped at a bakery hoping for bougatsa but it was sold out. We did pick up some bread. Not knowing if Evi would have good tomatoes yet, we bought some at a produce stand. Then, the long high drive along the turquoise far below to Agnonda. Maria welcomes us with hugs and more kisses (filakia), and gets the keys to show us to our favorite rooms over the line of seaside taverna. We look out onto our favorite pine-enclosed bay of amazing two-toned turquoise waters. Vicki was right; there is a fourdouna today, the new sound of wild, heavy surf on this usually quiet bay. We're thrilled with the newly refurbished rooms, AC, TV, new wooden shuttered doors, marble bathroom and kitchenette! We stroll across the street to the mini market to see Evi and pick up onions, beans and feta. We're psyched to find the Greek sausages, loukanika, for tomorrow's lunch. Always looking ahead, planning for the next meal, dreaming of the next feast, as good

Gourouni sisters must do! Floyd has been waiting for us to bring the fresh milk back so he can make our first cup of filtered coffee. We now sip it on the balcony and do a few crossword puzzles with the background music of surf and after every other word, glance up to make sure this isn't a dream. We are really here again; Agnonda, the jewel of Skopelos Island. The swallows are dancing with delight in the cool air before us, and down below, my favorite Parkinsonia tree's limey green is bending into the teal green of the water.

FLOYD

Trying to decide where to drive to first. Fotini tells us that her daughter is the favorite health-care worker of the nuns at the monastery of Agios Prothromos, so we'll check that out today.

GEORGIA

Across from the harbor of Skopelos Town is the monastery we've been looking at from the waterfront every time we come here, and now we've made the long, winding, scary drive to its gate. It dates from the thirteenth century and is still inhabited by three *athelfoules* ("little sisters," or nuns). We ring the bell at the gate, and a stooped black-clad nun waved us in from the wooden courtyard door. Dan and Floyd stayed outside. We whispered our way into the flowered courtyard, and the church door opened. What a jewel!

ELIZABETH

The tiny church felt really sacred. We put coins in the slot of the candle holder and lit small, thin yellow candles, thin as our birthday candles but longer. I said a silent prayer for all our family. I could smell that familiar fragrance of incense evoking numerous memories of being in church as a child, watching the scented smoke rise as the priest directed the censer towards each pew. I could hear the jingling, bell-like sound and imagined our prayers rising to heaven with the fragrant smoke. We turned to go and the tiny nun, who was actually shorter than I am (five feet tall), led us out to the court-yard and into the gift shop. There were many small souvenirs but the lovely, hand-painted icons captured our attention and we each purchased a few as gifts. She indicated that her eyesight was not good and opened the cash drawer for us to make our own change. It was hard to understand her Greek, since it appeared that she no longer had teeth. She was, however, extremely thankful and blessed us as we left this dark little shop.

DAN

Today we visited the oldest monastery that was recommended by Fotini. The ancient nun has been there for forty-seven years. Her superior, who is lost in her own world, has been there for fifty years! Anyway, we visit, take some pictures, and eventually after the girls made some small purchases at the gift shop, we escape. We visit two more on the way down the hill and stop on the waterfront for a coffee drink. We look for and find Fotini's daughter's crêpe place, called Barames, and enjoy some sweets. The way back to Agnonda was lovely with views of turquoise water between pine boughs, and when we got back I rewarded myself with a small swim in a little gravel beach, slightly longer than a bathtub, that lent access to the sea. I met everyone by the Nemesis Café. Georgia got a picture of me in my Speedo (not too flattering, of course) with my beautiful Eli by my side.

GEORGIA

We're having a creamy frappe at the Nemesis Ble, where the Greek blue canvas slingback chairs always beckon us. Watch the guys swim and skip rocks. Dan hears familiar reggae music. "Are we in Jamaica?" he asks. He's inspired to order a rum and coke.

Fotini just left for the church service with her silver tray piled high with a mound of koliva, that delicious concoction we remember getting at certain times in church. It was always a mystery, never really explained at the time, but now we learned it really is a carry-over from some ancient pagan rituals incorporated into the Christian church from its beginnings, as many fragments of old were intertwined with the new.

She invites us to come back later to share a bowl of it in honor and remembrance of our ancestors, too. When she returns at sunset, we three sit at one of the five tables she has set with blue-and-white-checked cloths for the dinner crowd right on the beach. From the taverna, she has carried over a tray with three small bowls of koliva, three snifters of cognac, and three small glasses of the juice from the boiling of the wheat. The familiar taste sensation of the soft cooked kernels of wheat, spicy with the cinnamon, cloves and sugar, is a delight. The juice, however, is another story. Not being accustomed to drinking this viscous gel, we were saved by the Metaxa! a sip-full of brandy makes the medicine go down. As we're sharing this moment, Fotini teaches us a new Greek word, *koutsoumbolyo*, meaning gossip, and we practice it! The sun goes down and we were bonded once again with this friend and her special hospitality, Fotini's kefi!

GEORGIA

A balcony breakfast of coffee, toast, and peaches from Fotini's trees. I'm savoring the memory of the crêpes we had at the Café Barames. They cooked especially for us a feta-and-bacon crêpe. It was garnished with tomatoes and peppers, making a rainbow of color on the side of its triangular fold, as if it were ready like a folded handkerchief to pop into a gentleman's pocket. Beautiful and scrumptious! The waters are still this morning, and we watch harbor business going on. Huge tankers are unloading building cement for all the new construction going on around here. Loaded dump trucks going back and forth on the narrow main street are all moving in slow motion. At the nearest end of the quay, a fishing boat docks and meets a fish truck to load up with the catch of the night. The fragrant aromas of food cooking from the tavernas below us are wafting up to entice us already for lunch, but we are off to find new beaches and new adventures! Our first destination is St. John's monastery on the other side of Glossa. We stop along the way to visit Klima, a bustling fishing village. I must photograph the rainbow of fishnets on the quay. We follow the map over a road that rivals any mountain road in Mani and descend into a tiny beach that connects to a gigantic boulder out in the ocean.

Here we see the stone-carved steps, leading up to a tiny white monastery floating at the top under an umbrella of pines. Many try to summit but return to say that the last few steps are carved out of the side of a cliff and too risky to try.

DAN

We find the road on the map to Glisteri Beach, a place many get to by a sea bus, like Tasso's boat from Skopelos Town.

ELIZABETH

As we drove around the northern part of Skopelos Island, we came upon a lovely beach with the seaside taverna called Palio Karnayio (Old Karnayio). The patio was set with blue chairs and tables covered with blue and white tablecloths. Through the grape-arbor patio cover, the dappled sunlight created a cool, inviting area open to the ever beautiful view of the brilliant blue sea. The white sandy beach had rows of comfortable chaise lounges, each with its own umbrella. So tempting was the water that Dan and Floyd went for a swim immediately while Georgia and I claimed a table for our lunch. We read on the menu that for the last twenty years, this taverna has been owned by the Kosma family, and Kyria Kyratso has made a name for herself with her wonderful cooking. She is well known for her stifatho, soups, fried cheese dishes, and roasted wild goat, which they raise on their own land. We were eager to try almost anything on the extensive menu. When Dan and Floyd returned from their refreshing swim, we all get serious about ordering lunch. Her onion pie was outstanding; a new and delightful taste sensation for us. Wandering through the building we discover that they also had a folk museum, with the family collection of artifacts presenting many aspects of everyday life of the people on Skopelos during the last two centuries.

The cool breeze that blew off the ocean through the grapevines was almost a caress, as we relaxed over a lovely gift of the dessert Kyria Kyratso gave us, warm and creamy galatopita, a classic Greek custard.

Onion Pie
Kremythopita
Serves 6–8

Caramelizing the onions before assembling this pie is the secret to its touch of savory sweetness.

6 T butter
6 medium onions halved and sliced ¼ inch thick
2 cloves garlic minced
2 T fresh dill chopped
Salt and pepper to taste

4 eggs
½ lb ricotta or cottage cheese
½ lb feta
½ lb filo, about 16 sheets
2 sticks of butter melted for the filo

Melt the six tablespoon of butter in a large skillet over medium low heat. Pile in the onions and cook, stirring now and then until onions brown and caramelize, about 45 minutes or longer. Add minced garlic and dill and cook 5 more minutes. Set aside and let cool. In a large bowl, lightly beat the eggs and mix in the ricotta and crumbled feta. To this bowl, add the cooled onion mixture and stir to combine the ingredients. Butter a 9- by 13-inch baking pan and lay one sheet of filo, brushing with melted butter. Repeat this process with seven more sheets of filo. Pour the onion mixture into the pan, spreading evenly over filo. Cover filling with the remaining filo sheets, brushing each one with melted butter. Cover and refrigerate for about two hours. Using a sharp knife, score the top few sheets into 12 large or 24 smaller pieces. Preheat the oven to 375 degrees F. and bake until golden, 30–40 minutes. Let rest for 5–10 minutes, then cut all the way through into squares and serve warm.

Sweet Custard Pie
Galatopita
Serves 8–10

Though this sounds like a dessert, this version of custard pie is sometimes eaten for breakfast.

6 c milk
6 large eggs
A pinch of salt
3 c sugar
1 c farina (cream of wheat)

1½ T vanilla
5 T unsalted butter
1 T cinnamon
½ c (1 stick) unsalted butter melted
10 sheets of filo dough

Bring milk just to a boil over medium heat, stirring constantly. Remove from heat and cover. In another pan, beat eggs with salt and 2½ cups of sugar until smooth. Add cream of wheat and mix well. Slowly pour in the hot milk, stirring constantly. Put the pan over medium heat, still stirring, and bring it just to a boil again (to the consistency of white sauce). Do not allow it to boil or it will curdle. Remove from heat and add vanilla and butter, one tablespoon at a time, stirring until it melts. Butter a 9- by 13-inch baking pan. Place one sheet of filo in the bottom of the pan and brush it with melted butter. Mix remaining ½ cup sugar with cinnamon and sprinkle over filo. Repeat layering all filo sheets in the bottom of the pan, brushing each with butter and sprinkling with cinnamon sugar.

Pour the egg mixture on top of the filo. Bake in a preheated oven at 400 degreesF. about 40 minutes until custard is set and browned on top.

DAN

It's raining in Agnonda! Yikes! Real full rain is pounding down. We have had our coffee and scrambles and then a deluge, which caused us to bring our clothes in off the line, turn our outside chairs over and grab a camera to record this historic moment. Rain! I know it is late spring, and our weather up to today has at least been dry. The last couple of days did include clouds and a threat or suggestion of sprinklings but nothing to wet the ground or cause rain gutters to spout, and the bay out front to look fuzzy as exceptionally large drops sting the water's surface.

Georgia was not feeling good last night and so we stayed in and Floyd and I, mostly Floyd, cooked the dinner of zucchini, orzo, and bifteki patties.
This morning we sleep in a bit. Considering the weather and Georgia's health, we decide not to look for a boat tour to another island. Today, of the fifteen yachts that were moored here yesterday, only three remain, and it is likely they will join their fellows and leave now that there is a break in the rain. The sun pops in and out, causing the harbor area to have a brilliant beauty one moment and shrouded in shadow the next. I wonder what would've happened if one of those freighters had come in yesterday to unload with the yachts in place. Who would have moved or given up?

It's a new day. Wine, feta, olives, and the usual Retsina on the balcony. The sun has set and once again Evia, Pelion, and the mainland look like various shapes of purple in the distance. After our nibbolakia (nibbling), we decide to go to Fotini's for dinner. Floyd and I have pork chops and Georgia and Elizabeth have meatballs. Very good. Eli says they're the most like her mom's that she's ever had, lots of mint. The fries are "fresca" and good, of course. We are, as usual, entertained by Fotini as she sits with us and we are her therapy. She tells much about the island life, with Georgia often trans-

259

lating in an undertone to Floyd and me as she goes along. Fun. It's late when we retire tonight. She has help tonight, a little guy named Stelio, who has helped for the last three years. We leave an extra tip on the table for him. Next week, two waitresses will arrive for the start of the real tourist season. They will live in the two RVs Fotini has out back.

GEORGIA

Tonight Fotini is in rare form. Since it is late spring, there are no tourists yet so she graces us by her presence at our table after grilling us fat, fabulous pork chops with the best fried zucchini and salad, and our first taste of tirosalata, a feta dip with green peppers and mayo in it. She makes us laugh so hard with her ramblings about life in general and hers in particular. We listen to her stream of consciousness. She remembers going to the olive pressings up in the high woods in November as a kid. The treat was to get fresh bread and dunk it in the first pressed oil. She tells us they make soap out of the dregs of the oil pressing. She's full of humor and wisdom, side by side. Her husband, Yiorgo, has left and gone back to the village near their Larisa home on the mainland, tending and supervising the workers in his vineyards, so we may not see him again this summer.

DAN

The chops are good but the stories are the real food that will last for years!

GEORGIA

Each time we dropped in to Fotini's we are given a song, an ancient proverb, or an island custom. Tonight it was interesting to hear that in the town of Larisa, her husband's hometown on the mainland, the males inherit from the family estate. So when she joined him at his parents' house as a young fiancée of eighteen, she was introduced to the family with drinks of a very dark wine which, she said, they could drink all night long and could wake in the morning with no ill effects, while she, the neefee (bride-to-be), was drunk every night! On Skopelos Island the women inherit and also, of course, must provide the dowry. She did for her daughters by giving them houses as part of their dowry. She also believes that a wife and husband's finances should be one, so she insisted that Yiorgo's name is on all of the property deeds she has! They just finished building their second mountaintop retreat, sweet houses that look down on the harbor town from a high ridge in Pefkias, a lovely pine-forested spit of land near the ovens where they dry the plums, "damaskina." We left her for about an hour to climb up the hill behind her taverna and visit her sister-in-law and husband's house, which is a luxurious apartment-rental complex complete with an eternity pool. It is called Lithanemo, meaning "the place the winds forgot," an appropriate name for Agnonda itself. Its southern situation is so well protected as a harbor that ferries, sailboats, hydrofoils, even freighters, all manner of boats find safe harbor from the north. We enjoy chatting with this charming woman, all three of us sharing smiles and tears about the death of her sister-in-law, Vasso, who had met our parents in California so many years ago, then by chance met us here on this island and discovered that!

ELIZABETH

Watching Fotini tonight, I am ever amazed at her spirit, her kefi. She is a statuesque woman with thick, black-as-coal hair mixed now with occasional silver strands. She looks much the same as she did on our first trip. She has that deep olive skin, classic, straight nose and dark eyes that seem to catch the light. She could have been one of the women we have seen in ancient frescoes or on museum pottery. Her personality is disarming and she sings Greek love songs while she takes food orders and tells you about the fresh catch of the day. Tonight the air is balmy, and there are sailing vessels docked here for an overnight stay. Their occupants wander in for dinner when, I'm sure, they hear her singing.

DAN

I will not go into a big discussion here but it is likely that the euro is the cause of much of the huge expense we are suffering while here in Greece. At this time (2006), one euro equals $1.25 (U.S.). Hotels that used to be eighteen dollars are around fifty to one hundred dollars. Food is about triple the cost of old, and travel on ferries has more than doubled. So with lodging, travel, and food increases, Greece is not the bargain it was seven years ago, in 1999. It will be interesting to see what we pay for this trip. It has still been great, however. Perhaps the weather will become nice in spurts. We're thinking of taking a drive this afternoon, maybe to the plum-drying regions of the interior. The girls will ask about which road to take. Floyd and I walk down the pier past the lone remaining yacht. I hear a pump, pump, pump sound and look over to see the discharge of their waste into the harbor, our harbor, where we swim! I wait until the Coast Guard man is free after the ferry leaves and tell him. Nothing is done, although he agrees it is wrong and anyone should know better. Unless he catches them in the act, there is little he can do. I think he does not want to confront the rich foreign couple on the boat. It would be justice if they were served fresh fish from this harbor, fried up for them tonight at dinner.

DAN

During what was going to be a siesta, I took a walk up the gravel road that split near the harbor sign to the left. I thought it might go up to some spectacular homes, but it turns out to be a through road from Agnonda to Cape Amarantos then joins the main route to town, totaling 3.6 kilometers. After that, it turns to the right for the coast again to a very narrow, scenic canyon beach called Dhakondo Schisma. I would like to see both but fear the girls want more monasteries. Perhaps we can mix the two.

FLOYD

The freedom and adventure we feel with our own car is unbelievable. We're off to tour the island.

GEORGIA

We've spent a few days doing business in town, like checking the schedule for departing boats and touring the island with our car. After not seeing us for a while, Fotini greeted us with "Hatheekateh!" You've been hiding!

DAN

Saturday at Fotini's she is singing an old island ballad about a daughter being as precious as gold. We are having what is supposed to be our last meal there, which is zucchini, souvlaki and meatballs. All delicious but the meatballs stole the show, well, except for Fotini herself. She must really be something when the place is very busy. Two groups of five get tables on the beach and as she comes back she's singing. They ordered a ton of really expensive langoustines, shrimp, et cetera. Of course she sings! I ask what type of tree that is down in the little churchyard and she says, "Telio, they

262

make tea with it. What else do you want to know?" Giggling she tells us that on the island here, especially in her taverna, she is the captain. But off the island she is shy and quiet. I cannot picture it, though I do believe her. The day is sunny, dry and cool. Out in the sea we watch a regatta going on with actual boats sailing! Every boat we have seen going by or into our harbor is just powering up by motor. Not a single sail have we seen until today. Afterwards, I swim two or three times in the bay, get dressed and then we take a small volta (walk) up the road slightly towards Limnonari. Floyd and I try hitting an orange mooring buoy with flat stones we've picked up (he comes closest), then the girls have to try, too. Comical! They do hit the water, at least.

GEORGIA
Before leaving, we stopped at Fotini's to say good-bye, but she had gone to run errands, so we asked her twin granddaughters to give her our thanks and our love until next time.

DAN
Dropping the girls off with our luggage in Skopelos at the closest spot to the Regina Hotel, Floyd and I returned the car to Spyro's rental. He was already coming to get us since we waved as we drove by and he did look concerned. Anyway, after discussion over how many days, we agree to nine days at €55 per three days, which equals €165. Floyd pays for this with his card and it takes Spyro ten minutes of phone calls and shuffling papers to get the transaction accomplished. After checking in with Vicki we go out to wander the town while Floyd gets a paper and reads it. It's sunny here on the waterfront. Blue sky and puffy white clouds. The girls have gone shopping and are now going to look for books at the Skopelos animal-care booth, where we bought books before. They each already had a chicken pita for a snack. We find the most comfortable-looking café chairs and have cappuccinos, and people-watch for a couple of hours, moving our chairs to stay in the sun, since we were under a nice mulberry tree which had leafed out. I go for a walk to the end of the quay and see dozens of sailboats coming in. As each crosses the imaginary line, the horn is sounded and their time recorded. It is the Northern Sporades Race, from Skiathos to Alonnisos to Skopelos. Back at the hotel we rest up from all of our sitting. The girls go to the dining room to get their last few promised recipes from Vicki. She is like a schoolteacher: "Okay now, students, get your pencils ready. What

263

else would you like me to tell you?" The girls are listening and taking notes furiously as I walk by to go to Floyd's room, where he is working on updating his journal. He asked, "Did we eat at the Akteon our first night on the island or in Athens?" Anyway, he is now at least on Skopelos in his journal.

GEORGIA

We finally got the hang of it—just sitting. At least this is what we like to think rather than admit we're tired of moving after so many weeks of traveling. We know how to find the best, cushioned chairs near the waterfront, moving from sun to umbrella-shade whenever we feel like it. Here we can count boats, study the tourists, the Greeks arriving for holiday on the first opening long weekend of summer. It's Holy Trinity, and even the local priests and residents of the town are strolling the promenade. Proudly pushing a baby in a stroller, a modern, hip Yiayia, clad in black but slim and wearing orange stiletto heels, smiles as she passes. A young dad holding the tiny hand of his little pink-dressed daughter, while on his other hand her sparkling red sequined purse swings in slow rhythm. He walks in little steps to match hers. Dan and Elizabeth have been to the Internet café to check their emails.

Before we left Agnonda, we were given a menu from a local taverna to take with us on the boat back to Athens. We smile as we read the menu and notice these common spelling mistakes that we see in many places.
Here are some entries from that menu:

Cheece and hum sanwitches
Vineyard of leafes
Nut pie
Varius wines
Rise with mussels
Pasta with winced meet
Cetsup
Spaghetti sos

Cheecy pie
Godfish in oven
Pork stake
Lamp on a stick
Votka
W heep creem
Anchonys
Fried sheese

Rost chicken
Big beans

We serve fool breakfast
Lamp Fricasse

DAN

Our last partial day here. We dragged ourselves down for breakfast. Vicki is incredibly busy with the full house to cook for, so we don't get our usual Skopelos Tiropita! The girls are getting one more recipe before we walk into town where we wait for our boat. We board the ferry on a rather blustery day. The sea looks rough.

Back to Athens

"Morning, sun-flooded, sun-lovely, the day.
Athens, a sapphire in the ring of earth."
— K. Palamas

ELIZABETH

This time we are on a ferry back to the mainland rather than the fast hydrofoil, then a bus to Athens.

GEORGIA

It seems like it was a long bus ride from Agios Konstantinos to Athens. As we entered the city from the north we got a chance to see an affluent neighborhood, an area on the outskirts of the city center, with some fancy-looking high-rise apartments, high-end clothing stores in the shopping district and only, it seems, Mercedes car dealerships. Couples stroll along the park-edged blocks, young boys on bicycles speed down the sidewalks so fast one lost a white paper mask he was wearing. We were refused by one taxi driver but kindly greeted and questioned by another who agrees, in excellent English, to take us to our Thission Hotel. We learn his family is from Evia, and he is the youngest in a ten-generation line of icon painters from the Byzantine era. Aptly, his surname is Zographos, meaning, the artist! He tells us in which churches we can view icons by his great-grandfather and grandfather. Today we will look for them. He was a gem. This morning I finished my toast and coffee surrounded by sparrows and mourning doves which share ham and the leftover chocolate croissant from our table under the green umbrella. Dan and Elizabeth are off for a last climb up to the Acropolis. These last two days back in Athens will take our travels full-circle, though not truly geometric, through Greece.

᷍᷍᷍

I remember the last time we were here when I was suffering with painful knees from dancing on the mountaintop of Roustika on Crete. I hobbled along, hurting but thankful that the pain came from dancing! Today we're in the same room at our favorite hotel, the Thission, facing the illuminated Acropolis, and the Parthenon glows in the sacred spot this spring night. Athens has streets and alleyways around the Plaka that are crowded with the old, the new, and the ancient. We were delighted to find a new taverna, called the Attalos, and from here we had another view of the Acropolis. The Parthenon is now on our right, and on our left, a small Byzantine chapel tower singing its bell song, Gypsy children trying to sell roses at each table, an old man playing the

269

harmonica as he strolled by us, his huge bundle of balloons bobbing in this Athenian spring breeze, a kid clicking over the cobblestones on his skateboard. Old, ancient, old, new, all in the same breeze!

DAN

By the time we nibble and sit and talk it is almost 2 a.m. for us when we check in and head to our rooms. We are number 34, one of our old favorites, and they are in 35, another of our old lovely rooms. Nothing inside has changed since our last visit and the view of the Acropolis from our room's balcony is just as glorious! I sit in bed writing in my journal with the door open to the outside world of the Thission District of Athens. Dogs bark, and cars and motorcycles sneak by the edges of the now pedestrian avenue. Now and then, still, there are conversations that hang in the air. Some sounds are right outside, others half a mile away.

ELIZABETH

It was so good to finally lie down. I don't remember anything once my head hit the pillow. I opened my eyes at 9:30 Saturday morning. Showered, dressed and went down to the outside tables where Georgia and Floyd and Dan already sat. Our breakfast was included in the €80-a-night hotel charge. It consisted of what the Greeks called "tost," which is a grilled ham-and-cheese sandwich. We also have a grilled chocolate croissant and a piece of poppyseed cake and really good filter coffee, which was a treat in itself.

DAN

I ended up walking down the avenue around the outside of the hotel through the ancient Agora and the Plaka. Neighborhoods are still quiet, but the place is beginning to stir, with people sweeping walkways and washing down stairs, and even now, beneath me, I can hear a masonry saw. Someone is cutting marble. It's 9 a.m. and the tourists are up and about and I must go back and see if the girls are up and if there really is a breakfast at our hotel. First I picked the poppies in memory of a very lovely and wonderful woman, Penelope "Poppy" Sardonis, my mother-in-law. Cheerful thoughts of her as I sit beneath the Acropolis.

FLOYD

Woke up around 8:30 after a restful sleep. Beautiful day, sunny, but not the usual Athenian heat. Before bed last night we went around the corner for a bite to eat at a candlelit café. I had coffee but it didn't affect my sleep. This a.m. I'm out for a morning coffee nearby, €3.60 for a cup! That's close to five dollars. Athens is closer in cost now to other famous cities, but still a bargain.

GEORGIA

Oh, what a beautiful morning as we wait for Elizabeth to wake up and come down for breakfast. Dan just got here from his early walk around the neighborhood.

ELIZABETH

We decided to take the bus tour of Athens, which was €5 each. Dan commented that it was cheaper than the taxi charge of €23 for the very short distance from Syntagma Square to the hotel.

As we sat at the Byzantino having lunch, Floyd spotted Tallie, a friend met on the plane, walking by, so she sat and chatted as we ate. She left looking for the restaurant her aunt had recommended.

FLOYD

Wandered to the Plaka and finally to the Byzantino for lunch. Food excellent as ever and we had a new meze, baked feta. The girls really raved about it, so I'm sure we will be having it again. Later, we renewed our acquaintance with Foti, one of the familiar owners who autographed Dan's print-out of the menu that he brought from home after finding this taverna on the Internet. Then Foti treated us to a fruit dessert, a great white plate of peponya and fraoutes, honeydew melons and strawberries

ELIZABETH

We loved the baked feta appetizer.

Baked Feta
Feta sto Fourno
Serves 7–8

The red pepper flakes are a perfect complement to the creamy cheese and herbs.

1-lb block of Greek feta cheese
2 t crushed red pepper flakes
1 T dried Greek oregano

3 T chopped flat-leaf parsley
3 T olive oil

Lightly oil an eight- or nine-inch shallow baking pan. Cut feta into about seven or eight equal slices, arranging them in the pan. Drizzle with olive oil, sprinkle with oregano and red pepper. Cover pan lightly with foil. Bake in a preheated oven at 375 degrees F., until feta begins to melt, about 15 minutes. Sprinkle with chopped parsley. Serve hot with bread.

GEORGIA

As we strolled home through the Thission neighborhood the noise was louder than Coney Island. Every café and elegant espresso bar was packed with young people especially enjoying the Eurovision competition. We found out later that the girl from Switzerland won. The double streets along the narrow square by our hotel, with colorful awnings and candlelit tables and glowing lamp posts, reminded me of van Gogh's painting of a similar scene, the colors of deep gold, cobalt blues, and accents of black. Our new eyes this trip notice the beauty more than ever.

We remember crossing Agios Pavlos Avenue teeming with wild Athenian traffic on our earlier trips in the 1990s. We used to marvel at the waiters from the line of hotels on the street next to the Thission, which have their table terraces across the road by the park entrance to the Keramikos, the ancient cemetery at the foot of the Acropolis. They literally would skip, jump, run, dance through the lines of moving cars, never missing a step, holding their food-laden trays high and smilingly keeping their calm! Once when we gingerly crossed after waiting for the pedestrian light, a gust of wind took Floyd's straw hat and dropped it behind us in the middle of the street just as the light changed and the cars started to whiz by! A young man on a moped stopped traffic as he jumped off, rescued the hat and brought it to Floyd. Our Athenian hero! These days the whole neighborhood called the Thission District is pedestrian-friendly. New cobblestones pave this boulevard and people stroll arm in arm, day and night, easily and safely from the cafés to the Acropolis without fear of the exuberant traffic! "Siga! Siga! Nice and slow!"

DAN

We see a crew working on the restoration of the Parthenon—a pleasure. The museum we have seen before, but if we see it again it will be in the new huge area below the site and across the street from the Herodian Theater. After more pictures of the Porch of the Maidens, called the Erechthion, we are ready to go. I climbed the steps of the huge rock overlooking the Thission area and the ancient agora, but as soon as I turned to leave, the rain started. We set off down the hill from tree cover to tree cover trying not to slip on the marble walkways that are slick enough even when dry. We make it to the hotel and go upstairs to visit with Floyd and Georgia and the rain stops.

Now we are on Floyd and Georgia's balcony drinking white wine and waiting for our nephew, Jason. We are in the Jay-watch mode. Both the girls are watching every taxi that pulls up. Two girls and a guy and they say, "Maybe he picked up a few girls," a bus and they say, "Maybe he's saving money," a fat guy with a girl and baby and they say, "Maybe he got married, has a baby and gained seventy pounds." Come on, girls, relax!

It is now morning and I sit at the shaded table in a very hot city even though there's a cool breeze, and have filtered coffee. Well, Jay didn't show up last night despite our best hopes and expectations. Elizabeth and I have to decide whether to use our last few days on day trips or just plain go somewhere. Leaving Floyd and Georgia will be hard. Their company is so enjoyable. Last night's dinner on the rooftop taverna, as well as the nightcap on their balcony, had a downbeat air to it. Poor Georgia, worrying about Jay and feeling responsible for our waiting around. Unless Jay shows up today, we will have to decide.

Jay has arrived! We were upstairs in Floyd and Georgia's room when someone knocked at the door and said, "Pizza Hut!" I actually was ready to say we didn't order any but then I recognized him. All right! We're having a few Amstel downstairs. Jay is telling us about Thailand, which he just left. Now we are talking cookbook talk. Another toast! Tonight we're eating on Thission's rooftop garden taverna again, relaxing with our wine, bread and conversation of books.

As midnight approaches, the full moon is struggling to rise from the tangle of cypress trees to the right of the Acropolis itself. The Parthenon and all else is lit with the tasteful glow of amber lights, and as I am propped up in bed just a bit, I can see clearly through our open sliding door.

ELIZABETH

This morning, Georgia and I have returned from a food-scouting trip and report that the fast-food place attached to the bus station looks fabulous so we go there for lunch. We split a gyro and Dan buys us micro-Amstel in mugs. We've decided to spend our last few days together in Nafplion.

Nafplion Return

Cicada Appetizers:
Catch grasshoppers, large ones preferably. Allow 4
grasshoppers per person. Fry in olive oil. Keep pan
covered while cooking so you don't lose them.
— Aristophanes

DAN

We purchase our tickets to Nafplion and nibble on various items while we wait for our bus. Floyd is reading one of the Greek newspapers and has seen that the Clippers have evened their series three to three with Elton Brand scoring 34 points. Our bus driver, thankfully, has good reflexes. Apparently a car pulled out in front of him just after we passed the Corinthian Canal. He swerved and missed him. That gave us all a good scare! We stopped shortly after that for a bathroom break and bought water that had partly frozen so it was nice and cold. It's a very hot day and although there is air-conditioning on this bus we barely feel it. Glad to get out of the city and, at least, near water. I have begun to read *Caught Inside* by David Duane, a gift from Jay along with a shirt from Thailand. Oops! The bus just broke down! Five Greeks, Jay and Floyd get off the bus to look at the motor! Can any of you do anything but watch? The driver gets it started, jumps in and we're going again, but we think we left someone behind!

ʃʃʃ

A lazy but persistent hot breeze pushes its way through the streets and alleys of Nafplion. The girls are shopping for a dress for Georgia and Floyd's granddaughter, Isabelle, while we merely sit at the table. I want to swim. Got trunks, will travel! Earlier, Jay and I swam, then went for refreshment at Mary's corner.

GEORGIA

I knew my friend, Anna, a teaching colleague, spent her summers in Nafplion, so as soon as we got there I started my search to find her. The concierge of the hotel she stayed at told me she spends her afternoons in the air-conditioned library. I found her there, bent over stacks of books, translating Plato into modern Greek, which she was studying in her retirement. She looked up the minute I said, "Yiasou, Anna!" We hugged and immediately went out to have a cool frappe under the plane tree on the platia. I introduced her to Elizabeth, as well as Jay, Dan and Floyd, who were just returning from their swim.

277

FLOYD

We planned a side trip to Epidaurus, the major Greek site of the ancient theater of the fourth century BCE. It is famous for its extraordinary acoustics and I look forward to testing that out.

ELIZABETH

We just got off the bus to Epidaurus and Georgia feels a bit faint. We went into the taverna called the Xenia right at the site and decided to have a snack. We were thrilled to find spaghetti with a simple Greek tomato sauce. As usual, after eating, we all felt better, especially Georgia. We are ready to climb to the top of the amphitheater while our husbands test the acoustics on the floor of the theater. They whispered "S'agapo, I love you!" (a few of the important Greek words we had previously taught them) and we could hear them!

The ticket to the site gives us access to the museum, the ruins of the Temple of Asclepius, the healing God, as well as the buildings there, like the hospitals and dwellings for the priest-physicians. We walked through the remains of the Greek baths, a huge gymnasium, and the outline of a stadium used for ancient games. On the bus back, we tell Jay all about our adventures traveling. Georgia and Floyd have made plans to take him to the homestead in Gythio tomorrow.

DAN

This morning, Floyd, Jay and I met for a swim and a walk around the peninsula. We found Mary's corner once again and savored the excellent souvlaki there. We walked back to the old town and who's sitting in the same chairs but Eli, Georgia, and Anna. Tomorrow, midday, Eli and I leave for Athens. We're sorry to leave but actually eager to get home. We decide to have an early dinner on the waterfront.

ELIZABETH

At this waterfront taverna, we watch the waiter carrying steaming bowls of some kind of soup to the table nearby. When he comes to take our order, we ask him what that was and he tells us it is one of their specialties, kakavia, a fish and vegetable soup. He goes on to say that the French take credit for this soup, calling it bouillabaisse, when it is actually a Greek dish introduced in ancient Marseilles by the Greek colonists there. They are both named for the pot they are cooked in, the Greek pot, kakavi, and the French pot bouilli. We all decide to order it with a loaf of fresh, hot Greek bread.

Fish and Vegetable Soup
Kakavia
Serves 4–6

A version of this soup is popular all over the Mediterranean.

½ c olive oil
1 large onion chopped
4 celery stalks chopped
3–4 carrots chopped
½ medium bell pepper chopped
1 clove garlic minced
1 T orange zest
Salt and pepper to taste
1 big pinch of red hot pepper flakes
1 c dry red wine

1 28-oz can diced tomatoes mixed
    with 1 T tomato paste
2 large potatoes chopped
2 bay leaves
½ t dry crumbled thyme
3 c water
2 lb cod or any firm white fish cut
    into small chunks
Wedges of 2 lemons for serving
½ bunch fresh flat-leaf parsley chopped

Heat the oil in a large saucepan. Add onion, celery, carrots, bell pepper, garlic, orange zest, salt and pepper and sauté for about 10 minutes. Add the wine and cook for a minute. Stir in the tomatoes and tomato paste, potato, bay leaves and thyme. Add the water and bring to a boil. Simmer for about one hour. Add the fish and cook gently until fish is opaque, about 3–5 minutes. Do not overcook. Add lemon juice and parsley and remove the bay leaves. Serve hot.

GEORGIA

The waiter is a fountain of information about ancient Greek foods. When I returned home, I read some descriptions of ancient recipes, described by ancient Greek philosophers, writers and chefs. I found in one of my own Greek cookbooks a number of ancient recipes researched and recorded by the author. Greeks of all ages have considered cooking more of an art than a science. No exact measurements for ingredients or cooking times were given, only brief and simple directions. Here are a few of my favorites:

Cicada Appetizers by Aristophanes

Catch grasshoppers—large ones, preferably. Allow 4 grasshoppers per person. Fry in olive oil. Keep pan covered while cooking so you don't lose them.

Shrimp by Ananius

Find the fattest shrimp in the market. Do not bother to haggle with the fish mongers. They are too independent and will ignore you. Order your cooks to boil the shrimp with salt, leaves of bay tree and marjoram. Serve hot on a fig leaf.

Baked Fish by Archestratus

Buy the best fish you can find, preferably from Byzantium. Sprinkle with marjoram. Wrap fish in fig leaves. Bake. Have slaves serve it on silver platters.

Pudding of Barley by Nicander

Boil some kid or capon. Pound 2 or 3 handful of barley groats in a mortar until like fine meal. Mix in a little olive oil. Pour meal into boiling broth after first having removed the meat. Cover pot to allow groats to swell. When pudding has cooled, eat it using hollow pieces of bread as mystron (spoons).
This seems to be the first mention of the use of a spoon in food references.

Boned Oysters by Chares of Mytilene, Lesbos

Use only the large Asiatic oysters caught in the Indian Ocean, Black Sea, or the Persian or Arabian Gulfs. Use the delicious white meat only. Discard the round, white bone sometimes discovered inside the shell—or give it to some Persian. They seem to prefer these bones to gold; they call them pearls.

Farewell to Athens

Yia Hara! (*To Joy!*)
—*Greek toast*

DAN

That time has come to say our good-byes at the square. Anna takes our picture. Floyd, Georgia and Jay walk us to the bus station. Hope they have a great last week. We get on the bus to Athens. When we arrived Eli and I went to our rooms and crashed for a while. Elizabeth went shopping while I went to Hadrian's Arch and the temple of Zeus, the largest ever. The temple has the greatest column, which fell in the wind, so you can see how it was pieced together.

I now sit in the shade of the plane trees, poplars and grape-vines at the Thission's Taverna. It is deserted but for two others...where are they from? California. Grads from USC and our son Clint's fraternity. He remembered Clint's name from the list he had to memorize as a pledge. This is another Greek thavma, or one of those twilight zone moments. Went to the Byzantino in the Plaka for our last dinner in Athens: Kotopoulo, patates sto fourno, spanakopita, horta, and salata.

ELIZABETH

At the Byzantino for our last dinner here, I finally ordered the spanakopita because it looked so good. I was disappointed, however, because it didn't have any onions in it and an overriding spinach taste. I realize how different some of the dishes we make ourselves can be, because of the region it may come from or the family. I didn't finish it because I was full and didn't like it enough to be my usual gourouni self. When the waiter came to clear the dishes, he was most disturbed to see I had left it on my plate and asked me why. When I told him I prefer spanakopita with onions, he said they do not put onions into their mixture because so many tourists don't like onions. I thought that was a questionable excuse but kept my opinion to myself. He gave us a raki to make up for it, which we appreciated very much. It left us with a good feeling about our favorite taverna.

DAN

We said good-bye to Maria, the concierge, and took a cab to the airport. Had bougatsa at the kiosk and waited for our flight home. I see what I am doing here: I am, with even the written word, lingering in Greece. Athens is really indispensable for the visitor, unless one is interested only in a particular area. The museum and ruins really are grand and set you up for the more remote spots. How refreshing to leave the crowded city, though we had breezy weather while we were there… almost ideal.

Unlike the Gourouni Sisters' view of the food served, the Pirouni Brothers give it the acid Amstel test: How much is the large Amstel and how cold?

Remember the bus driver who would not let us off the bus unless we promised to look at his mother's room for rent? The girls went while we sat and had a beer. They told him no because their husbands insisted on air conditioning. We stayed in the Edelweiss Hotel in Kalambaka. At most tavernas they keep tabs on what you are spending by bringing the receipt in a shot glass each time you order something…often give us complimentary raki or Metaxa.

ELIZABETH

We board the plane, dragging our feet for our last moments on Athens soil. I'm looking forward to getting home again, but feel as though I still have strings attached, pulling me back. I will miss this wonderful place. After three trips here, we definitely have special memories that will keep us coming back in our minds and conversations.

DAN

The humongous Olympic Airline jet slogged its way though gray and white clouds like an old ex-champ punching his way through a wet wall of newspaper. Water blurred our windows until we finally saw the rough Atlantic below us. We banked into JFK shuddering as we were hit with the low winds, grinding down our landing gear. We held on and leveled off while Greek women were crossing themselves. The flight attendants were seated and no longer smiling. Elizabeth's nails were practically piercing my palm when we unexpectedly experienced a perfect landing. Applause! We arrived in lots of rain—a storm named Danny! Although it has been twenty-four hours since we left Greece, we arrive home the same day we left Athens.

GEORGIA

Today we had to say farewell to Dan and Elizabeth, our best travel companions. What a magnificent time we had together exploring Greece—laughing, marveling, toasting, and feasting. We raised our last glasses of wine to clink and exclaim, "Yia mas! To our health." The final leg of this journey for Floyd and me will be to accompany Jay to the family homestead in Gythio. Mother's cousin, Angeliki, once again awaits us in her classic Greek kitchen with a splendid table laden with a scrumptious feast. It feels profound to me to be introducing our son, Jay, the next generation of the family, to the unbroken chain of philoxenia, Greek hospitality, in the land of our ancestors. We found our roots at last, and planted another seed.

And if someday you seek your roots, your journey to your own Ithaca, remember these words of the Greek poet, Constantine Cavafy and linger long:

Ithaca

When you set out on the voyage to Ithaca,

pray that your journey may be long,

full of adventure, full of discovery . . .

Hope your road is a long one.

May there be many summer mornings when,

with what pleasure, what joy,

you enter harbors you're seeing for the first time . . .

Ithaca gave you the marvelous journey.

Without her you wouldn't have set out . . .

Yia Hara!

RECIPE INDEX

Please check our website for color photos and more recipes: www.beyondbaklava.com

Georgia Cone
27 Randolph Avenue
Randolph, VT 05060

Elizabeth Songster
23522 Cavanaugh Road
Lake Forest, CA 92630

References

The Classical Cookbook, A. Dalby and S. Grainger, J. Paul Getty Museum, CA 1996

The Complete Greek Cookbook, Theresa Karas Yianilos, Avenel Books, New York 1970

Culinaria Greece, Marianthi Milona, Editor, Konemann 2004

The Flavors of Greece, Rosemary Barron, William Morrow & Co, Inc. New York 1991

The Foods of the Greek Islands, Aglaia Kremezi, Houghton Mifflin Co., New York 2000

The Food and Wine of Greece, Diane Kochilas, St. Martin's Press, New York 1990

The Glorious Foods of Greece, Diane Kochilas, Harper Collins Publishers Inc, New York 2001

Greek Cookery, Nicholas Tselementes, D.C. Divry, Inc. New York 1972

The Italian Country Table, Lynne Rossetto Kasper, Scribner, New York 1999

The Penguin Book of Greek Verse, Introduced and Edited by Constantine A. Trypanis, Published by The Penguin Group, London

The Simple Art of Greek Cooking, A.Spanos and J. Spanos, The Putnam Publishing Group, New York 1990

Sofi's Aegean Kitchen, Sofi L. Konstandinides, Clarkson N. Potter, Inc., New York 1993

Thank You

We thank these important people for the help they gave us:

Barbara Carter
Diane Comas
Anne Black Cone
Tessa Cone
Erin Dickerson
Mary Dulac
Holly Jennings
Cindy Lelliott
Ashley Ludwig
Mike Nicholson
Lou Sardonis
Emily Songster
Patrick Texier
Sara Tucker

We especially thank our husbands, Dan and Floyd, who took this journey with us, for their enthusiasm, companionship, sense of humor, journal contributions and love.

We thank all of our family for their love and support.

"Yia Hara! To Joy"

16162300R00162

Made in the USA
Charleston, SC
07 December 2012